The Quest for El Cid

The Quest for El Cid

Richard Fletcher

OXFORD UNIVERSITY PRESS
New York   Oxford

Oxford University Press

Oxford   New York   Toronto
Delhi   Bombay   Calcutta   Madras   Karachi
Petaling Jaya   Singpore   Hong Kong   Tokyo
Nairobi   Dar es Salaam   Cape Town
Melbourne   Auckland

and associated companies in
Berlin   Ibadan

First published in Great Britain by Century Hutchinson Ltd.,
London, in 1989.
First published in the United States by Alfred A. Knopf, Inc.,
New York, in 1990

First issued as an Oxford University Press paperback, 1991

Published by arrangement with Alfred A. Knopf, Inc.

Oxford is a registered trademark of Oxford University Press

Fletcher, R. A. (Richard A.)
The quest for El Cid / Richard Fletcher.
p.   cm.
Includes bibliographical references and index.
1. Cid, ca 1043–1099.   2. Spain—History—711–1516.   I. Title.
[DP99.F57   1991]
946—dc20   90-22382
CIP
US ISBN 0-19-506955-2 (pbk.)
UK ISBN: 0-19-285244-2

4 6 8 10 9 7 5 3
Printed in the United States of America

Contents

List of Illustrations

Acknowledgements

The preliminary research for this book was aided by a grant from the Hélène Herroys Literary Foundation which made possible a journey to Morocco in 1987, and by contributions from the University of York to my travelling expenses in Spain in 1986 and 1988: to both institutions I offer my thanks.

I am grateful to Mr John Parker, Professor George Scanlon and Dr David Wasserstein for advice in connection with translations of Arabic texts and their interpretation. Professor Colin Smith has not only been prodigal with offprints of his many admirable articles on Cidian matters, but also very kindly lent me the works devoted to the life and writings of Ramón Menéndez Pidal which are listed in the bibliographical note to Chapter 12. In one of the more bizarre encounters which have contributed to the making of this book, Mr Charlton Heston shared with me – at a moment of some personal inconvenience, in the dressing-room of an English provincial theatre only a few minutes before he was due on stage – his recollections of Menéndez Pidal in his role as historical adviser in the making of the film *El Cid*. Professor Bernard F. Reilly generously sent me a copy of his study of the reign of Alfonso VI in advance of its publication, a timely present which considerably assisted me in my final revision of the text of this book. To all I express my hearty thanks.

It seems a long time since the moment when, sitting in the rubble of a half-built conservatory on a hot August night in 1975, I first gave spoken utterance to my hope one day to write a book on El Cid. Without the help of her with whom I shared this confidence the job could never have been done. This book is for her.

RICHARD FLETCHER

Nunnington, York
November 1988

Genealogies

THE ROYAL FAMILIES OF
LEÓN-CASTILE AND ARAGON

The genealogy is much simplified.
It should be borne in mind that the kingdom of Navarre was partitioned between
the rulers of Castile and Aragon after the murder of Sancho IV in 1076.

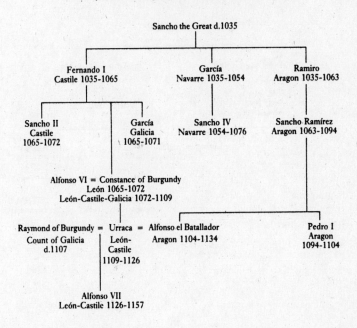

Sancho the Great d.1035

Fernando I
Castile 1035-1065

García
Navarre 1035-1054

Ramiro
Aragon 1035-1063

Sancho II
Castile
1065-1072

García
Galicia
1065-1071

Sancho IV
Navarre 1054-1076

Sancho Ramírez
Aragon 1063-1094

Alfonso VI = Constance of Burgundy
León 1065-1072
León-Castile-Galicia 1072-1109

Raymond of Burgundy = Urraca = Alfonso el Batallador
Count of Galicia   León-   Aragon 1104-1134
d.1107   Castile
                   1109-1126

Pedro I
Aragon
1094-1104

Alfonso VII
León-Castile 1126-1157

Rulers of the
Taifa of Valencia

Those who ruled Valencia are indicated by capital letters.

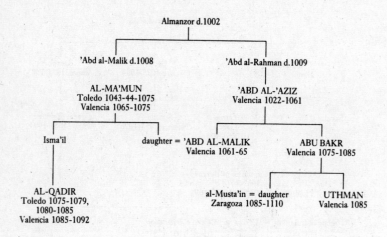

Almanzor d.1002

'Abd al-Malik d.1008

'Abd al-Rahman d.1009

AL-MA'MUN
Toledo 1043-44-1075
Valencia 1065-1075

'ABD AL-'AZIZ
Valencia 1022-1061

Isma'il

daughter = 'ABD AL-MALIK
Valencia 1061-65

ABU BAKR
Valencia 1075-1085

AL-QADIR
Toledo 1075-1079,
1080-1085
Valencia 1085-1092

al-Musta'in = daughter
Zaragoza 1085-1110

UTHMAN
Valencia 1085

THE BANU HUD OF

ZARAGOZA

The genealogy is much simplified.
Rulers of Zaragoza are indicated by capital letters.

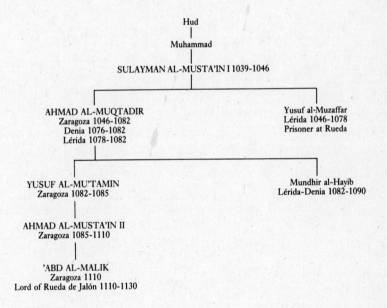

Hud
|
Muhammad
|
SULAYMAN AL-MUSTA'IN I 1039-1046

AHMAD AL-MUQTADIR
Zaragoza 1046-1082
Denia 1076-1082
Lérida 1078-1082

Yusuf al-Muzaffar
Lérida 1046-1078
Prisoner at Rueda

YUSUF AL-MU'TAMIN
Zaragoza 1082-1085

Mundhir al-Hayib
Lérida-Denia 1082-1090

AHMAD AL-MUSTA'IN II
Zaragoza 1085-1110

'ABD AL-MALIK
Zaragoza 1110
Lord of Rueda de Jalón 1110-1130

✳ Part One

I

✴ The Problem and the Method

In the summer of the year 1099 there died in the city of Valencia, on the eastern seaboard of Spain, a man whose name was Rodrigo Díaz but who is better known to posterity as El Cid. *Cid* is derived from the Arabic word transliterated *sayyid*, meaning 'lord' or 'master': it was originally used only of a certain line of the Prophet's descendants but later came to be used more widely as a courtesy title, as it still is in the forms *Sidi* or *Si* in many parts of the Arabic-speaking world today. El Cid therefore means 'the lord', 'the leader', 'the commander', 'the boss', 'the gaffer': it is equivalent, perhaps unpalatably, to *Caudillo, Duce* or *Führer*. Unlike the latter three words, however, *el Cid* was never used as an official title during its holder's lifetime. We do not indeed even know for certain whether it was used of him at all during his lifetime, though there is every likelihood that it was. It is a fair if unprovable assumption that this is how Rodrigo's followers would have referred to him. The term's first appearance in our surviving records is in a Latin poem composed in celebration of the conquest of Almería, in south-east Spain, by the emperor Alfonso VII of León-Castile in 1147. The anonymous author, assumed to have composed his verses soon after the triumph they celebrate, twice in the space of a few lines referred to Rodrigo as *meo Cidi*, 'my Cid', in such a fashion as to make it plain that he expected his audience to know at once to whom he was referring. The use of the possessive is arresting and prompts speculation. If a man can refer informally to 'my lord' it stands to reason that other men may have other lords to whom they will refer in the same terms. In Rodrigo Díaz's lifetime there were in Spain and elsewhere many lords, leaders, commanders or bosses. In his day

3

he was not unique but one of a type. Who were these military bosses of the eleventh century? What sort of world did they operate in?

However, if there were many *cids* there is only one national hero of Spain (and more particularly of Castile), El Cid – the crusading warrior who waged wars of re-conquest for the triumph of the Cross over the Crescent and the liberation of the fatherland from the Moors. There is a disjunction here between eleventh-century reality and later mythology. In Rodrigo's day there was little if any sense of nationhood, crusade or reconquest in the Christian kingdoms of Spain. Rodrigo himself, as we shall see, was as ready to fight alongside Muslims against Christians as vice versa. He was his own man and fought for his own profit. He was a mercenary soldier. In modern Anglo-American usage the term 'mercenary' carries pejorative overtones. It is true that the mercenary soldiers of today – for example, in post-colonial Africa – are not a very savoury bunch. Their eleventh-century predecessors may have been equally unappealing: we must not romanticise the Cid. Be that as it may, the word 'mercenary' will be used in this book in the neutral sense of 'one who serves for pay'. Rodrigo made his living out of warfare: he was a professional soldier. He was a highly successful one too; more so than many, less so than a few. From modest origins among the aristocracy of Old Castile he so prospered that he ended his life as the independent ruler of a principality which he had won for himself in that region of eastern Spain known as the Levante, whose capital is Valencia. How did he do it? How and why did posthumous legend transform him into what he had not been during his life? Why does the image thus created retain its vitality in Spanish national mythology?

These are some of the questions which this book will discuss. In so far as it has an argument, it is that the Cid can usefully be interpreted in the context of his own time with the aid of only those sources of evidence which are contemporary (or nearly so) with him. So commonplace an aim may occasion surprise among those not acquainted with Cidian studies. But it is peculiarly difficult, in the case of the Cid, to disentangle history from myth.

To write about the Cid is also, inevitably, to write about his most influential modern biographer, Ramón Menéndez Pidal. In the course of a very long life – at his death in 1968 he was four months short of his hundredth birthday – Don Ramón made contributions of lasting significance to the study of Spanish philology, literature and history. As far as the study of the Cid is concerned his masterpiece is his book *La España del Cid*, first published in 1929 and many times reprinted. Highly acclaimed on its publication, an instant bestseller, the work has been more influential than any other in shaping a view not just of the age of the Cid but of the Spanish Middle Ages in general and of their significance in the history of Spain, of

Europe and of Christendom. When he was in his eighties Menéndez Pidal was invited to act as the historical adviser in the making of the film *El Cid*, and the overall interpretation of the hero as presented by Charlton Heston was in its main lines his: through the medium of the screen Menéndez Pidal's Cid has been made known to millions throughout the world.

For the last sixty years all historians of eleventh-century Spain have laboured in the shadow cast by this great and eccentric work. I have called *La España del Cid* 'eccentric' because that is what it *is*. As I shall attempt to show in a later chapter, there is a certain sense in which Menéndez Pidal's book is a tract for his own times disguised as history. (The same could be said of many distinguished historical works.) A patriot whose native land was going through troubled times, he presented his countrymen with a national hero in whom they could rejoice and to whose virtues they should aspire. For Menéndez Pidal there was no disjunction between history and legend. The Cid of history was as flawless in his character and deeds as the Cid of legend.

At several points in this book I shall be critical, either explicitly or implicitly, of Menéndez Pidal's interpretation of the Cid and his age. It is only just to put it unambiguously on record, before going any further, that however much my version of the Cid may differ from his, I continue to regard Ramón Menéndez Pidal as one of the foremost medievalists of modern times whose scholarship must always command respect. Nevertheless, this rendering of the Cid rested, to simplify matters, on two foundations, the one technical and the other rhetorical. The technical one was a matter of scholarship. Menéndez Pidal was an accomplished and respected scholar. He argued persuasively that certain texts which presented the Cid in an apparently legendary perspective did in fact embody reliable historical information, either because they were composed earlier than critics had thought or because fragments of earlier texts could be discovered embedded in later ones. The rhetoric of his case lay in his repeated assertion that there was something 'truly' national and Spanish about the Cid. He wrote at a time – which in some quarters has not yet passed – when Spanish historians were preoccupied with identifying and delineating the essence or soul of Spanishness. It formed an important topic of national debate. (Lest we dismiss this too quickly as mere crankiness it is worth reminding ourselves that our forebears devoted much energy to debating the truly national and English character of, say, King Alfred.) Because of this preoccupation he was disposed to match the Cid with analogues drawn from other epochs of Spain's past, before or after the eleventh century. The context that he furnished for the Cid was therefore, so to say, a 'vertical' one, the panoramic backdrop of Spanish history unfolding from a remote antiquity to the present; rather than the 'horizontal' one, formed of the doings of other eleventh-century Europeans in other lands.

It should by now be clear that my modest aim of restoring the Cid to his context by following a different method of enquiry is more worthwhile, even necessary, than it might have seemed when first enunciated a few pages back. The reader must become familiar with the distant but not irrecoverably remote world of the eleventh century before the career of Rodrigo Díaz can become intelligible. The quest for El Cid most fittingly begins with an attempt to reconstruct the social and political scene of the Spain into which he was born, which shaped the attitudes and expectations of a man of his rank and type. This attempt will involve delving far back into the centuries which preceded the eleventh. Large parts of the Iberian peninsula fell under Islamic control in the eighth century: some sketch of the history and culture of these regions will first be essayed. The focus will then shift to the very different world of the modest Christian principalities of northern Spain, with special attention to Rodrigo's own homeland of Old Castile. It is desirable, also, to enlarge our context by looking beyond the Pyrenees. The Cid has too often been interpreted in a distortingly narrow, merely Spanish perspective. But eleventh-century Europe at large was full of warrior-adventurers. To try to characterise some of the features of aristocratic life which were common to the noble classes of Christendom at that time is to liberate Rodrigo from the shackles of patriotic hero-worship and to assist, it is hoped, a juster appreciation of him as a man of his time – a remarkable one, certainly, but not unique. So much for the contextual matter. At that point, a pause for breath. Some may, indeed, wish to skip over the chapter of interlude which surveys the sources on which our knowledge of the historical Cid is based; others may be interested to know what they are, and where their strengths and limitations seem to lie. For it is on these that the narrative treatment of Rodrigo Díaz's career which follows must rest. Finally, I shall turn to examine – very selectively – the growth and persistence of the legends about El Cid from the twelfth century down to our own day.

So much for the method adopted. A few words need to be said about what this book is not. In the first place, it is not a biography in any normal sense of that word. The historian of the eleventh century is inescapably constrained by his sources which with a very few exceptions portray their subjects with a stiff, wooden flatness that allows no display of idiosyncrasy. Eleventh-century people are as formalised in the written sources as they are in the Bayeux Tapestry. We possess no personal, informal documents about the Cid. We shall never know whether he was tall or short, patient or quick-tempered, approachable or withdrawn, austere or self-indulgent, or anything else we might like to know about him as a personality.

The sources do indeed suggest certain traits of his character, but I have deliberately refrained from drawing these out, preferring to leave this exercise to the reader. This book, then, is not and could not have been an 'exposé' of the 'real' man. Such an undertaking is for the psycho-historian or the historical novelist, not for the historian.

Secondly, this is not a book intended for an academic readership. This does not mean that it is not meant to stand up to academic scrutiny: I hope it will, but whether it does so or not is for others to judge. I mean simply that there are certain respects in which the book lacks the sort of paraphernalia which a fully academic study of the Cid would come equipped with. Let two examples suffice. The chronology of public events in eleventh-century Spain is at many points uncertain and in consequence a matter of scholarly contention. I have followed what seems to me the most plausible and defensible reconstruction, without dwelling on the difficulties involved, because it seemed to me that to have so dwelt might prove distracting for the reader. Thus, for instance, the Almoravide intervention in Spanish affairs which I have placed in 1089 is dated by some enquirers to the preceding year: but the present work does not seem a fitting place for laborious justifications for my choice of the latter date. Or again, I have decided to keep scholarly apparatus to a minimum by jettisoning references in footnotes and supplying in their place short and informal bibliographies, chapter by chapter, to direct the enquirer to my sources. I have not been unmindful of 'that pestilent fellow the critical reader', as H. W. Fowler called him, and believe that it should be possible for him, with a little persistence, to track down my citations from the sources should he so wish.

Thirdly, this book is not the work of an author who has approached this subject, as many others have done, by way of the study of Spanish literature in general and in particular through study of the great vernacular epic devoted to the exploits of the Cid, composed probably about a century after his death and known to posterity as the *Poema de Mio Cid* – a work which occupies in Spanish literature roughly the sort of celebrity held by *Beowulf,* the *Chanson de Roland* or the *Nibelungenlied* in English, French and German. Rather, it is a treatment of its subject by a working historian who happens to be interested in medieval Spain but who is equally interested in the history of other parts of the medieval Christian and Islamic world.

My first encounter with the Cid was at the age of about seven, in the pages of a book called *Wonder Tales of World Heroes* by the Reverend J. Crowlesmith. The book had belonged to my father at the same age, as his name and a date on the flyleaf indicated, and its dog-eared condition suggested that he had enjoyed it. The same volume is now giving pleasure to my children. I have not been able to discover anything about Mr Crowlesmith. It is no mean achievement to have pleased three generations of children. I have to confess that his chapter on the Cid interested me a good deal less than his accounts of other heroes – easy favourites for me were 'Cuchulain the Hound of Ulster' and 'Grettir the Strong' – but, looking back from nearly forty years later, I suppose that some seed was planted and for this I have cause to be grateful to Mr Crowlesmith.

Germination was slow. In 1963, as an undergraduate, I went on holiday to Spain and visited Burgos, the northern Castilian city near which the Cid grew up, which has always shown a strong proprietary interest in him. The elderly monk who showed me round the nearby monastery of Cardeña, hallowed as the mausoleum of the Cid and his family, referred reverently but confusingly to 'El Thith'. It was in the wake of this journey that I read the *Poema de Mio Cid* for the first time, with immense enjoyment, in the admirable verse translation by W. S. Merwin (J. M. Dent, London, 1959) which had earlier been broadcast on the Third Programme of the BBC. It is a work that deserves to be reprinted. It fed in me a budding interest in the medieval history of Spain. At that time there were few books on the subject in any language that I could then read, and my mentors at Oxford were of little help.

After graduation I embarked on research into certain aspects of the ecclesiastical history of Spain in the eleventh and twelfth centuries. A number of factors brought me back to the Cid. One was the necessity of reading all the narrative sources which were composed in the Christian kingdoms of Spain during that period. This led me to read for the first time the remarkable early biography of the Cid known as the *Historia Roderici*. The other was the need, in studying the diocese of Salamanca, to find out all I could about Jerónimo, its first bishop after the re-establishment of the see, formerly companion of the Cid and Bishop of Valencia. After the evacuation of Valencia in 1102 he returned to the kingdom of León-Castile and was given the bishopric of Salamanca which he governed until his death in 1120. This led me to consult for the first time Menéndez Pidal's *La España del Cid*, in which the author devoted a few pages to Jerónimo. I found it a work of absorbing fascination.

As far as research was concerned, I was kept busy first in preparing a doctoral thesis, then in revising it for publication and subsequently in writing another book which arose out of earlier work, on a twelfth-century archbishop of Santiago de Compostela. The writing of the last-named book was completed in 1982. However, a chance discovery made ten years earlier had brought the Cid and Cidian studies to my close attention as never before. In the spring of 1972 I had come across some documents in the cathedral archive of Segovia which struck me as having some modest bearing on the hotly debated question of the date at which the *Poema de Mio Cid* was composed. In testing this surmise and in working up an article for an academic journal I was again driven to read the sources bearing on the career of the Cid, but this time with a more attentive scrutiny. It was while I was putting the finishing touches to this article, in the summer of 1975, that the thought drifted across my mind that I might one day try my hand at a book on the Cid. The casual inclination hardened into a decision, but other commitments delayed the project. No sooner had I completed the book on Compostela than I was invited to write one on the Anglo-Saxons, and that was not finished until the end of 1985. I could not set pen to paper for this book until the following year.

Perhaps the delay was salutary. For the purpose of teaching a course on the Cid and his age during the last three years I was compelled not simply to re-read all the books bearing upon it but also to translate many of the original sources for the use of those without a knowledge of Latin. Nothing so wonderfully concentrates the mind upon a text as the business of translating it. In translating those materials, and later in expounding, defending, modifying or elaborating my interpretation of them, I hope that I have learned much.

Of this initially unplanned and unconscionably long pregnancy the book that follows is the child.

2

✶ Al-Andalus

Long ago, in the early years of the seventh century of the Christian era, there lived a middle-aged businessman who started to behave rather oddly. He took to wandering about by himself in the deserted countryside outside his native city. He heard voices talking to him when no one was present. He saw an angel standing in the sky. The same angel visited him in a dream and almost suffocated him with a brocaded textile until the sleeper spoke the words:

> Recite: in the name of thy Lord who
> created, created Man of a
> blood-clot.
> Recite: And thy Lord is the most
> generous, who taught by
> the Pen, taught Man that
> he knew not.

When he woke, he later recalled, it was 'as though these words were written on my heart'.

The city was Mecca and the man's name was Muhammad. As a result of these mysterious goings-on, the course of the world's history was changed.

The distinguished French orientalist Ernest Renan (d. 1892) once made the bold claim that Islam was born and grew 'in the full light of history'. Muhammad, it seemed, was more accessible to us than, say, Jesus (about whom Renan wrote a notoriously controversial study published in 1863). Certainly, on a superficial view, the sur-viving evidence relating to the life and teaching of Muhammad would seem to support such a claim, for it is ample and diverse –

the revelations contained in the Koran, several early biographies of the Prophet, accounts of Islamic expansion by early Arab chroniclers, the comments of contemporary Christians writing in Greek or Syriac. However, the interpretation of this evidence poses formidable difficulties. Scholars today are inclined to be much more circumspect than Renan. A recent judgement by a distinguished academic, Fergus Millar, is that the rise of Islam was 'one of the most profoundly unintelligible series of events in history'. The contrast between these two opinions reflects not simply a century's painstaking scholarship but a larger change in European morale. The breezy optimism of the nineteenth century has given way to the cheerless resignation of the twentieth.

The origins and growth of Islam are indeed exceedingly difficult to explain; but the facts are not in dispute. Muhammad's preaching began soon after his earliest revelations in about 610. In 622 he left Mecca for Medina, the famous *Hijra* or migration which has ever since featured as Year I in the Muslim calendar. By the time of his death in 632 the community which he had founded had come to embrace many of the tribes which inhabited the Arabian peninsula. A new power had been born. In the following generation the caliphs who succeeded to the Prophet's leadership – and the Arabic word *khalifa* means simply 'successor' – unleashed the military energies of the tribesmen upon the settled peoples of the Fertile Crescent. At that date the area was dominated by the two superpowers of the ancient world, the Persian and Roman empires. Between 633 and 651 Persia was defeated by Islam and overrun in a series of lightning campaigns: Islamic dominion in the East reached into modern Afghanistan. In the early seventh century the Roman empire had consisted of the eastern and southern Mediterranean lands stretching from Greece and the Balkans through Asia Minor, Syria, Palestine, Egypt and on through North Africa to distant outposts in modern Morocco. (It is often referred to as the Byzantine empire, a name derived from the settlement which underlay the empire's capital city, Constantinople, but its rulers referred to themselves as Roman emperors. The western provinces of the empire had been taken over by Germanic invaders at an earlier date.) Between 634 and 638 Palestine and Syria were conquered by the Islamic armies. Egypt followed in the years 640–2, and in the following year Arab forces began to stream into the provinces that form the modern state of Libya.

Thus within twenty years of Muhammad's death his followers had destroyed one ancient empire and hacked great chunks off another. Mighty cities such as Antioch and Alexandria had fallen into Muslim hands. The most sacred sites in Christendom, the Holy Places of Jerusalem and Palestine, had been lost: not for over four centuries would Christian armies attempt to recover them.

The western expansion of Islam did not halt with Egypt and Libya. Soon the Arab armies were pushing on into what is now modern Tunisia and Algeria. The city of Kairouan, to the south of modern Tunis, was founded in 670. Raids were launched ever further to the west: they reached Tlemcen in western Algeria in 675; in 683 the leader of one such raid penetrated to the Atlantic near Agadir in southern Morocco. The Arabs had reached the limits of the known world. However, the Islamic conquest of the Maghrib - western North Africa – was to prove a much slower business than the extraordinarily rapid Middle Eastern conquests. For in the far west the Arabs came up against the dogged resistance of the Berbers. The Berbers in earlier centuries had stubbornly resisted attempts to assimilate them to the culture of the Romans. The Greeks and Romans of the ancient Mediterranean had called all foreigners 'barbarians', a word designed to parrot their uncouth speech. Only in the Maghrib has the label stuck from that day until this: 'Berber' is derived from *barbari*, barbarian. The political reach of the Western Roman emperors had once indeed extended beyond Caesarea (Cherchell, west of Algiers) across an ever-narrowing coastal strip through the province of Mauretania Tingitana, past its capital, Tingis (Tangiers), and down the Atlantic coast to Sala (Salé, outside Rabat); and a precarious imperial dominion in the area round Septem (Ceuta), restored by Justinian in the sixth century, survived until the end of the seventh. But the characteristic marks of Roman civilisation were absent. Towns were few and small. The official religion of the late Roman world, Christianity, had made scarcely any impression. The Berbers had not wanted to be civilised by the Romans, nor did they want to be conquered by the Arabs. In the event they were conquered by the Arabs, but slowly, over a period of about forty years (c.670–710) and with difficulty; and their assimilation into the emergent Islamic culture was even more gradual than that.

It is important to stress this point, for the so-called Arab or Islamic conquest of Spain in the early years of the eighth century was only partly Arab or Islamic: it was mainly Berber. It came about in this fashion. In the year 711 Musa, the Arab governor of the province of Ifrikiya – that is, the Maghrib – sent a raid across the Straits into Spain under the command of one Tarik (who is said to have given his name to his landfall: *jebel Tarik*, 'Tarik's rock', Gibraltar). The force despatched was small and the expedition was intended simply as an exploratory raid. In the lower valley of the River Guadalquivir, perhaps not far from Medina Sidonia, Tarik encountered in July an army under the Visigothic King of Spain Roderic or Rodrigo. The king had been far away in the north of Spain at the time of the invasion, campaigning against the Basques. The army at whose head he faced the invaders had been hastily gathered; the troops were tired and probably not numerous. In the engagement which followed Roderic was decisively defeated and killed, leaving no obvious successor. Tarik hastened to take possession of the capital city, Toledo. These wholly unexpected events brought Musa over to Spain with a much larger army shortly afterwards. In a series of campaigns between 712 and 715 he and Tarik conquered most of the Iberian peninsula before they were recalled to Damascus by the caliph. Their successors completed the job: by 720 the whole peninsula was under the control of the invaders. The Islamic presence in Spain, which in one shape or form was to endure for the better part of a millennium and to leave a deep impress upon Spanish culture, started almost by accident, the chance success of a single battle.

This in itself will tell us something about the kingdom which Tarik and Musa conquered. A long tradition of patriotic Spanish historical writing – still very much alive in some quarters – has sought to present these events in a moralising perspective. A scapegoat had to be discovered who could be blamed for the collapse of the Visigothic kingdom. King Roderic, it was later rumoured, had seduced the daughter of a certain Count Julian who had then invited Tarik to Spain to be the instrument of his revenge upon the king. The story is a myth. Others have argued that there was something decadent about the Visigothic kingdom in the later seventh and early eighth centuries. The conquest could then be presented as a consequence of, even a punishment for the shortcomings of Spain's ruling élite; its aftermath would bring about purification through endurance, followed by the Phoenix-like ascent of a new, clean, vital spirit dedicated to the ennobling task of national resistance and renewal. It is a reassuring patriotic myth; in short, for the historian, eyewash.

There was nothing decadent about the Visigothic kingdom of Spain. The Visigoths had invaded and conquered Spain in the 470s. They were a West Germanic people who had already lived within the confines of the Roman empire for about a century, in the course of which they had adopted many of the trappings of Roman civilisation, notably the Christian religion. They admired Roman ways and adopted them very thoroughly. Visigothic Spain was the most Romanised of the successor-states to Roman dominion which emerged in the provinces of Western Europe. Soon after the Visigothic conquest, in 483, an inscription was carved at Mérida recording the repair of the Roman bridge over the River Guadiana; it had been undertaken by a local Visigothic official at the request of the Catholic bishop, Zeno. The episode symbolises the Goths' determination to maintain the apparatus of Roman civilisation. In matters of government, economy and culture broadly conceived, there was a much greater degree of continuity from Roman to post-Roman in Visigothic Spain than there was in Frankish Gaul or Anglo-Saxon England. The name of King Recceswinth may sound uncouthly in our ears;

but it was he who, as Flavius Reccesvintus Rex, issued in 654 the most sophisticated code of law produced in early medieval Western Christendom. His predecessor King Sisebut (d.621) was a learned man who wrote Latin verse and prose with accomplishment. The Latin culture of seventh-century Spain, of which Isidore, the polymath bishop of Seville (d.636) was the leading light, was the richest in Western Europe. A distinguished series of archbishops of the primatial see of Toledo presided over a succession of church councils which issued legislation impressive in both bulk and quality for the guidance of the Spanish church. The churchmen of the seventh century were diversely active: they elaborated a splendid liturgy; they founded numerous monasteries; they wrote theology; they pressed Christian observance vigorously upon a rural population which was still only partly Christianised. A rich artistic culture is suggested by the regrettably few surviving buildings, sculptures and pieces of jewellery which have come down to us from the Visigothic period.

This is not to claim that all was harmony in Visigothic state and society. In common with the remainder of the Mediterranean world it is probable that Spain was beginning to experience a long-drawn-out economic malaise from about the year 600. Its symptoms, principally urban dereliction, are being uncovered by archaeologists. Its causes remain obscure, though the most important of them may have been the arrival of bubonic plague on the shores of the Mediterranean in the middle of the sixth century, to be endemic for the next couple of centuries or so. The effects of this malaise could have been debilitating. Like other early medieval monarchies, Visigothic kingship was basically unstable. No clear conventions governed the succession to the throne, and faction-fighting among the higher aristocracy who backed rival claimants was common. It appears that Roderic was confronted by rivals in the north-east of the kingdom in the years 710–11, who may directly or indirectly have contributed to his defeat. The kingdom was less united than our sources might seem to suggest. It is significant that at the time of Tarik's invasion King Roderic was hundreds of miles away, engaged in trying to subjugate, like many Spanish rulers before and since, those notoriously unsubmissive people, the Basques. Another minority in Spain was the Jewish community, apparently fairly sizeable in the cities of the east and south (which were always more prosperous and sophisticated than those of the west and north). For reasons that remain unclear, the Jews were subjected to savage persecution at the hands of the Visigothic authorities, especially towards the end of the seventh century. Their sufferings led them to look on the hosts of Tarik and Musa as deliverers and they may have contributed to the swiftness of the conquest.

The Romano-Gothic culture of Spain was comprehensively

wrecked in the eighth century. The popular image of Moorish Spain is of a land of abundance and tranquillity, where mosques and palaces stood in populous well-governed/ cities girded by irrigated fields and orange groves, and courtiers discussed poetry in cool gardens. Perhaps this image was realised now and again, in a few places and at a later date. The reality of the eighth and ninth centuries was altogether different. There are three points which require emphasis. First, the social and political history of this period was extremely turbulent. Second, the emergence of a distinctively Islamic society in Spain was gradual. Third, the steps towards what was indeed to become a splendid civilisation were hesitant and slow.

Among the invaders, the Berbers provided the rank-and-file and a much smaller number of Arabs the leadership. How many of them were there? The latest estimate suggests that at least 150,000 to 200,000 Arab and Berber warriors migrated to Spain in the eighth century. These figures should be multiplied severalfold to allow for wives, children, slaves and other dependents. In other words, it is possible that something like a million immigrants settled in Spain during that period. Among them the Arabs may have been outnumbered by the Berbers in a proportion of as much as ten to one. In the settlement that followed the conquest the Arab minority kept all the richest territories of the south for themselves, allocating to the politically less powerful Berber majority the less rewarding lands of the centre and the north. Not surprisingly there was friction between the two groups. In the 740s the Berbers rebelled against the Arabs and civil war broke out. The fighting lasted intermittently for about twenty years. The Berbers themselves were very far from being united. Theirs was a tribal society in which the fundamental social unit was the qawm ('fraction' or 'clan') consisting of several hundred 'tents' or families. These clans have left their mark on many Spanish place-names; for example, the little Aragonese town of Mequinenza, in the valley of the Ebro downstream from Zaragoza, derives its name from the Berber qawm Miknasa. The cohesion of any one qawm was maintained by what anthropologists call endogamous marriage, that is, marriage within the group, However, women from one qawm could be assumed into another by marriage to one of its members; and they would bring their bridewealth with them. The attraction or capture of women was one of the most important ways in which one qawm could increase its wealth and prestige at the expense of others. Another was through the rustling of livestock on which the Berbers' predominantly pastoral economy largely depended. Both sorts of rivalry could lead to prolonged and violent intertribal feuds. Political authority above the level of the elders of each qawm was unknown. Berber society was 'segmentary'. Constant tribal warfare was the norm.

Further to complicate matters, there were dissensions within the

Arab élite, and the confusion was worse confounded by the stirring events of the middle years of the eighth century, when in 745–50, the Umayyad caliphal dynasty of Damascus was displaced by the rival dynasty of the Abbasids (who were descended and took their name from Muhammad's uncle al-Abbas). The first Abbasid caliph was known by the soubriquet al-Saffah, 'the shedder of blood', because of his ruthless pursuit and elimination of members of the displaced Umayyad family. One of its members, however, escaped his clutches, a young man named 'Abd al-Rahman, who after a series of hair-raising adventures managed to make his way to the Maghrib. From there he crossed to Spain in 756. He staged a military coup, displaced the last of the governors nominally loyal to caliphal authority, and proclaimed himself amir of al-Andalus (the Arab name for that area of the Iberian peninsula under Islamic control). From this date onwards Spain was to remain politically independent from the seats of Islamic authority in the Middle East.

'Abd al-Rahman's dynasty was to rule in al-Andalus for two and a half centuries. It threw up some very able rulers who presided at Córdoba over one of the most richly creative civilisations ever seen in Europe. But all this, it must be emphasised, lay in the future. Precariously, surviving at first, the new rulers only gradually enlarged the scope of their territorial authority; and the obstacles to their progress came not only from the resistance of the Berber tribesmen but also from recurrent feuding within the family and some bloody disputes over the succession to the amiral office.

The development of an Islamic society within Spain was brought about, obviously enough, by the conversion of large numbers of people to Islam. It is likely that few among the Berbers were Muslims at the time of the invasion; and then, of course, there were the indigenous Christian and Jewish inhabitants of the Peninsula. At what rate did people undergo conversion from a previous religion to the faith of Islam? Recent research has been directed to answering this difficult question. Its results, though necessarily somewhat speculative given the nature of the evidence, suggest that in Spain only about eight per cent of the population were Muslims by the year 800; that the proportion had crept to about twelve and a half per cent by 850; that it then leapt to about twenty-five per cent by 900 and fifty per cent by 950, before peaking at about seventy-five per cent round the year 1000. The period of most intense transfer of confessional allegiance was therefore between c.850 and c.950. The statistical material – it is based mainly on patterns of name-giving – which yields this conclusion is arguably reinforced by other sorts of evidence. Under Islamic law, Christians and Jews, as 'Peoples of the Book', are tolerated. The Christian communities who continued to live under Islamic rule in al-Andalus were known as Mozarabs. In the middle years of the ninth century a number of

Mozarabic Christians at Córdoba, worried by the increasing attraction of Arabic culture and Islamic faith for their co-religionists, deliberately sought martyrdom by publicly insulting the Prophet and his teaching. The timing of this bizarre episode is plausibly a result of the growing number of converts to Islam. So too the migration of large numbers of Mozarabs from al-Andalus to live under Christian political authorities elsewhere which was a feature of the period, especially between c.870 and c.940; a response, apparently, to the rapid Islamicisation of Andalusi society. Architectural evidence points in the same direction: successive enlargements of the great mosque of Córdoba – one of the glories of Islamic art – presumably afforded shelter to a consistently growing congregation of worshippers.

Steady conversion, followed by the gradual integration of the converts into the full status of believers under Islamic law, was one of the principal foundations upon which the slowly growing power of the amirs of Córdoba rested. The converts provided, so to say, a new social constituency. Its members were defined by religion and culture rather than by ethnicity and tribal loyalties; they formed a public with a stake in stability; and they could serve government in useful, peaceful ways as clerks or tax-collectors or lawyers. (In these roles, indeed, so could those who did not go over to Islam, the remaining Mozarabic Christians and the Jews.)

The tacit bargain struck was advantageous to the new men who served the amirs, for they could grow wealthy in the service of the state. This suited their masters too, for cash relationships dissolve older tribal loyalties: salaried bureaucrats and professional soldiers make more reliable props of government than vendetta-ridden clansmen. Such relationships were made possible by the developing economy of al-Andalus. The long trough of economic recession which the Mediterranean world as a whole had apparently experienced between c.600 and c.800 came to an end, to be succeeded by a slow improvement of the economic climate in the ninth century. Both the causes and the stages of this economic recovery remain mysterious; but a recovery we must postulate, if only to explain the wealth and buoyancy of the tenth century.

In the year 948 an Arab traveller named Ibn Hawkal visited Spain. About twenty years later he composed a geographical handbook, ambitiously called the *Description of the World*, which included an account of Spain based on his travels there. He was an intelligent and observant man, and if we wish to discover what al-Andalus was like in the tenth century we can do no better than to put ourselves in his hands.

Ibn Hawkal was struck in the first place by the general prosperity of al-Andalus:

There *are* uncultivated lands, but the greater part of the country is cultivated and densely settled . . . Plenty and content govern every aspect of life. Possession of goods and the means of acquiring wealth are common to all classes of the population. These benefits even extend to artisans and workmen, thanks to the light taxes, the good state of the country and the wealth of its ruler – for he has no need to impose heavy levies and taxes.

He correctly saw an indicator of this prosperity in the great amount of money in circulation. From the eighth century the only coin struck in Muslim Spain was the silver *dirhem*, but in the 920s 'Abd al-Rahman III inaugurated a period of bimetallism by undertaking the minting of gold coins called *dinars*. The ratio was seventeen *dirhems* to one *dinar*, which was in line with the ratio in the rest of the Islamic world and in the Eastern Roman empire – in itself an indication that al-Andalus was now part of a larger commercial community. The state mint at Córdoba exercised control over the weight, fineness and design of the coinage. The volume of coin in circulation seems to have been very large, and this is another indicator of commercial prosperity, for only a favourable trade balance could account for the inflow of bullion to sustain an ample monetary circulation.

In the last resort Andalusi prosperity was based upon agriculture. Ibn Hawkal was much impressed by what he saw:

The land is well irrigated, either by rain from which you get a good collection in the spring, or by canals of which there is a superb network, extremely well looked after.

Irrigation in medieval Spain was of two sorts. The simpler was gravitational: the downward flow of water from its source in river or cistern was also controlled by means of a network of canals and sluices. The more complex was powered: water was raised artificially from its source by means of a wheel fitted with scoops or buckets, and then distributed as required. This was the mode of irrigation celebrated by, among others, the poet Ibn Waddah of Murcia (d. 1136) in his poem 'Waterwheel':

Oh the one weeping while the garden laughs,
Whenever it spills o'er it its flowing tears:
What startles one who looks at it is this:
The lion's roar and the writhing of serpents!
It fashions silver ingots from the water of the pond,
And makes them grow in the gardens in the shape of *dirhems!*

Rarely if ever has market-gardening been so eloquently celebrated. There has been much dispute over the origins of Spanish irrigation technology. It seems likely that powered systems – especially those in which a horizontally-set wheel moved by human or animal power was geared to a vertically-set hydraulic wheel – were introduced from Syria in the ninth century. Nearly all the language of irrigation in modern Spanish is of Arabic origin: for example, the two words most commonly used to denote a hydraulic wheel, *noria* and *aceña*, are both derived from Arabic. Both, incidentally, have left their mark on the place-names of Spain, for example La Nora, near Murcia. Some of the irrigation systems of al-Andalus displayed great ingenuity. Mobile river-mills sound the most remarkable of all. The famous twelfth-century geographer Idrisi reported mobile mills on the rivers Ebro and Segura at Zaragoza and Murcia respectively. They were mounted on moored rafts which could be moved to take advantage of the fastest flowing parts of the current.

Ibn Hawkal was particularly impressed by the mules of Spain, which were used for traction and portage. He reckoned that they were even better than those bred in other areas notable for excellent mules, such as Armenia and Georgia. The most famous studs were on the island of Majorca. Majorcan mules would sometimes fetch 150 or even 200 *dinars*.

Ibn Hawkal does not tell us much about crops, but we can supply this lack from other sources. Foremost among these is the work known as Recemund's *Calendar*. Recemund was a Mozarabic Christian, a native of Córdoba, who enjoyed a successful career as a civil servant under 'Abd al-Rahman III and ended his life as bishop of the Christian community at Elvira (the name of the town which antedated Granada). About the year 960 he sponsored a work known subsequently as the *Calendar of Córdoba* which is rich in information about agricultural routines, techniques and crops. Recemund's *Calendar* contains our earliest record of a number of crops introduced to Spain by the Arabs: for example, rice, sugar cane, aubergines, watermelons and bananas. Some of these depended on irrigation. Rice, for instance, was a speciality of the region round Valencia where irrigation systems were already sophisticated: not for nothing is paella a Valencian concoction. There were many other new crops, not mentioned by Recemund but attested in other sources of the tenth and eleventh centuries; for instance, hard wheat, cotton, spinach, artichokes, oranges, lemons and limes.

We can dimly make out what seems to have been an agricultural revolution in al-Andalus during this period. An increase in productivity was made possible by more intense exploitation of the land. Irrigation, in particular, enlarged the growing season of the year – you can raise four vegetable crops a year on well-tended irrigated land in Mediterranean Spain – and eased dependence on unpredictables such as the weather. Higher and more stable incomes were the result, and with greater prosperity came greater confidence.

This in its turn, together with the light taxation noted by Ibn Hawkal, and the free market in land and labour, encouraged agricultural innovation and experiment. These were facilitated by the unitary cultural world of classical Islam in which travel was easy and knowledge could be diffused rapidly. And that world was indeed big. Málaga exported figs to Baghdad. A story told by the eleventh-century historian Ibn Hayyan of the vizir Almanzor (d. 1002) started, 'An eastern merchant who traded in jewels once came to Córdoba from Aden . . .' A Jewish merchant who lived in Cairo about the year 1000 traded dye from India to Spain. One of his contacts could well have been such a man as Abu-Abdallah al-Andalusi, a merchant of Denia to the south of Valencia, of whose annual round trip to Egypt and Sicily we hear in an early eleventh-century letter. The tombstone of an Alexandrian merchant has been discovered at Almería.

More varied crops did more than just diversify gastronomy. (Think of the bleakness of a world without lemons or spinach.) A better, more varied diet means a healthier population. Hard wheat, the main constituent of pasta, grows in drier conditions than soft (bread) wheat and stores for a prodigiously long time because of the low water content of the grain. Al-Razi (d. 955) tells us that around Toledo it would keep in store without decay for upwards of sixty years; it was transmitted in inheritance from father to son like other property. Crops such as this helped to stave off the threat of famine. Prosperity meant earlier marriage, larger families, diversification, opportunity, leisure.

The upward demographic drift propelled by a flourishing agrarian base explains the populous cities of al-Andalus and their busy economies. Ibn Hawkal tells us that Córdoba was nearly half the size of Baghdad, which in his day was probably the biggest city in the world. Córdoba's population might have been, at a conservative estimate, in the region of 100,000 in the tenth century, which would have put it on a par with the other great cities of the Mediterranean world, Constantinople, Palermo or Cairo. It was probably at least five times the size of the biggest cities of Northern Europe (among which London may already have been the largest). After Córdoba the second city of al-Andalus was probably Seville, with a population of perhaps 60,000. Toledo might have been half that size. Valencia, Granada and Málaga could have mustered 15,000 to 20,000 apiece: Badajoz, Lisbon and Zaragoza perhaps 12,000 to 15,000. These figures are the merest approximations – for our surviving sources do not permit reliable estimates – but they at least are useful for purposes of comparison. Córdoba, the seat of government, far outstripped all other Spanish cities in the tenth century, though possibly not, as we shall see, in the eleventh. The most populous and richest cities were by and large those of the south and east. By contrast, those of the north and west were fairly modest. Toledo was the exception which proves the rule.

This was a world of booming towns. Almería was founded by 'Abd al-Rahman III in 955: within fifty years it had probably entered the 'Top Ten' and we have already seen evidence of its far-flung trade. Among the industries of al-Andalus, Ibn Hawkal was especially struck by what we would call, broadly speaking, luxuries – textiles, ivories, ceramics, metalwork, fine wood- and leather-work. Spanish linen was exported to Egypt. Silk of various grades from the thick and coarse to the very fine was woven, and much sought after. When the vizir Almanzor wanted to reward the Christian noblemen who had accompanied him to sack the town of Santiago de Compostela in 997 he distributed to them '2285 pieces of the silken stuff called *tiraz* of various patterns and colours'. Enough is displayed in the world's museums today of the luxuries produced in al-Andalus to give us some sense, however vague, of what has been lost. Other commodities we can only read about: the musical instruments which were a speciality of Seville, for instance, or the paper produced in the only paper-factory in Europe at Játiva.

Some commodities of trade were even less likely to withstand the assault of time: few things as perishable as the human body. Slaves were imported into Spain and a high proportion of them were re-exported. Here is Ibn Hawkal again:

> An important export commodity is slaves, young men and women, who are brought in from Francia and Galicia; also Slav eunuchs. All the Slav eunuchs in the world come from Spain. They are castrated in this country; the operation is performed by Jewish doctors.

When John, abbot of Gorze in Lorraine, was sent by Otto I of Germany on an embassy to Córdoba in 953 he took as his guides merchants of Verdun; when Recemund of Elvira was sent from Córdoba to the court of Otto I three years later (for reasons connected with John's earlier mission), so did he. These merchants of Verdun were almost certainly slavers, for it is yet another contemporary, Bishop Liudprand of Cremona – who met Recemund in Germany in 956 – who tells us that the Verdun merchants made huge profits from the slave trade. We can piece together from various scraps of evidence a fair amount of information about this unappealing traffic (which was, incidentally, almost certainly the biggest single trade in early medieval Europe). The main source of slaves was the great swathe of untamed territory stretching eastwards from Germany, the lands of the Slavs. (Our word 'slave' is derived from the ethnic designation *Sclavus*, 'a Slav': cf. French *esclave*, etc.) The primary collectors of slaves were probably in the main Scandinavian. The slaves were distributed to east or west; for the western markets Prague was the great staging-post. Then the merchants of Verdun (and doubtless other towns) took over and a long journey by land and water to Spain ensued. It would be easy and misleading to suppose that the fortunate ones were those who died en route. The slaves who were imported into Spain and stayed put there – for many were re-exported to North Africa – were not on the whole used for menial labour. Great numbers of them were drafted into the Andalusi armies. Smaller but still considerable numbers were trained for government service, in the bureaucracy or the household offices of the court. In either of these careers they could rise to positions of influence, and a few became very powerful. We shall see more of them later on.

This buoyant and diverse economy underpinned the government of the three men in whose reigns the might of al-Andalus attained its zenith: the amir 'Abd al-Rahman III who ruled from 912 to 961, and took in 929 the religious title of caliph; his son the caliph al-Hakam II (961–76); and the vizir al-Mansur, more familiar as Almanzor, who ruled in all but name through the puppet caliph Hisham II in the years 981 to 1002. The centre of government was at Córdoba on the River Guadalquivir. From the eighth century the amirs had had their principal residence in a palace next to the great mosque in the south-west quarter of the city, underlying the present episcopal palace, near the Roman bridge over the river. 'Abd al-Rahman III started to build a new palace at Madinat az-Zahra, about three miles to the north-west of Córdoba, in 936. When it was completed some fourteen years later, he moved the court and all the government offices there. The buildings were pillaged and destroyed early in the eleventh century, but contemporary descriptions and excavations conducted about eighty years ago give us a fair idea of what the new palace was like. Of course, it was much more than a palace: it had barracks, a mosque, gardens, lodgings for civil servants and visiting dignitaries, workshops, baths, merchants' quarters, and so forth. The caliphal palace proper was very big and very grand; the Versailles of al-Andalus. The daily allowance of bread for the fish in its ponds was said to have been 12,000 loaves. It contained mechanical devices designed to impress and overawe the beholder. Here is a description of one of the most famous of them:

Another of the wonders of az-Zahra was the Hall of the Caliphs, the roof of which was of gold and solid but transparent blocks of marble of various colours, the walls being likewise of the same materials . . . There was in the centre of the room a large basin filled with quicksilver; on each side of it eight doors fixed on arches of ivory and ebony, ornamented with gold and precious stones of various kinds, resting upon pillars of variegated marble and transparent crystal. When the sun penetrated through these doors into the hall, so strong was the action of its rays upon the roof and walls that the reflection only was sufficient to deprive the beholders of sight. And when the caliph wished to frighten any of the courtiers that sat with him, he had only to make a sign to one of his slaves to set the quicksilver in motion, and the whole room would look in an instant as if it were traversed by flashes of lightning; and the company would begin to tremble, thinking that the room was moving away.

The caliph surrounded himself with an elaborate ceremonial which was daunting for visitors who were unaccustomed to it. When John of Gorze's embassy was granted an audience it was considered a mark of the highest favour that 'Abd al-Rahman III so far relaxed protocol as to allow John to kiss his hand. Most visitors had to prostrate themselves before the caliph and present their requests from that posture.

'Abd al-Rahman III had a standing army of about 30,000 men; under Almanzor it may have reached 50,000. The principal munitions factory at Córdoba could produce 20,000 arrows a month and 3000 tents every year. Stud-farms for the breeding of the cavalry's horses existed in the lower valley of the Guadalquivir, in the rich pastureland round Seville. Dockyards at a number of sites from Tortosa in the north-east to Alcácer do Sal near Lisbon supplied fleets which patrolled the coasts. The caliphs made strenuous efforts to control communications. Their chancery issued newsletters giving the official account of their annual campaigns. Their postal service relied upon specially trained runners imported from the Sudan. They seem also to have used pigeons and heliograph for transmitting messages. Their justice was strict, and its sanctions as exemplary and draconian as Islamic law permits. Public crucifixion was the lot of those whom 'Abd al-Rahman III judged guilty of treasonable responsibility for his defeat at the battle of Simancas in 939.

The government of the caliphs of Córdoba in the tenth century thus displayed many of the familiar techniques of autocracy. It was impressive, but one is bound to wonder how effective it was. Spain has always been a country of markedly fissile tendency, where a single political authority has had the greatest difficulty in imposing its will upon the provinces. This is not owing to any stubborn streak of cussedness or pride in the Spanish character. It arises simply from the size and physical conformation of the Peninsula. The Islamic rulers of Spain in the tenth century faced the same sort of problems as their Visigothic predecessors. The centralism of tenth-century Córdoba was as fragile as that of seventh-century Toledo. That we tend to overlook this is owing to two principal reasons: first, we know so much more about the capital than the provinces – largely because the caliph's propagandists have made sure of this; second, the most distinguished modern historian of tenth-century Islamic Spain was the French scholar Evariste Lévi-Provençal (d. 1956), who was culturally attuned to centralism and regarded the provinces as shabby and distasteful. It's all the more important, therefore, to have a look at them.

The units of local administration in al-Andalus, as in other parts of the Islamic world, were known either as *kuwar*, 'provinces' (singular *kura*), or as *tugur*, 'marches' (singular *tagr*). Each *kura* was administered by a civil governor known as a *wali*. The *wali* was appointed from Córdoba, though he was often a member of a family of local notables, and he had at his disposal as it were, a model of the caliphal government in miniature for the administration of his province. With luck and good management the *wali* could run his own show with little or no interference from Córdoba, his province potentially a little state of its own. The marches – the Arabic term means 'front teeth' – were the frontier provinces and in the tenth century there were three of them: an upper or eastern march based at Zaragoza, a middle march based at Medinaceli, and a lower or western march usually centred upon either Coria or Coimbra. The marches were by definition further from the capital at Córdoba and correspondingly less easy to control than the *kuwar*. They were geared to the defence of an exposed frontier and were administered not by a civil governor but by a *ka'id* or general. They were bigger units of government than the provinces to their south, but poorer and more sparsely populated. Their characteristic units of settlement were the fortified towns known as *kal'a* – a term which has survived in many Spanish place-names such as Alcalá or Calatayud – and the castles of which some magnificent examples still stand, such as that at Gormaz in the modern province of Soria, dated by an inscription to 965. The marcher generals and their families were even less amenable to central control than the civil governors of the provinces. The annual caliphal campaigns on their northern frontiers, ostensibly expeditions against the Christians of the north, were probably as much tours of inspection intended to cow the boisterous marchers. This was about as far as Córdoba's authority went. Here too then, in the marches, lay the potential for independent principalities.

In the event the centralised authority of Córdoba *did* crumble away and the unitary caliphate was succeeded by a number of successor-states in the early eleventh century. This process created the political world in which the Cid grew up. The leadership story is very complicated: in what follows I present a simplified version.

On the death of the caliph al-Hakam in 976 his ten-year-old son Hisham succeeded him. Power lay with a triumvirate of the late caliph's ministers who acted as regents. Among them one stood out, an able, ambitious and unscrupulous civil servant named Muhammad ibn Abi 'Amir. During the years 976–81 he contrived to eliminate his two rivals. From 981 until his death he was the ruler of al-Andalus in all but name. It was in that year that he took the title al-Mansur, usually westernised to Almanzor, 'he who is victorious by the will of God'. He had already built a new palace complex to the east of Córdoba, Madinat az-Zahira, 'the glittering city', obviously intended to rival in splendour 'Abd al-Rahman III's construction to the west, and it was thither that he transferred all the government departments in 981. The financial basis of Almanzor's position was weak. Al-Hakam was said to have left a colossal reserve of treasure – forty million *dinars* – in the treasury at Córdoba at his death. But Almanzor cut taxes to curry favour, balanced on an intricate network of bribery, poured money into buildings and hugely increased the size of the army on which in the last resort his power rested. It was perhaps the pressure of financial need which led to the campaigns against the Christians of northern Spain for which he is most famous; though Almanzor himself took care that he should be presented first and foremost as a champion of Islam:

> He wrote with his own hand a Koran which he always carried with him on his campaigns, and in which he used constantly to read . . . He also took with him his grave-clothes, thus being always prepared to meet death whenever it should assail him. The winding-sheet was made of linen grown in the lands he inherited from his father, spun and woven by his own daughters.

The verses on his tomb adopted a more triumphalist tone:

> The traces he left behind will tell
> thee who he was, as if thou
> sawest him with thine own eyes.
>
> By Allah, the succeeding generations
> will never produce his equal,
> nor one who knows better how to
> defend our frontiers.

Almanzor died in 1002. His son, 'Abd al-Malik, succeeded to his position and retained power until his early death in 1008. It was then that serious trouble started: for the heritage that Almanzor left behind him went far beyond ephemeral military glory and a reputation for piety. The policies of Almanzor and his son had two fatal flaws. In the first place, they had effectively displaced the caliph and in so doing weakened the already somewhat hazy intellectual basis upon which the Spanish caliphal institution rested. If one adventurer had been able to shove aside constituted authority, then so could another. This was the reflection that occurred to several people in and after 1008. In acting upon it, often with results that proved fatal to themselves, they initiated a period of extreme political instability precisely where this would have the gravest effects – in the centre, at Córdoba. The second fatal legacy of Almanzor's rule was the mushroom growth of the army. In addition to the financial strain, this expansion introduced new peoples into al-Andalus; for Almanzor recruited among the Berbers of the Maghrib and the Slavs imported from central Europe into Spain. Almanzor's troops were not assimilated into Andalusi society but remained an alien element, resented by the population who had to pay for them. Their generals felt more personal loyalty to the house of Almanzor than to what was left of the Umayyad caliphal dynasty. In the chaotic turmoil of the years after 1008 they came forward to play a sinister political role.

For twenty-three years after 1008 factions diversely made up of Umayyad loyalists, supporters of Almanzor's dynasty, Slav or Berber generals and bureaucrats of native Andalusi stock fought for control of what was left of the centralised government laboriously constructed by 'Abd al-Rahman III. Disintegration of unitary political authority was the most important process of this period. Symbolically, the city of Córdoba *and* the caliphal palace at Madinat az-Zahra *and* Almanzor's at Madinat az-Zahira were all sacked in the course of the years 1009–13. The last of a succession of short-lived, incompetent and powerless caliphs, Hisham III, was sent packing in 1031. He was too insignificant to be required to sign an act of abdication, let alone to be worth executing. The caliphate of Córdoba as an institution was finished for ever.

3

✸ The Breaking of the Necklace

During the period of anarchy in the public affairs of al-Andalus between 1008 and 1031, as the centre failed to hold, Spain's centrifugal, fissile tendencies were able to develop unchecked. The poet al-Shaqundi, looking back at this process from the early thirteenth century, wrote of 'the breaking of the necklace and the scattering of its pearls'. The frail unity of al-Andalus disintegrated into a number of regional successor-states known to historians as the taifa kingdoms – the name is derived from the Arabic word *ta'ifa*, which means 'faction' or 'party'. The ruler of one of these states, 'Abd Allah of Granada, has left us a description in his remarkable book of memoirs of what happened:

> When the Amirid dynasty [i.e. Almanzor's] came to an end and the people were left without an *imam* [the use of this word recalls the divine sanction claimed by the Umayyad caliphs] every military commander rose up in his own town and entrenched himself behind the walls of his own fortress, having first secured his own position, created his own army, and amassed his own resources. These persons vied with one another for worldly power, and each sought to subdue the other.

Each taifa kingdom was typically based on a town which had previously been the capital of a province or march, such as Seville or Zaragoza, where there already existed a machinery of local administration and a degree of regional solidarity which an opportunist could exploit. Initially, in the period of maximum confusion down to about 1040 or so, there existed some three dozen of these petty principalities. But the big fish swallowed the little ones, and by the mid-century half-a-dozen larger states stood out as pre-eminent:

Seville and Granada in the south, Badajoz to the west, Toledo in the centre, Valencia on the east coast, and Zaragoza in the northeast. We are presented with a political scene in mid-eleventh century Spain, the age of the Cid's boyhood and youth, in some ways reminiscent of pre-Alexandrian Greece or Renaissance Italy or the Germany of the Enlightenment: diverse principalities in a state of constant rivalry with one another.

Looking more closely at this teeming scene, let us consider a sample of these taifa states, starting with the principality of Valencia. There were two brothers named Mubarak and Muzaffar. These were not their original names. They had been captured as children in a Christian country – possibly, though not certainly, somewhere in Eastern Europe – sold as slaves in Spain, castrated, and brought up in the religion and culture of Islam. So far, the story of countless thousands in the tenth and eleventh centuries. They became the slaves of a man named Mufaris, himself also a slave, who became chief of police at Almanzor's palace of az-Zahira. Their master's unsavoury but very powerful job seems to have introduced them – literally – to the corridors of power at the palace. We know nothing about the next stages of their career, but we may assume that they acquitted themselves well and prospered because by 1010 they were jointly in charge of the irrigation of the *huerta* – the belt of irrigated land – of Valencia; that is to say, they controlled the city's water and food supply. By a coup of whose details we know nothing they made themselves masters of Valencia and its region and ruled there jointly from 1010 until 1018. Their administration was said to be harsh. It was alleged that they exacted 120,000 *dinars* in taxation every month; a gigantic figure which is only just credible. And then Mubarak died in a riding accident. The Valencians rose against Muzaffar and killed him. They then chose, though by what procedures we do not know, a certain Labib, again a former slave, as their ruler. He had been governing Tortosa, up the coast, in about 1015–16: possibly he had organised the rising against Muzaffar. Meanwhile, there was growing up in Zaragoza a grandson of the great Almanzor. He was the son not of 'Abd al-Malik (d. 1008) but of the latter's half-brother, Almanzor's second son – by a Christian Spanish wife, incidentally – 'Abd al-Rahman, who was killed in the violence at Córdoba in 1009. Born in 1007 and thus only two at the time of his father's death, the child 'Abd al-'Aziz was taken for safekeeping to distant Zaragoza where he was brought up. During and as a result of the collapse of Almanzor's dynasty, a number of its prominent slaves and servants gravitated to Valencia as refugees. In 1022 they approached 'Abd al-'Aziz secretly and offered him the headship of the principality. The young man, then aged only about fifteen, accepted. With Zaragozan help a coup was staged and Labib displaced. 'Abd al-'Aziz reigned prosperously over Valencia for nearly forty years. We shall meet him again.

In the second place consider the taifa principality of Granada. This is a misnomer, for at its inception the city of Granada did not exist. The capital of the province was Elvira, some six miles away to the north-west, in the flat lands that form the *vega* or cultivated plain that skirts the rock which is the nucleus of present-day Granada. The *vega* of Elvira was much fought over in the disturbances of the early eleventh century; a land without government, awaiting a protector. The opportunity was seized by one of Almanzor's generals, a Berber named Zawi, who took over the province in about 1013: he claimed, as those who achieve power through *pronunciamiento* usually do, that he had acted at the Elvirans' request. Zawi prudently moved the seat of his power to a more defensible site, and Granada began to arise on its mountain. Shaky though his position was at first, Zawi founded a dynasty that ruled in Granada for nearly eighty years. Its last king, 'Abd Allah, the great-great-grandson of Zawi's brother, composed the memoirs already alluded to which are the principal source of information about the family. Of 'Abd Allah, and the unhappy circumstances in which he composed his memoirs, we shall have more to say later.

The taifa of Zaragoza presents a different experience again. The city was, it will be recalled, capital of the upper march under the rule of the Umayyad caliphs of Córdoba. Since the late ninth century it had been governed by a family known as the Tujibids in nominal subjection to Córdoba but for much of the time in effective independence. In the early eleventh century the family simply stayed on as local rulers after the removal from the scene of the last shreds of central authority. In 1039 a rival local family, the Banu Hud or Hudids, whose power seems to have focused upon the Tudela area, staged a coup. The Tujibids were displaced and a new ruler, Sulayman ibn Hud, ruled in his turn. The Hudid dynasty reigned at Zaragoza until 1110. The Cid's dealings with its members were to be close.

These three different leadership transfers – the bureaucrats who organised a takeover, the general who posed as a protector, the family of local bosses who stayed on – do not exhaust the ways in which the taifa principalities emerged, but they are fairly representative. What these three examples also show is how vulnerable individual rulers were. And not just individual rulers, but frequently their kingdoms too. Take the case of Denia, to the south of Valencia. Here a kingdom was set up in about 1012 by a certain Mujahid, formerly a slave in the service of Almanzor. His authority embraced the Balearic Islands and his rule seems largely to have been based on sea power: in 1015–16, for example, he launched a daring though ultimately unsuccessful raid on Sardinia. He reigned over Denia for thirty years and passed his kingdom on to his son Ali who reigned for another thirty. Denia looked secure, but it was suddenly swallowed up by the Hudid ruler of Zaragoza in 1076. Or consider the case of Seville, whose rulers absorbed successively the taifas of Mértola, Huelva, Niebla, the Algarve, Algeciras, Silves, Morón, Ronda, Arcos, Carmona, Segura, Córdoba and Murcia, to become by the 1070s the most extensive and powerful of all the taifa kingdoms.

As against this, there were some taifa states and dynasties which survived unmolested by their neighbours. Two examples are the principalities based on Alpuente and Albarracín, respectively about forty and about eighty miles to the north-west of Valencia, among the mountains which divide the Ebro valley from central Spain in the modern province of Teruel. In Alpuente a locally prominent family, the Banu Qasim, took power in 1009–10 and held on to it for nearly a century; likewise the Banu Razin who have given their name to Albarracín. These two little states are chiefly notable for the longevity of their rulers: 'Abd Allah II of Alpuente ruled from 1043 until 1106 and Abu Marwan governed Albarracín from 1044 until 1103. They were both men who, already well-stricken in years, would find themselves recipients of the unwelcome attentions of the Cid: but both survived him.

Alpuente and Albarracín maintained their independence, perhaps, because they were not attractive to predators. Then as now, the wild country where they lay can have been neither populous nor rich. But in this they were unusual. Generally speaking the taifa kingdoms were rich. Though the economic life of al-Andalus must have suffered during the disturbances of the years between 1009 and 1031, there are signs that recovery was swift. The taifa rulers were the heirs to the wealth of al-Andalus under the caliphate. One among many signs of considerable spending power may be seen in the public works undertaken during this period. At Valencia 'Abd al-'Aziz built walls round the city and had a stone bridge constructed over the River Turia. At Granada the Zirid dynasty carried out similar public works. Many other examples could be quoted.

The wealth of the taifa kings enabled them to indulge the activity for which they are best remembered, the patronage of literature, learning and art. Of course, other factors alongside wealth were influential in this context. Patronage was a traditional princely activity, shedding lustre on the patron and his court. Competition grew up between courts: which prince could attract the most gifted poets or the most learned scholars, commission the most lavish palace, lay out the most elegant gardens? We should also reckon with the pressure of the distant past. Ibn Ghalib of Córdoba (d. 1044) wrote a work called 'Contentment of the soul in the contemplation of the ancient remains found in al-Andalus'. Contentment for the antiquarian perhaps, but not necessarily for the ruler. Near Seville there still stood the fourth largest amphitheatre of the Roman world. (It was destroyed by the corporation of Seville in the 1730s to furnish stone for the embankment of the River Guadalquivir.) By what monuments was an eleventh-century ruler to be remembered? There was also the pressure of a more recent past. 'Abd al-Rahman III's palace outside Córdoba might have been razed to the ground, but everyone still remembered its splendour. Emulation of the past was a spur to princely patronage in the eleventh century. There is a sense too in which the passing of the caliphate released provincial energies. Cultural as well as political life had been centralised in the tenth century. In the eleventh, the removal of that heavy hand which had sought to direct artistic endeavour towards Córdoba released a surge of creative energy in the provinces. By a happy chance the conditions were propitious for a flowering of the arts in Spanish Islam such as had never occurred before and was never to occur again.

Not a great deal has survived the assaults of fashion and neglect over the nine centuries that separate us from that golden age: enough, however, to suggest how dazzling it must have been. What survives is made up of some architectural fragments, decorative sculpture in marble or wood, textiles, manuscripts, metalwork, glass, ceramics and ivory carvings. The latter in particular were (and are) justly prized. Consider for example the casket illustrated in Plate 1. It is of wood decorated with panels of ivory – probably East African ivory – carved in open work with friezes of foliage, birds and animals. The inscription at the lower edge of the lid reads in translation:

In the name of God, the Merciful, the Compassionate. Perpetual blessing, complete favour, enduring health, ample felicity, glory and prosperity, benefits and excellence, fulfilment of hopes to its owner, may God prolong his life. One of the things made in the city of Cuenca by order of the chamberlain Husam al-Dawla Abu Muhammad Isma'il ibn al-Ma'mun . . . in the year 441 [1049–50 AD]. The work of 'Abd al-Rahman ibn Zayyan.

Cuenca possessed an important school of ivory carving during this period. The chamberlain who commissioned this piece was a member of the ruling family of the taifa of Toledo: his father al-Ma'mun ruled at Toledo from 1044 to 1075. The casket is now in the Museo Arqueológico Nacional in Madrid. At an earlier date it had belonged to the cathedral church of Palencia in Old Castile. It is likely that it had made its way there, directly or indirectly, as plunder or tribute. We do not know when the bishopric of Palencia had acquired it, but it is a reasonable guess that it had come into the hands of King Alfonso VI of León-Castile (1065–1109) about the time of his conquest of Toledo in 1085 and had been given by him to the bishop of Palencia. Such caskets were valued in Christian ecclesiastical circles as storage places for precious objects, especially relics. Sometimes they were 'Christianised'. The panel from a casket illustrated in Plate 2 has received this treatment: the original panel can be attributed on stylistic grounds to the same workshop of Ibn Zayyan of Cuenca, c.1050; at some much later date a Christian angel was set into it, ruining its elegant design but making a confessional statement. Not all such containers were rectangular in shape. In the cathedral treasury of Narbonne, for example, there survives a little round casket of about the shape and size of a small tea-caddy, also the product of the Cuenca school of carvers as its Arabic inscription testifies. There are similar ones in the cathedrals of Pamplona in Navarre and Braga in northern Portugal, both of them originally made for 'Abd al-Malik (d. 1008), the son of Almanzor. Caskets survive in other media: of wood plated in silver, for instance, like the casket commissioned by the caliph al-Hakam II for his son Hisham between 965 and 976, which is now in the cathedral of Gerona in Catalonia.

Textiles have not withstood time so well. One fragment of silk that has is illustrated in Plate 3. The design in the larger roundels shows harpies on the backs of lions; the circular frames feature men attacked by griffins. The smaller medallions bear inscriptions reading 'This is one of the things made in Baghdad'. But it is a lie. The design and weave are of characteristically Andalusian rather than Persian type, and the spelling of the inscription is peculiar to the Western Mediterranean sector of the Islamic world. The piece was almost certainly woven in southern Spain. The inscription 'made in Baghdad' was designed to mislead, presumably to deceive a customer; just so can 'workshop of Chippendale' or 'attrib. Hepplewhite' work wonders for the price of an eighteenth-century desk or chair. This piece of silk is now in the Museum of Fine Arts in Boston, but once it belonged to a Castilian prelate, Pedro, bishop of Osma, who died in 1109. After his death he was venerated as a saint, and the vestment of which this piece of silk was once a part was deposited in his tomb in the cathedral of Burgo de Osma.

Some of the taifa rulers were themselves scholars. Al-Muzaffar, king of Badajoz from 1045 to 1068, is said to have compiled a work in fifty volumes, now lost, which 'treated of universal knowledge, being a repository of art, science, history, poetry, literature in general, proverbs, biographical information and so forth'. Al-Mu'tamin of Zaragoza (d.1085) composed a work on mathematics. Mujahid assembled at Denia a team of scholars who devoted themselves to the textual study of the Koran. Al-Ma'mun of Toledo – the father of the chamberlain who commissioned the casket discussed above – was a patron of scientific studies who commissioned the celebrated astronomer al-Zarqal to construct a clypsedra or water-clock which became one of the wonders of al-Andalus. It was situated in a building on the banks of the Tagus outside Toledo and consisted of two large basins which filled and emptied themselves of water every lunar month in time with the waxing and waning of the moon. It is said that some fifty years after the Christian re-conquest of Toledo by Alfonso VI in 1085 his grandson Alfonso VII of León-Castile, curious to learn how it worked, had it dismantled; but his artificers were unable to reconstruct it, so one of the great technical triumphs of Islamic science was lost. The story may or may not be true: it has at any rate a certain symbolic value. We owe the tale to the historian al-Maqqari whose nineteenth-century translator, Gayangos, claimed to have seen the remains of the basins in 1836.

Poetry was cultivated avidly in the taifa kingdoms. Here is an anecdote which vividly re-creates this intensity. Abu Amru ibn Salim of Málaga, leaving his house one day to go to the mosque, fell in with his friend Abu Muhammad. Ibn Salim continues:

I sat by his side; and on his entreating me to recite him some verses, I repeated the following of an Andalusian poet:

> They stole from morning the colour
> of her cheeks; they borrowed
> from the arak tree its slender
> and delicate form.
> Innumerable jewels shone brightly
> on their bosoms; and they took
> the glittering stars for a
> necklace.
> Not content with the slenderness of
> the spear and the agility of the
> antelope, they still took from
> the latter the tender eye and
> the undulating cheekbone.

No sooner had I uttered the last syllable of the latter verse, than to my great astonishment I heard my friend give a piercing shriek, and I saw him fall senseless to the ground. Having run to his assistance I found him in a swoon, and it was not until an hour had elapsed that he again came to his senses: when he said to me, 'Excuse me, my son, for there are two things in this world against which I have no strength, namely the sight of a pretty face and the hearing of good poetry.'

Panegyric poetry, naturally enough, was much to the taste of the taifa rulers. This is how al-Ma'mun of Toledo was hailed by the poet Ibn Arfa' Ra'suh:

Hold fast to the love and drink to
the health of the Possessor of
Dual Glory [i.e. al-Ma'mun]
Who supports the lands of the East
and the West,
And who gives succour to believers, a
descendant of Ya'rub,
The lofty king, who humbles sultans,
Who leads cavalcades, and is the lion
of the battlefields,
He is a king whose heart is braver
than the lion's,
Just as his finger is more generous
than the rain clouds.

Or again: one day al-Ma'mun was sitting drinking with some court-iers, talking of the other taifa kings and improvising verses about them, when Ibn Arfa' Ra'suh spoke up:

Stop talking about kings and sons of
kings, because
He who sails on the sea does not
yearn for rivers.
There is none as noble as al-Ma'mun
in this land;
See what you've heard about him
confirmed by the fact!
Oh you Unique, without an equal in
glory, the man
Whom your hand has favoured yearns
not for rainfall!
You arose on our sky like a sun,
hence no eye
Looked up to a star or the moon for
leadership:
You appeared to us like the *wusta*
among kings,
Hence we did not make a halt at
small-sized pearls.

A *wusta* is the big, central pearl in a necklace – with which, perhaps, the poet was rewarded.

Successful panegyric could make a poet's career. This was the good fortune, initially at least, of Ibn 'Ammar, perhaps the greatest Andalusian poet of the eleventh century. Several strands of the life and thought of the taifa period intermingle in his story. He was born near Silves, on the southern coast of what is now Portugal, in 1031. His family was undistinguished but managed to give him a good education. As a young man he drifted eastwards, attracted to the court of al-Mu'tadid, the ruler of Seville (1041–2 to 1068–9). Under al-Mu'tadid's rule the taifa of Seville was just embarking on that programme of expansion which would bring it to pre-eminence among the taifa states. In 1053 he had invited the rulers of Ronda, Arcos, Morón and Jérez to Seville on a peaceful diplomatic visit. While they and their companions were taking a bath before attending the reception in their honour, al-Mu'tadid had every aperture of the bath-house stopped up, so that they suffocated inside it. He hung their heads on the wall of his citadel as trophies. Himself an accomplished poet, he celebrated this triumph in verse:

> Now I conquered you, O Ronda,
> So you are my kingdom's necklace . . .
> I shall make an end of my foes,
> If my time does not end early,
> Through me their error will perish,
> So Right Guidance shall grow stronger!
> How many rivals did I kill,
> Steadily, one after another:
> Of their heads I made a garland
> Adorning the edge of the side wall!

In the wake of these events Ibn 'Ammar reached the court of al-Mu'tadid, to whom he addressed a long panegyric. It is the finest such composition of the period. Here is a translation into modern verse:

> Pass round the bowl; the breeze of morn
> Is blowing free and wide,
> The nightbound stars, now travel-worn,
> Have tossed their reins aside.
>
> Behold how yonder camphor, our
> Great gift from rising dawn,
> Gleams, as from heaven night her dower
> Of amber has withdrawn.
>
> The meadow, that fair maiden, wears
> Her robe of every hue
> The flowers, and a necklace bears
> Bejewelled all with dew.
>
> The roses, like some modest girl's
> Shy blushes, blossom red;
> The tossing myrtles hang like curls
> About her lovely head.
>
> Against the garden's gown of green
> A silver wrist doth gleam:
> In virgin purity serene
> Flows on the silent stream.

Now as the breeze its surface bright
Disturbs, there seems to glow
My monarch's sword, that puts to flight
The legions of his foe.

Abbad's great son, whose bounteous hand
Alleviates all lack,
Keeps ever green the grateful land
Although the skies be black.

And he bestows, for virtue's meed,
A pure and lovely maid,
A horse of mettle and of breed,
A gem-encrusted blade.

A monarch he who, when the kings
Of earth come down to drink,
They dare not venture to the springs
Until he leaves their brink.

More fresh than dew his bounty lies
Upon the hearts of those
Who weary, sweeter to the eyes
Than slumberful repose.

He strikes the flint of ardent fame;
The fire of battle he
Quits never, save to light the flame
Of hospitality.

A king as virtuous as wise,
As charming as discreet,
A garden lovely to the eyes
With fruitfulness replete.

The Kauthar of his gifts to me
Is boundless; I know well
That with his liberality
In Paradise I dwell.

Since fruitful branches most delight,
As you observe most clear,
Their monarchs' heads you featly smite
To fructify your spear.

Observing beauty evermore
In scarlet robes arrayed
Most sweetly, with their champions' gore
Your breastplate you have sprayed.

Accept this tribute, if it please,
A garden drenched with showers
And visited by morning's breeze,
Until it bore these flowers.

> I wove for their embroidery
> Your fame, a golden thread,
> And o'er my verses cunningly
> Your fragrant praise I shed.
>
> Who dares contend with me thereon,
> Since I your name have brought
> For aloes-wood, to lay upon
> The brazier of my thought?

(The Kauthar, which occurs in the thirteenth stanza, is one of the streams of Paradise.)

This poem made Ibn 'Ammar's fortune. He was taken on as one of al-Mu'tadid's salaried court poets. He became the close friend of the crown prince Muhammad – later to be known as al-Mu'tamid, ruler of Seville from 1068–9 until 1091. When Muhammad was sent by his father to learn the skills of rulership by governing Silves, Ibn 'Ammar was sent with him as an adviser. A distinguished career seemed to be opening up before him. But then disaster struck. In 1058 al-Mu'tadid sent him into exile. By what slight or misdemeanour he had offended we do not know for certain: it was rumoured that he and the crown prince had had an affair, and references in some of Ibn 'Ammar's poetry seem to confirm this. For whatever reason, he had to depart from the taifa of Seville. After short stays at the courts of Almería and Albarracín he finally settled at the Hudid court at Zaragoza. He remained in exile there for about ten years, from time to time addressing self-piteous verses to al-Mu'tadid in an attempt to soften his heart:

> Rainclouds are weeping – over me,
>   indeed!
> Turtledoves are wailing – over me,
>   indeed!
> For none but me the stars are clothed
>   in mourning,
> For none but me they stand bewailing
>   the dead!

His appeals did not succeed. But when al-Mu'tadid died in 1068–9 and was succeeded by al-Mu'tamid, Ibn 'Ammar was recalled to Seville and resumed his career as courtier and adviser. All was calm for a further ten years. But in 1078 a much more serious rift occurred between the poet and the royal family of Seville. Ibn 'Ammar kept on urging his master to attack the taifa state of Murcia in the southeast of Spain. It was widely believed, and probably correctly, that he wanted to get hold of Murcia for himself and rule there as an independent prince. In 1078 he was sent against Murcia at the head of an army. In order to increase his strength for the campaign, Ibn

'Ammar engaged the military assistance of the count of Barcelona against the payment of 10,000 *dinars*: without the knowledge of al-Mu'tamid he sent the latter's eldest son al-Rashid as hostage to Barcelona as security for the payment. Eventually Murcia fell. Its ruler, Muhammad ibn Tahir, fled to the court of Valencia where he found asylum with Abu Bakr, the son of 'Abd al-'Aziz. Meanwhile, in Murcia, Ibn 'Ammar

> behaved atrociously: he rode roughshod over the people, broke the laws of God, and became an inveterate wine-bibber so that in the end he brought upon himself the odium of its inhabitants. He managed a show of obedience to al-Mu'tamid though in fact he was in revolt. It was no secret that he ran al-Mu'tamid down and lampooned him for things of which he was innocent, in the way that villains and rascals do.

The words are those of a very hostile witness who had earlier suffered at the hands of Ibn 'Ammar, 'Abd Allah of Granada: but the truth of the accusations can be confirmed from other sources. In short, Ibn 'Ammar had first endangered the life of his prince's son and heir and then gone on to show alarming signs of insubordination by acting to all intents and purposes as an independent ruler. Al-Mu'tamid, helpless back in Seville, responded by directing his own very considerable poetic talents into the composition of a lampoon which ridiculed Ibn 'Ammar's family origins. Stung by this, Ibn 'Ammar riposted with an even more savage reply in which he mocked the prince, his favourite wife and their sons. Abu Bakr of Valencia contrived to get a copy of this written in Ibn 'Ammar's own hand and forwarded it to al-Mu'tamid. This was an insult which the ruler of Seville could never forgive. At about the same time Ibn 'Ammar was betrayed in Murcia by one of his local allies and forced to flee. Valencia being closed to him and a return to the taifa state of Seville out of the question, he headed north to Toledo, tried to find refuge at the court of Alfonso VI of León-Castile and then sheered off to Zaragoza where he spent the years 1081–4 in the service of the Hudids. (In the course of these years he cannot have failed to meet another exile at the court of Zaragoza, the Castilian Rodrigo Díaz.) In 1084 he was captured by a trick and sold by his captors to al-Mu'tamid. He entered a plea for clemency in a last and characteristically accomplished poem to his old friend, but it did him no good. Al-Mu'tamid in person killed Ibn 'Ammar – with an axe which had been a present from King Alfonso VI – in the winter of 1084–5.

We know a great deal about Ibn 'Ammar partly because he features prominently in the memoirs of his enemy 'Abd Allah, and partly because his celebrity as a poet ensured him a place in the writings of other chroniclers and compilers of biographical dictionaries. His career is instructive. It shows how highly poetic talent was valued in the taifa principalities and what rewards a skilled practitioner might command. His travels in exile show how easy movement was from court to court and across the religious frontier. He hired troops from Alfonso VI as well as from the count of Barcelona: money could buy Christian mercenary soldiers for campaigning in al-Andalus. The upheavals in his career conjure up the factions, rivalries, rebellions and betrayals which characterise the political history of this period more markedly than that of most others. His acquisition of Murcia shows what opportunities might open up to the ambitious, unscrupulous adventurer. In certain respects, indeed, Ibn 'Ammar's career presents suggestive parallels to that of El Cid.

'He broke the laws of God and became an inveterate wine-bibber.' In this Ibn 'Ammar was far from unique. There is abundant evidence that a good deal of drinking went on in eleventh-century al-Andalus, contrary to Koranic precept. Much of the poetry of the period celebrates the enjoyment of wine:

> The wine has coloured his cheeks,
>   like a rising sun shining upon
>   his face:
> The West is his mouth, the East is
>   the lively cup-bearer's hand.
> When the sun had set behind his mouth
>   it left upon his cheeks a rosy
>   twilight.

It may be objected that poetry is not necessarily good evidence for practice. But more prosaic sources may be cited. 'Abd Allah was remarkably candid in his memoirs about the drinking habits of his father and grandfather. An intriguing sidelight on the Mozarabic community is cast by the revelation that in Toledo well-to-do Muslims were accustomed to drop into Christian monasteries to take a glass of wine. Perhaps this practice lies behind the confession of the poet Ibn Shuhayd that he had once spent a night in a Christian church in Córdoba where he had drunk wine. Monasteries thus appear to have provided the same sort of access to alcohol for the laxer sort of Muslim that westernised hotels do in some Islamic countries today. Other forbidden indulgences were provided for Muslims by Christians. The distinguished jurist al-Turtushi (1059–1126) wrote a pamphlet entitled 'Concerning the prohibition of the cheese of the *Rum*' (the last word, literally meaning 'Romans', being a normal term among writers in Arabic for 'Europeans' or 'Christians'). Evidently 'Christian cheese' was attractive to Muslim palates. What is not clear is how it infringed Islamic dietary requirements.

There may even have been a degree of religious syncretism in eleventh-century al-Andalus. It is surprising to find that the use of the Christian calendar was widespread among the Andalusian Muslims and that some of them at any rate observed Christian religious festivals. One instance of their veneration of a Christian shrine has even come to light.

Plausible explanations and justifications for these tendencies may be found. For example, the Christian calendar is suitable for the marking of many economic operations throughout the year, since it is tied to the seasons in a way that the Muslim lunar calendar with its 354-day year is not. Additionally, there is a body of evidence which suggests that Islamic observance was somewhat easy-going in eleventh-century Spain. Two further practices which might scandalise the orthodox may be cited. One was the belief in astrology. 'Abd Allah of Granada believed that Almanzor owed his success to the ascendancy of Pisces and Sagittarius at his birth. He recorded that astrologers had correctly foretold the death of a ruler of Toledo in 1075. He read a prediction by a celebrated astrologer who had died in 1055 that the taifa kingdom of Denia would fall in 1076: it did. He put it on record that al-Mu'tamin of Zaragoza 'was a scholar who had studied books of magic as well as horoscopes' and therefore could foretell the day of his death. He saw peril to the rulers of Seville in Ibn 'Ammar's operations at Murcia because of an astrologer's predictions. The concluding chapter of his memoirs included a lengthy discussion of his own horoscope. It also contained an even lengthier defence of astrology. Its tone, at once guarded and jaunty, is well conveyed in this extract:

> Some astrologers have said: 'Why should we be charged with heresy? For we have not denied the existence of the Creator and have simply talked about created things, each of which has been described in so far as it is within the grasp of man's knowledge to describe them. It is just the same as describing a man or trees or a mountain.' A sage is said to have been seen with the Koran on his right-hand side and an astrolabe on his left-hand side. On being asked why he had seen it necessary to combine the two, the sage replied: 'In the Koran I read God's words, while in the astrolabe I reflect on God's creation. Astrology is a form of worship.'

Not all agreed with 'Abd Allah.

> I strongly advise you to shun astrological prognostications, for he who believes in them is outside the fold of the Faith and is just another heretic.

Strong words: they were uttered by a famous Andalusi *faqih* of this period, Abu'l Walid al-Baji, in a collection of prescriptions for the guidance of his sons. The *faqihs* were the doctors of Islamic law, guardians of orthodoxy and right observance. They were looked up to with respect by the community at large and their opinions on such issues as this were heeded attentively. It would be a foolish ruler who alienated them.

The other instance is of a very different type. It concerns the position of the Jews in Andalusi society, and specifically their role in the government of the taifa states. Jews who rose to high positions of trust in the service of the taifa rulers can be traced at Almería, Granada, Seville and Zaragoza; also, with less certainty, at Albarracín and Valencia: so the phenomenon was not uncommon. The most remarkable career was that of Samuel Ha-Nagid of Granada. Born at Córdoba in 993, he left the city at about the age of twenty on account of its sack, which seems to have included attacks on the Jewish community there. After a spell in Málaga he settled in Granada where he entered the service of Zawi's nephew Habus. On the death of the latter in 1038 Samuel was instrumental in securing the succession for his son Badis – 'Abd Allah's grandfather – against the claims of a brother. From then until his death Samuel was, in effect, the first minister of the taifa state of Granada. He regularly commanded Granadan armies in the field. (It has been pointed out that 'he was probably the first Jew [apart from the Khazars] to command troops for nearly a thousand years'.) He was also a scholar who corresponded with other Jewish learned men in the Mediterranean world, and an accomplished poet. After his death in 1056 his son Joseph succeeded to his father's position at the Granadan court.

It was a violation of Islamic law for a Jew to exercise civil or military authority over Muslims. Samuel Ha-Nagid had been attacked on these grounds by Ibn Hazm of Córdoba, the greatest Muslim scholar of his day. Samuel's son was attacked in a savage poem by the Granadan *faqih* Abu Ishaq, addressed to Badis, urging him to kill his minister and put an end to Jewish influence in the affairs of Granada. In 1066 there were anti-Jewish riots in Granada, perhaps stirred up at least in part by Abu Ishaq's poem: Joseph was murdered, and large numbers of his fellow Jews with him. Matters did not take such a violent course elsewhere, so far as we know. However, contemporary opinion seems to have been critical of the taifa rulers for their employment of the Jews in their service. It was further evidence of their slackness in religious observance.

It would one day matter very much to the taifa rulers if accusations of irreligious behaviour were laid against them by their subjects before one particularly exacting and puritanical tribunal – the Islamic fundamentalist sect known as the Almoravide movement, which grew up in Morocco during the middle years of the eleventh century. The punishment meted out to certain taifa rulers by the Almoravides, as we shall see, was final. But before that they had to contend with other enemies to their north – the Christian principalities of Spain.

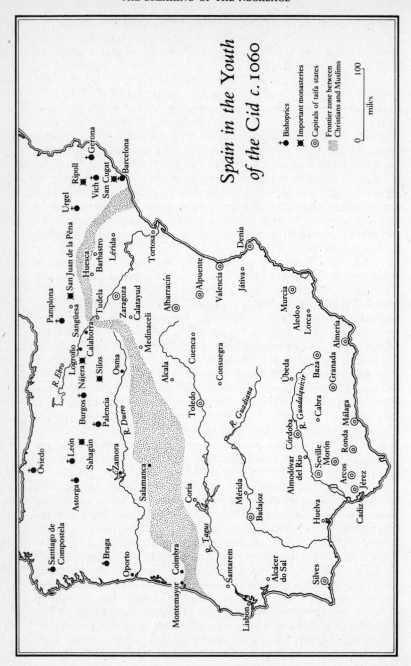

Spain in the Youth
of the Cid c. 1060

† Bishoprics
✠ Important monasteries
⊙ Capitals of taifa states
Frontier zone between
Christians and Muslims

0   100
└────────┘
miles

4

✳ The Heirs of the Visigoths

The Arab and Berber invaders of the eighth century extinguished
the Visigothic monarchy but they did not destroy every nucleus of
native resistance. The early history of the small Christian principalities that emerged in the north of the Iberian peninsula is ill-
documented. The three zones where these states originated, a
western, a central and an eastern, differed markedly, and far-reaching consequences for the future history of Spain were to follow
from this diversity. The tiny polities that grew up in the eighth and
ninth centuries would develop in time into the larger and more
sophisticated kingdoms of the eleventh, which constituted the political landscape of Christian Spain during the Cid's lifetime.

In the north-west the invaders had reached the Bay of Biscay and
installed a governor at Gijón, the port of Oviedo in the Asturias.
That damp and foggy coastline cannot have been congenial to them
or to their camels; furthermore, between the mountains of the Cordillera Cantábrica and the sea lay broken, wooded countryside in
which resistance movements could flourish. In 718 (or possibly 722)
a battle was fought at Covadonga, east of Oviedo at the foot of the
Picos de Europa, which tower there to over 8500 feet. A party of
rebels defeated and killed the governor of Gijón, and in the wake
of this reverse the invaders evacuated their northernmost province
and retired south of the Cordillera to the plain of León. The action
itself was probably a small-scale affair of no great military significance. In the course of time patriotic myth-making would transform
it: the leader of the rebels, Pelayo, would become a national hero and
his victory at Covadonga the first step in a Christian re-conquest.
But this is legend rather than history. What Pelayo's victory did
make possible was the emergence of a small Christian kingdom in

the Asturias whose rulers were able to consolidate their hold upon that region and the northern parts of Galicia to their west during the years of confusion into which al-Andalus was plunged by the Arab-Berber strife of the next few decades. The kingdom was small and insecure; its institutions were rudimentary, its economy simple, its culture unsophisticated. It was subjected to constant harassment from the amirs of Córdoba in the second half of the eighth century. However, it survived.

In the course of the ninth century its character began to change. One cause of this was probably economic. Little as we know of these matters, it seems likely that the population grew denser, that agricultural exploitation became more effective and that trade quickened. These changes must have been very gradual, so gradual as to be barely perceptible to contemporaries, but some such order of changes must have occurred as the precondition for what came next. A second cause was the immigration of Mozarabic Christians from the south. This was taking place in a trickle from the late eighth century, which became a torrent about a century later. The Mozarabs were important to the Asturian kingdom for the culture they brought with them. The nucleus of the kingdom lay in an area which had been little touched by Romano-Visigothic civilisation, but now the Mozarabs imported to it the cultural traditions of the Visigoths. They established monasteries and centres of learning where these traditions were cherished and elaborated. They encouraged the Asturian kings to shape a new image of themselves. Alfonso II (791–842) fixed his capital in the city of Oviedo, where he built a palace and churches. He introduced there the ceremonial of Gothic rule as it had once existed in Toledo. He and his successors may, like the Gothic kings, have held church councils in his capital; they certainly, like the Gothic kings, collected relics of the saints who might act as their protectors and intercessors with God. Alfonso III (866–910) sponsored the composition of chronicles which laid stress on the theme of continuity from the Visigothic through to the Asturian kingdom.

A third cause, or perhaps just a symptom, of change lay in the contacts which were made between the Asturian kingdom and other parts of Western Christendom. Alfonso II had had diplomatic relations with the Frankish kingdom under Charlemagne (768–814) and his son Louis the Pious (814–40). The intellectual preoccupations of the court of Alfonso III were akin to those of the Frankish court under Louis's son Charles the Bald (840–77), and it was presumably from the Frankish rulers that Alfonso III derived notions about *imperium* – 'empire' or 'imperial rule' – which were to lead to the adoption of the title of emperor claimed by some of his tenth- and eleventh-century successors.

During this period the kingdom gradually expanded to the south of the Cordillera Cantábrica. The shift of its centre of gravity on to the rich tablelands of the Spanish *meseta* was recognised by the movement of the capital from Oviedo to León early in the tenth century. From then onwards its rulers were styled kings of León. And there, for the moment, we may leave them.

The Basque country was the central zone where a principality, later to be known as the kingdom of Navarre, emerged in the eighth and ninth centuries. If the early history of the Asturian kingdom is ill-documented, that of Navarre is scarcely documented at all, and its origins are shrouded in obscurity. We start from the given fact that historically the Basques have resisted assimilation to other cultures. Their language is like no other. Its place-names, uncouth to our eyes and ears, lie thick on the ground of their homeland: Orzanzurieta and Echalecu, Urdax and Egozcue, Esterencuby, Louhossoa and Astigarraga. The impact of Roman culture on the region had not been negligible, but it had left a fainter impress on the Basque lands than it did on eastern or southern Spain. Pamplona was a Roman town astride the road that led out of Spain towards Bordeaux, but it was a place of modest size and little importance. Hispano-Roman landed families built their country houses in the valleys of the upper Ebro and its tributaries to the south of Pamplona: and some of them must have been very grand, judging by the superlative mosaics from Arróniz now to be seen in the Museo Arqueológico Nacional in Madrid. But such landowners were not attracted by the Pyrenean region. Christianity made slow headway among the Basques. There was a bishopric at Calahorra by about 400, and there might have been one at Pamplona too by the fifth century, though it is not reliably attested until 589. The great Aquitanian missionary-bishop Amandus preached to the Basques in the middle years of the seventh century, but with little if any success. Parts of the Basque provinces may still have been pagan as late as the eleventh century.

During the sixth and seventh centuries the Basque tribes were expanding southward into Spain and northward into the south-west corner of Gaul (to which they have given their name, Vasconia, Gascony). We have already seen that at the time of the Arabo-Berber invasion the last of the Visigothic kings was on campaign in the north, trying to contain them. This preoccupation was inherited by his Islamic successors. In 755 an Arab army sent against the Basques was defeated. Perhaps this was some sort of Navarrese Covadonga. We shall never know, for practically nothing is known of its context.

Preoccupation with the Basque problem was shared by the kings of the Franks. During the middle years of the eighth century the Carolingian rulers of Francia, Charles Martel and Pippin III, were pushing down into Aquitaine in an attempt to give some substance to Frankish claims to dominion there. Necessarily, they came up against the Basques. The most famous encounter occurred in 778 when Pippin's son Charles – later to be known as Charlemagne – was returning from a military campaign in Spain. The rearguard of his army, commanded by Roland, was ambushed by the Basques in the pass of Roncesvalles and annihilated. Though a defeat of little military significance, it was long remembered and gathered to itself accretions of legend which eventually found literary form in the grandest of Old French epics, the *Chanson de Roland*. In 781 Charles placed his son Louis in charge of a sub-kingdom in Aquitaine. Louis attempted to set up marcher counties in the western Pyrenees. One of these was in the valley of the River Aragón; another could have been based at Pamplona which the Franks captured in 806. However, it proved unsurprisingly difficult to get the Basques to co-operate and after a Frankish defeat at a second battle of Roncesvalles in 824 direct Carolingian intervention came to an end. (Louis and his successors had in any case more pressing cares back in the northern half of their kingdom.) In these circumstances a small independent kingdom based upon Pamplona emerged during the second quarter of the ninth century under a native chieftain named Iñigo Arista. His descendants ruled the kingdom of Pamplona and exercised at the least an intermittent suzerainty over the county of Aragon until the early tenth century. They were then supplanted by another local dynasty whose first representative was a king named Sancho Garcés I (i.e. Sancho son of García) who ruled from 905 to 925. We shall hear more of him shortly.

Frankish expansion southwards had brought the Carolingians to the eastern end of the Pyrenees as well as the western: a region of strikingly different character. Here were the rich coastal lands which stretched from the Spanish Levante to the delta of the Rhône – the civilised Mediterranean world. Greeks and Phoenicians had founded trading settlements here as early as the sixth century BC. The Romans had fostered the growth of cities such as Tarragona, Barcelona and Narbonne; villas had sprung up in the countryside, Latin had displaced indigenous languages, and Christianity had arrived perhaps within a century after the death of Jesus. It seems probable that the Arabs and Berbers had wrought less damage here than they had further south. Louis of Aquitaine conquered Barcelona in 801 and the area between the city and the Pyrenees was divided up into counties, the standard unit of local administration in the Frankish empire: Barcelona, Gerona and Empuries on the Mediterranean seaboard; then Cardona, Vich and Besalu; Cerdanya and Urgel, which bordered on present-day Andorra; then further inland Pallars, and beyond that, marching with Aragon, Ribagorza. As the Frankish empire disintegrated and the Carolingians lost direct control of the area, the Catalan counties drifted into a *de facto* independence. Among the many families of local aristocrats who emerged as petty dynasts, one was very gradually to make itself supreme. Its first prominent member was a man unforgettably named Wifred the Hairy, who by the time of his death in 898 had concentrated in his hands the counties of Barcelona, Gerona and Vich. His descendants would slowly extend their dominion over all of what the Franks had called the Spanish March, until the count of Barcelona governed the whole of Catalonia. But these days lay far ahead of Wifred's lifetime. He and his heirs continued for at least another century to think of themselves as being formally a part of the Frankish kingdom. They dated their official documents by the regnal years of Frankish kings. The monastic houses of Catalonia continued to seek confirmation of their title-deeds from Frankish rulers long after the day when those rulers had lost all effective power over Catalonia. Bizarre this may seem, but it made sound cultural sense. Then, as at other epochs in her history, Catalonia's contacts with the Mediterranean world of France and Italy were stronger than those with the Iberian hinterland.

By the early part of the tenth century, approaching the time of El Cid, there had thus grown up three embryonic Christian principalities, or groups of principalities, in northern Spain. To their diversity of economic and social organisation imposed by landscape and climate were added differences in historical antecedents, legal institutions and cultural loyalties. What they shared was a common enemy across the religious frontier.

To write of a 'common enemy' and a 'religious frontier' is to risk misrepresenting the reality of the ninth, tenth and eleventh centuries. It is therefore important to stress that the frontier was not a line but a zone or no-man's-land with constantly fluctuating edges. Some scholars have argued that in the central and western parts of the Peninsula the zone was in the most literal sense a no-man's-land; that along, roughly speaking, the valley of the River Duero and its tributaries, systematic depopulation had occurred in the eighth century so that the region was devoid of permanent human settlement until the conquest and resettlement of the area by the kings of León between c.850 and c.950. (It should be emphasised that a similar case has not been argued for the Ebro valley in the east where it is acknowledged that settlement was maintained throughout this period.) The argument has been pressed too far, and on too slender evidence. The valley of the Duero can never have been completely depopulated. However, it is likely that the population shrank drastically, especially in the towns such as Oporto, Zamora, or Salamanca; and that with the collapse of urban life the apparatus of orderly administration and defence gradually withered and died. The frontier zone in the tenth century probably was to a great degree a land without civil government. In 1012 the monks of the Catalan monastery of San Cugat could describe their nearby frontier region as a place of 'great fear and trembling . . . a desert place browsed only by wild asses and deer and other animals' where 'evil men' were to be found; and it is likely that the Navarrese and Leónese thought of their frontier in much the same way.

'Bad men' skulking in the no-man's-land of the frontier were not the only persons to be encountered there. The frontier zone was permeable, penetrable. All sorts and conditions of people travelled in it during the tenth and eleventh centuries. There were merchants bringing slaves from the north or textiles from the south; Mozarabic Christians migrating to new homes on the plain of León; diplomats such as John of Gorze; transhumant shepherds passing seasonally to and fro with their flocks; pilgrims to Christian shrines such as the tomb of St James at Compostela; criminals on the run; scholars on their way to Córdoba in quest of the learning of the Orient. However, the people who traversed it most regularly were soldiers: Muslim armies raiding the Christian principalities, and Christian armies defending themselves and retaliating.

This image of Christian and Muslim locked in conflict is cherished by traditional Catholic and nationalist schools of Spanish historians. But it is misleading. The reality was more complicated. To grasp it we could do worse than look at what actually occurred on one of these campaigns. 'Abd al-Rahman's expedition against Pamplona in 924 is an apposite example. Our principal source of information is the account transmitted by the eleventh-century historian Ibn Hayyan (d. 1076). Although he was writing a century and a half after the events described he had access to strictly contemporary sources among which the most significant, in all likelihood, was an official newsletter composed for public circulation immediately after the campaign; so his witness has authority. There is also a panegyric poem celebrating 'Abd al-Rahman's campaigns by the contemporary court poet Ibn 'Abd Rabbihi.

In the years immediately preceding 924 there had been much fighting in the upper Rioja region. Sancho Garcés of Pamplona had managed to wrest Calahorra and a number of lesser places from Muslim control, and in 923 he had seized the castle of Viguera, about ten miles south of Logroño. The campaign of 924 was undertaken by way of reprisal.

'Abd al-Rahman and his army left Córdoba on 24 April. He made his way up the Levante coast through Murcia, Valencia and Tortosa, putting down rebellions, and then struck up the valley of the Ebro past Zaragoza to Tudela where the Tujibids, lords of the upper march, joined him with their troops. On 10 July he left Tudela and advanced up the Ebro towards Calahorra. Sancho had evacuated the place: the Muslims demolished and fired it. They then headed north, burning crops, gathering booty, destroying fortresses and homesteads, until they reached Sangüesa on 17 July. By now they had moved away from the open country of the Ebro valley into broken, hilly scrubland where they were more vulnerable. Sangüesa was the birthplace of King Sancho and its destruction

> hurt his pride. He got together a force from wherever he might until he had assembled a certain number with which he thought that he could offer battle to the Muslims. The [Muslim] army could see heavily-armoured cavalry on the hilltops. On the night of 21 July 'Abd al-Rahman ordered the troops to be drawn up in formation and put on full alert. Early in the morning the march was resumed in this fashion, with utter trust in Allah. The army passed by those hilltops and crags, while the enemies of Allah waited an opportunity to attack the flanks or rearguard of the Muslims.
>
> While the army was in the midst of this broken country, next to a river named the Ega, a band of infidel cavalry charged down from the hills against the lightly-armed Muslim troops and there was a short skirmish. 'Abd al-Rahman ordered the men to halt and dismount, pitch his tent and prepare for combat. The Muslims fell on their enemies like ravening lions, crossing the river and hurling themselves upon them *en masse*. They dislodged them from their position and continued the attack until they had put them to flight and made them fodder for swords and spears, pursuing them towards the steep slopes of a nearby hill which the Muslims scaled with Allah's help, killing many there and strewing the ground with corpses. The cavalry continued the action along the flat ground, taking booty and every kind of livestock and equipment. They disengaged weighed down with plunder and without loss, except that Ya'qub b. Abi Jalid at-Tuzari . . . fell a martyr there, Allah granting him a happy death. Many heads of infidels were gathered, but could not be sent to Córdoba because of the danger and distance of the journey.

The action seems to have taken place between Sangüesa and the Foz (or defile) de Lumbier, through which the invaders must next have passed. They continued on their way, laying waste the country through which they passed, until they reached Pamplona on 24 July.

> Finally they got to Pamplona, the city which gives its name to the region, and they found it abandoned and deserted. 'Abd al-Rahman himself entered the town, traversed its streets, ordered all its buildings to be destroyed and the venerated church of the infidels to be demolished: everyone assisted in the task and they razed it to the ground.

The Muslims withdrew after the sack of Pamplona. They made their way back, continuing to burn and plunder, harried by Sancho's troops but successfully fighting them off. The most northerly Muslim outpost, the fortress of Valtierra, was reinforced. 'Abd al-Rahman was back in Tudela on 2 August after a round trip of some three hundred miles in twenty-four days. He reached Córdoba on 26 August.

The campaign of 924 was a punitive raid directed at Sancho Garcés in retaliation for the defeat at Viguera the year before. It did a great deal of damage but it left the frontier where it had been: the Navarrese held on to Calahorra and the upper Rioja. In other words, it was a frontier skirmish of little military significance. For Córdoba, considerations of security were paramount. The government there wanted trouble-free frontiers. Such gains as were made lay in plunder, ransoms, slaves and satisfaction, but not in land. Territorial gain was no part of the war-aims of 'Abd al-Rahman III. Thus superpowers deal characteristically with a little local difficulty on their borders. It should be noticed that the campaign was also one of internal policing, directed against the rebels in the Levante and designed to demonstrate to the marcher lords of Zaragoza, the Tujibids, who was in charge.

It has been suggested that the campaigns of Almanzor against the Christian states in the late tenth century were marked by a different tone, one of fanaticism and religious hatred. It is true that he frequently struck at specifically ecclesiastical targets: the monastery of San Cugat in 985, the Leónese monasteries of Sahagún and Eslonza in 988, the church of Santiago de Compostela in 997 or the Riojan monastery of San Millán de la Cogolla in 1002. Yet the first two-thirds of his life, before the campaigns, do not suggest that he was a religious fanatic. He employed Christians in his armies. He respected the shrine of St James. It seems likely that he attacked churches more because they were rich than because they were Christian. Like the Vikings, who did the same, he needed loot.

'At length divine mercy deigned to lift this scourge from the Christians . . . and Almanzor was seized by the Devil, who had taken possession of him while he lived, at Medinaceli; and he was buried in hell.' So a chronicler writing in León in about 1120. By that date ideas about a crusading re-conquest were beginning to gain currency in Spain. People were coming to believe that relations between Christians and Muslims were necessarily and justly hostile, that Christian warfare against Islam bestowed positive spiritual merit on the participant, and that the Muslims should be driven out of Spain. Were such ideas widely current a century or more beforehand? It is difficult to be sure, but on the whole it seems improbable. To assert this is to question a cherished national myth which still finds passionate defenders in Spain, so it is important to be quite clear about the claims that are being made. It is not claimed that Christian and Muslim lived side by side in harmony: of course they did not. The warfare of the tenth century, of which the Pamplona campaign of 924 is a good example, left a trail of suffering and resentment in its wake. Nor is it claimed that the notion of a re-conquest of Spain had not yet occurred. At the court of Alfonso III, where the memory of the Visigothic kingdom was kept green, one anonymous writer of the 880s whose work has come down to us looked forward eagerly to the imminent end, as he trusted, of the Islamic presence in Spain. It *is* claimed, rather, that in the tenth and eleventh centuries ideas about a Christian re-conquest were neither clearly articulated nor widely shared. How then did the heirs of the Visigoths regard their Islamic neighbours?

The most striking feature about Christendom's reaction to Islam was incomprehension. At least, that is what we call it today. Early medieval Christians would have been scandalised to have their reactions characterised in this manner, but we live today in an atmosphere of religious pluralism. Christianity is one religion among many, and so is Islam. For the early medieval Christian such thoughts were in the strict sense of the word unthinkable: they would not have been able to make any sense of the last sentence. For a start, they did not have a word for 'religion' as used there. In early medieval Europe the Latin term *religio* meant what we understand by 'regular' or 'professed' religion, i.e. the monastic life. The most widely used term for 'religion' was *fides*, faith. The faith was Christian. Of course, peoples existed who were not Christian but – and this is crucial – they posed no intellectual problem or challenge. The Jews had been offered the revelation but had rejected it: that was their look-out. There were still plenty of pagans about but they would all be converted one day – the Bible said so – and so they were not a source of disquiet. All others were deviants from Christianity; heretics. It was easy to interpret Islam as a Christian heresy. After all, it had so much in common with Christianity – belief in a single God, reverence for the patriarchs and the Virgin Mary, veneration for Jerusalem, and so forth. And yet it had perverted Christianity: in its theology by denying the Incarnation and the Trinity, and in its ethics, notoriously, by its toleration of polygamy. That was enough: manifestly, a Christian heresy. Greek scholars of the Eastern Mediterranean took up this intellectual stance very quickly after the emergence of Islam in the seventh century and transmitted it to Western Europe where it remained dominant for many centuries. One can see why it suited people so well. It explained Islam neatly and convincingly, and it made further investigation unnecessary. The largest ingredient of the early medieval incomprehension of Islam was unconcern.

In Spain, as elsewhere, there was very little writing *about* and absolutely no debate *with* Islam. Spaniards made no attempts to convert Muslims to Christianity. They evinced no interest in the sacred writings of Islam. The Koran was not translated into Latin until the 1140s, and though the work was done in Spain the impulse to do it came from a French monk, Peter the Venerable, abbot of Cluny. This is the more remarkable in that there were considerable numbers of Christians in Spain for whom Arabic was the first language, the so-called Mozarabic Christians who lived under Islamic rule in al-Andalus. The Isaac Velázquez who translated the Gospels into Arabic in Córdoba in 946 presumably did so for the sake of his co-religionists who had no Latin. The priest called Vincent who translated a textbook of canon law into Arabic in 1049–50 and dedicated his translation to a Christian bishop called 'Abd al-Malik – see unknown – presumably did so because the bishop's clergy were readier at Arabic than at Latin.

But if the beliefs of the Muslims were of no interest, they were credited by their Christian neighbours with other attributes which were. Foremost among these was wealth; another was knowledge. By the middle years of the tenth century the intellectual culture of Muslim Spain was becoming sophisticated, principally owing to reception in Spain of the accumulated learning of Middle Eastern Islam, which in its turn rested on the scientific and philosophical corpus of Greek and Persian antiquity. Learning was taken seriously at the court of 'Abd al-Rahman III and his son and successor al-Hakam, the latter himself a distinguished scholar. In the year 949 the Byzantine emperor Constantine Porphyrogenitus – another learned ruler – sent a splendid manuscript of the work of Dioscorides, the most famous pharmacologist of antiquity, as a present to the caliph of Córdoba. 'Abd al-Rahman assembled a group of scholars to study it. They included a Greek monk named Nicholas sent by the emperor at the caliph's request, a Greek-speaking Arab from Sicily and half-a-dozen Andalusi scholars who may have included the Jew Hasdai ibn Shaprut, who was the caliph's own physician and a scholar noted for his scientific interests. In this anecdote we can sense the intellectual vitality of tenth-century Córdoba.

Sooner or later the Christian scholars of Western Europe would be attracted to the learning to be found in Spain, which was so vastly superior to their own resources. A later scholar, Plato of Tivoli, who was making translations of Arabic astronomical works at Barcelona in the 1130s, lamented 'the blindness of Latin (i.e. Western) ignorance'. Rome, he wrote, has been 'for long inferior not simply to Egypt and Greece but also to Arabia'. By Plato's day a flood of translations was starting to be released from Spain, and their irrigation of the parched fields of European science and philosophy would in time yield a spectacular harvest. Back in the tenth century only the first tentative trickles can be detected. Small and hesitant though they were, however, they have significance as portents of what was to come and as indicators of the stirring and drift of men's minds. Take for example Gerbert, a native of Aurillac in the Auvergne, who went to Spain in search of learning in the 960s. A French chronicler of the mid-eleventh century tells us that Gerbert went as far as Córdoba 'in quest of wisdom', but this seems unlikely. What is certain is that he spent some time at the monastery of Ripoll in Catalonia. Ripoll had been founded by Wifred the Hairy, it was a well-endowed house and it had used its wealth to build up, among other things, a splendid library which was particularly strong in mathematical and astronomical works. Gerbert made good use of it. He also encountered other people with intellectual interests besides the monks of Ripoll. Some years after his return to France he wrote from Rheims to a certain Lobet of Barcelona asking for a copy of a work on astrology 'translated by you'. We know from other sources that Lobet was archdeacon of Barcelona, and though we cannot now identify the work which Gerbert wanted to borrow we do know that Lobet translated another work from Arabic concerned with the use of the scientific instrument known as the astrolabe. Gerbert himself later composed a work on the astrolabe which seems to derive from a similar work (probably not Lobet's) written in Catalonia in the late tenth century.

The astrolabe was an instrument of critical importance in Europe's intellectual advance. It permitted all sorts of astronomical observations to be made with hitherto unmatched accuracy; it made possible rapid and accurate terrestrial measurements, for example of height and distance; it could be turned to navigational use and it could serve as a clock. The astrolabe was invented in antiquity, but the Arabs were the first to grasp its potential and elaborate its design. Knowledge of it was quickly diffused throughout the Islamic world. Astrolabes made in Muslim Spain have survived: for one made in Toledo in 1067 see Plate 5. Whether or not Gerbert was personally responsible for introducing Latin Christendom to the astrolabe, it is certain that by the middle years of the eleventh century there was a flourishing interest in the astrolabe and its uses in Western Europe. This interest was particularly strong in the schools of Northern France and the Rhineland and from there it spread to, among other places, England. Our first testimony to the use of the astrolabe in England comes in a vivid piece of writing by Walcher, prior of Malvern, who died in 1125. He had been in Italy in 1091 where in the small hours of the morning of 30 October he had watched a lunar eclipse.

When I got back to England I enquired about the time of the eclipse and a certain brother told me this: he said that he had been very busy during the day before the eclipse and did not get home till late at night. When he had had supper, he sat a while, and then a servant, who had gone out, came rushing back saying that something horrible was happening to the moon. Going out he noticed that it was not yet midnight, for the moon had still some way to go before it was in the south. I thus perceived that several hours separated the time of the eclipse in Italy and in England, since I saw it shortly before dawn while he saw it before midnight. But I still had no certainty about the time of the eclipse and I was distressed about this, because I was planning to draw up a lunar table and had no starting-point. Then unexpectedly in the following year on 18 October, during the same lunar cycle, the moon . . . underwent another eclipse. I at once seized my astrolabe and made a careful note of the time of full eclipse . . .

'I at once seized my astrolabe.' There, in the account of a lunar eclipse watched in England in 1092, we can glimpse something of what the Arabic learning of Spain had to offer to Christendom.

Not all Muslim inhabitants of Spain looked favourably upon the transmission of this learning. Ibn 'Abdun, who composed a treatise on the administration of the city of Seville about the year 1100, advised that 'you must not sell learned books to Jews or to Christians . . . because they at once translate these scientific books and attribute them to their own people'. The context makes it clear that books on medicine in particular were intended here. But there was no stemming the flow. Exotic learning was to be had in Muslim Spain and Christian intellectuals were going to get it.

Many people felt the same about wealth. Muslim Spain already had a reputation for wealth in distant parts of Western Europe by the middle years of the tenth century. Hrotswitha of Gandersheim, the extraordinary German poetess of that period, referred to Spanish Muslims worshipping idols of gold. The northern French audience of the *Chanson de Roland* in the eleventh century was constantly reminded that the Muslim king Marsile of Zaragoza commanded vast reserves of gold. The ignorance about Islamic religious practice betrayed by the poem's reference to the worship of idols is characteristic but the belief that gold was plentiful in al-Andalus was founded on reality. The gold coinage minted there from the 920s onwards is our best evidence for this plenty. We shall have something to say in a later chapter about the source from which the bullion came, in trans-Saharan West Africa.

Inside Spain, the gold drifted northwards into Christian hands partly by means of commerce but also – especially significant after about the year 1000 – as payment for troops. We may be sure that the Leónese and Galician noblemen who enlisted in Almanzor's armies were rewarded with cash as well as with the exotic textiles which he distributed to them after the attack on Compostela in 997. On four occasions in the early eleventh century (1010, 1013, 1017 and 1024) Catalan armies intervened in the confused warfare in southern Spain which brought about the fall of the caliphate of Córdoba. In 1010, for instance, the count of Barcelona, Ramón Borrell, and his brother the count of Urgel were engaged by Wadih, a Slav retainer of Almanzor, to support his candidate for the office of caliph. Wadih undertook to pay the counts 100 *dinars* each day and the wages of their troops on campaign. They took their obligations seriously – the year 1010 was called 'the year of the Catalans' by

Islamic chroniclers – and in the campaigning of that summer the count of Urgel and no less than three fighting bishops (Barcelona, Gerona and Vich) were killed. The influx of gold during these years had far-reaching effects upon Catalan society. Among other things it powerfully assisted the counts of Barcelona to draw ahead of other rivals for power among the counties of the Spanish March. Another Christian leader who intervened to his profit in the Andalusian strife of these years was Count Sancho of Castile (995–1017).

Sooner or later foreign military adventurers were going to start coming to Spain to seek their fortunes. Despite earlier contacts between Asturian and Carolingian rulers, despite the cultural links between Catalonia and Francia, the fact remains that in many ways the principalities of Christian Spain were somewhat isolated from their Western European neighbours during the ninth and tenth centuries. Various factors began to dissolve this isolation from the late tenth century onwards. One of these was the coming of ever larger numbers of people as pilgrims to the shrine of St James at Compostela in the extreme north-west of the Iberian peninsula. At some point in the first half of the ninth century a body believed to be that of the apostle St James the Greater was excavated at the place now known as Santiago de Compostela. ('Santiago' simply means 'Saint James'.) Although it is in the highest possible degree unlikely that St James or his disciples ever so much as set foot in Spain either alive or dead, the ninth-century churchmen of Galicia were convinced that they had found the mortal remains of the apostle. A local cult started at the site of the tomb. In the course of time influential persons began to encourage it, notably King Alfonso III and his successors as kings of León during the tenth century. Miracles, it was believed, were worked at the shrine. Devotion to the holy place of St James grew and spread, and pilgrims were drawn from ever-widening circles.

At the same time churchmen were coming to present pilgrimage as one of the more important religious exercises in which laymen of the aristocratic and knightly classes should participate for the safety of their souls. This concern was particularly strong among the monks of the great Burgundian abbey of Cluny and its dependent houses in France, whose links with the nobility and gentry were especially close. Thus the encouragement of pilgrimages to Compostela assisted in diffusing awareness of opportunities in Spain among the feudal aristocracy of France. Significantly, the earliest known direct connection between Cluny and Spain occurred during this period. It was in about 1025 that a certain Paternus, abbot of the Aragonese monastery of San Juan de la Peña, went to Cluny to become acquainted with the monastic way of life there. When he returned he brought a handful of monks with him to help disseminate Cluniac observance in Spain. These early Cluniacs seem to have had little influence, but their coming established a connection which was to become very important later in the century.

The initiative in entering into relations with Cluny had come from King Sancho of Navarre, the great-great-grandson of that Sancho Garcés who had suffered at the hands of 'Abd al-Rahman III in 924. This later Sancho, remembered as *el Mayor*, 'the Great', ruled from 1004 to 1035. By means of war and diplomacy he built up an extensive if short-lived empire which by the time of his death stretched from the mouth of the Gironde to the mountains which separate León from Galicia. He established lordship over the Pyrenean counties of Aragon, Sobrarbe and Ribagorza. He extended his authority over Gascony as far as Bordeaux in the 1020s. By right of his wife, the daughter of Count Sancho of Castile, and profiting from a suspiciously timely assassination, he absorbed the county of Castile in 1029. In the last few years of his life he pushed his lordship westwards to embrace the plain and city of León. Never again was the suzerainty of a king of Navarre to extend so far.

Sancho the Great's empire did not outlast him. León and Gascony north of the Pyrenees rapidly shook off his authority. Sancho himself had provided for the partition of his other lands, to create three kingdoms for his sons. To García went Navarre, to Fernando Castile and to Ramiro Aragón. Of the three, Fernando was to make the biggest mark. The initiatives he took during his reign in relations both with the Muslim princes of the taifa states and with Cluniac churchmen in France were to be of great and continuing significance for many years after his death. But before we turn to them we must look more closely at the region of which he became king in 1035. There is another reason for such an examination. Castile was the homeland of the Cid and it was during Fernando's reign that he grew up there.

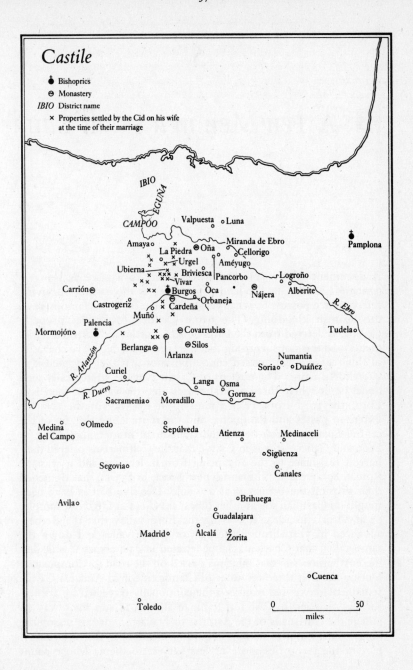

Castile

- ♠ Bishoprics
- ⊖ Monastery
- *IBIO* District name
- × Properties settled by the Cid on his wife at the time of their marriage

IBIO

LEGUNA

CAMPÓO

Valpuesta   ○ Luna

Amaya ○   Miranda de Ebro
    La Piedra ⊖ Oña
    × Urgel   ○ Cellorigo
Ubierna   × × Améyugo
    × ×× × Briviesca
    × × × Vivar Pancorbo   ○ Logroño
Carrión ⊖   × × × Oca   ○ Alberite
    ♠ Burgos   Nájera
Castrogeriz   × × ⊖ Orbaneja
    × Cardeña
    Muñó   ×
Palencia ♠   ×
Mormojón ○   × ×
    Berlanga ⊖ ⊖ Covarrubias   Tudela ○
    ⊖ Silos
    Arlanza
        Numantia
    Soria ○ ○ Duáñez
Curiel ○
    Langa Osma
    ○ ○
Sacramenia ○ Moradillo ○ Gormaz ○

R. Arlanzón

R. Duero

R. Ebro

Medina   ○ Olmedo   Sepúlveda ○   Atienza ○   Medinaceli ○
del Campo
        ○ Sigüenza
Segovia ○   Canales ○

Avila ○   ○ Brihuega
    Guadalajara ○
Madrid ○   Alcalá ○ Zorita ○

        ○ Cuenca

Toledo ○   0   50
        miles

5

A Few Men in a Small Land

A document of the year 800 which refers to a place as being *in territorio Castelle*, 'in the land of Castile', is the earliest surviving reference we possess to what was to become the most famous of all the Spanish kingdoms. The name Castile or Castille, properly *Castilla*, is derived from the Latin *castella*, 'castles' or 'fortified settlements' and it is not surprising that the armoured, defensive character of this region so impressed contemporaries that they adopted it as a territorial name. The nucleus of Castile was the strategically vital nodal point where three natural routes met: the valley of the River Ebro, the road from France into Spain by way of the western Pyrenean passes and Pamplona, and the route along the top of the central Spanish *meseta* below the Cantabrian mountains leading to León and Galicia. It was in Castile that the Celtiberians offered their fiercest resistance to the advancing Roman legions, and it was the Roman conquest of Numantia, near Soria, in 133 BC that tightened their grip on the Peninsula as a whole. Decisive battles have been fought on Castilian soil at other times; at Nájera in 1367 for example, or at Vitoria in 1813. It was up the Ebro valley that the Berbers advanced in 714; through the pass of Roncesvalles and down the same valley that Charlemagne penetrated in 778; across Castile and the northern *meseta* that pilgrims passed on the road to Compostela. During the first three centuries of Islamic rule in al-Andalus Castile remained an exposed frontier zone continually traversed by armies, such as that led by 'Abd al-Rahman III in 924, on their way to pillage the Christians of the Asturias or Navarre. For this reason the kings of the Asturias set up a subordinate county in the easternmost part of the territories more or less subject to them, whose count was charged with responsibility for organising its defences. Such were the origins of the political entity of Castile.

According to legends which were apparently current by the twelfth century, on the death of King Alfonso II of the Asturias in 842 the Castilians elected two 'judges' to govern them, Laín Calvo and Nuño Rasura. The legend of the judges has more to tell us of the Castilians' self-image at a later date than of the realities of the ninth century: they liked to think of themselves as sturdy, independent, resourceful, democratic. But reliable evidence about ninth-century Castile is meagre. The first historical figure we can trace with any degree of certainty is a Count Rodrigo who is attested in the year 852. He may have been related to the royal family and he seems to have died about the year 873. Successive counts may be traced with increasing confidence thereafter. Behind the shield of their defence the elements of a more civilised social life began to emerge – the resettlement of the countryside and the growth of villages and towns; the establishment of a bishopric and the foundation of monasteries and parish churches; the growth of exchange and the appearance of markets. Slowly Castile began to expand from its original nucleus about the headwaters of the Ebro, south towards the valley of the Duero and south-east into the Rioja.

The hero of early Castilian history is Fernán González, count of Castile from about 931 until his death in 970. Legends of his exploits seem to have started to circulate soon after his death, and much later on, in the thirteenth century, an epic poem about him was composed. Yet even when the trappings of legend are stripped away, we can still discern a man whose achievements were lauded by his contemporaries: 'the most glorious count' and 'the illustrious count', as two writers referred to him in 941 and 945. In a charter given in his name the count is made to refer to himself in an even more imposing manner: *ego quidem gratia Dei Fredenandus Gundisalviz totius Castelle comes*, 'I indeed Fernán González by the grace of God count of all Castile'. This royal style may have been deliberately intended to indicate a claim to Castilian political independence. Fernán González has indeed been held up to generations of Spanish schoolchildren as the founder of Castilian independence.

The reality was less straightforward than the resounding phrase suggests. Fernán González fought dutifully alongside his lord the king of León against 'Abd al-Rahman III at the battle of Simancas in 939; when he rebelled in 943–4 the king could deprive him of office and imprison him for a time. However, Fernán González shrewdly contrived to profit from two features of the political scene in the middle years of the century: the consolidation of a stronger monarchy in Navarre and a phase of political instability in the kingdom of León in the 950s and 960s. He was able to conduct what was in effect an independent foreign policy. He married a daughter of the king of Navarre and arranged a marriage for his son and heir to a daughter of the Pyrenean county of Ribagorza. He played off Navarre against León. Inside Castile he usurped royal prerogatives, exercising these rights to encourage the growth of the institutions of ordered civil life. In 940, for example, he resettled the former Roman site of Sepúlveda, well to the south of the River Duero. Sepúlveda was to remain for over a century a precarious outpost, but it registered Castilian territorial ambitions, staking out a claim on the *meseta* of central Spain. By the time of the count's death in 970 Castile was to all intents and purposes an independent principality, and this independence was fortified under the government of his son and grandson, García Fernández (970–95) and Sancho Garcés (995–1017). A dynasty had emerged.

Nature has not favoured Castile. The country is high and bare, though it may have been more thickly wooded in the early Middle Ages than it is today. As a local proverb puts it, the climate swings between the extremes of winter and hell, playing upon the words *invierno* (winter) and *inferno* (hell). Place-names such as Villafría, 'cold settlement', tell their own tale. Yet the counts of the ninth and tenth centuries succeeded in attracting settlers to this inhospitable land. Many of the immigrant settlers came from the Basque country. They have left their trace on the landscape in the form of place-names such as *Villa Vascones*, 'Basque settlement', which occurs in a document of 945. In the higher reaches of the valley of the River Oja, where it runs down from the Sierra de la Demanda towards Santo Domingo de la Calzada, there is a whole cluster of Basque village-names – Ezcaray, Uyarra, Zorraquin, Azarrulla and others – and most of the minor names (fields, streams, hills, etc.) are Basque too. In manuscripts copied at the nearby monastery of San Millán de la Cogolla there are glosses in Basque, and the thirteenth-century poet Berceo, who was an inmate of it, could assume a knowledge of Basque in his audience. In 1235, King Fernando III of Castile permitted the people of this region to plead in Basque in the law-courts. It looks as though the area was deliberately 'planted' with Basque settlers by authority of the count, and it is tempting to associate this with the foundations of the nearby castle of Grañón in 899. Settlers came also from the south, Mozarabic Christians who left al-Andalus to live among their fellow Christians in the north. They can be recognised by their Arabised names which evidently caused difficulties for Castilian scribes and produced such bizarre formations as the Abolgomar who lived near Cardeña about the year 900 and the Abogaleb who was a monk at Berlangas in about 950. Abogaleb's monastery contained the relics of the Christian child-martyr Pelayo, killed at Córdoba in 921, almost certainly brought there by Mozarabic immigrants, and some of its tenth-century manuscripts contain marginal notes in Arabic.

Settlement was hard work. Its atmosphere is captured in one of the earliest Castilian charters we possess, the document from the year 800 in which occurs the first reference to Castile by that name. A certain Abbot Vitulo and his brother Erwig were resettling land in the Mena valley in the extreme north of Castile:

> We found the area abandoned . . . we built churches there; we cultivated; we planted; we built there houses, cellars, granaries, wine-presses, mills; established orchards for apples, vineyards and other fruit-bearing trees . . .

It was a slow business, unrewarding in the short term, and often dangerous. Many though the settlers were, we are probably correct in assuming that the Castile of the Cid's youth was sparsely populated. A famous line from the poem about Fernán González describes the tenth-century Castilians as 'a few men gathered together in a small land'. This is how they thought of themselves, or rather how their thirteenth-century descendants liked to think of their forebears. Well into the second half of the eleventh century rulers were continuing to encourage new settlement. In 1071, for instance, King Sancho II could grant land to a follower with 'freedom to lay out buildings and settle the estate with the men who shall come to you from all parts'. Large tracts of land were still untamed, roamed by wild pigs and cattle, wolves and probably bears. (An eighth-century Asturian king had been killed by a bear.) They were roamed also by voluntary or involuntary drop-outs from human society such as hermits or outlaws. When Juan de Ortega was trying to set up as a hermit in the Montes de Oca in the early twelfth century he was frequently troubled by robbers who stole the materials which he had gathered for building a chapel.

Settlers were attracted by grants of privileges, undertakings which were no doubt given verbally at first but in the course of time came to be reduced to written form in documents known as *fueros*. (Castile, like other regions of Christian Spain, regulated its affairs according to the norms of the Visigothic law-code promulgated by King Recceswinth in the seventh century. One impulse among others to the writing down of the *fueros* was that they embodied modifications of Visigothic legal custom.) The earliest surviving *fuero* whose text has any appearance of reliability – for it will be obvious that the temptation to forge 'early' grants of privilege often proved too strong to be resisted – is that granted to the settlers of Castrogeriz by Count García Fernández in 974. Its clauses evoke the society of this embattled frontier province.

> We grant these good customs to the mounted soldiers, that they shall enjoy the status of noblemen . . . and let each man settle his land . . .

and if anyone should kill a knight of Castrogeriz let him pay compensation for him of 500 *solidi* . . . the men of Castrogeriz shall not pay tolls . . . and let the clergy have the same privileges as the knights . . . if a knight of Castrogeriz does not possess a fief [of land] he shall be exempt from military service unless the *merino* [a royal official] supply him with his wages and maintenance . . . if a man shall be proved to have borne false witness let the council of Castrogeriz have his teeth.

It was a rough, stark world where status mattered, justice was uncomplicated and war never far away.

Other documents reveal a little of the economic activities which sustained these unruly cavalrymen. We learn from one, for example, that in 943 the monks of Cardeña paid 400 sheep in return for grazing rights near Sacramenia. This is a very interesting reference, first in its hint that the monastic flocks were big, second in its implication that transhumant pasturing was already of importance in the Castilian economy: Cardeña is just outside Burgos and Sacramenia is about sixty miles away, far to the south beyond the River Duero (not very distant from Sepúlveda, which Count Fernán González had resettled in 940). Already it seems that we should be thinking of the annual passing and re-passing of flocks of sheep on the *cañadas* or sheep-walks of Castile, herded no doubt by dogs as fierce and shepherds as taciturn as they are today. And not only sheep. To our mental picture of early medieval Castile we must add cattle and cattlemen and all that goes with them – beef for the better-off, plentiful good leather, trade for the blacksmith in horseshoes and branding-irons, horse-coping and cattle-rustling. A short narrative attached to the text of the *fuero* of Castrogeriz is singularly revealing.

In those days [the reference is to 1017–35] there came Diego Pérez and seized our livestock and took himself off to Silos: we went after him and attacked his houses and estate, and killed fifteen men and did a great deal of damage; and we brought our livestock back by force . . . In the time of King Fernando [1037–65] Nuño Fáñez and Assur Fáñez came and took our livestock to Villa Guimara, and we went after them and sacked their houses and reclaimed our beasts . . . In the time of King Alfonso [1065–1109] the *merino* of the *infanta* Urraca came and drove our cattle off to the *infanta's* residence at Villa Icinaz; and we went after him and wrecked the house and the estate, and drank all the wine we could find there and what we could not drink we tipped out on to the ground . . . And another time we went with Salvador Mudarra after one Pedrero to Melgarejo; and he hid in the mansion of Gudesteo Rodríguez and we broke into the house and found him there, and we took him to the bridge at Fitero and forced him to jump into the water and there he was killed . . .

It should also be remembered that the proximity of the frontier held out the possibility of the easy disposal of stolen livestock. Here is another tale, in a very different literary genre.

> There was a man named Stephen, a native of the village called Sojuela which is a possession of [the monastery of] San Millán the holy confessor of Christ, situated near Nájera. Prompted by the Devil, the root and author of all evils, he gathered round him a band of very wicked men, with whom he took to robbery in the forests and hills and wherever he could, in his rapacious greed inflicting all the damage he could on the people who lived round about . . . [On one occasion] they entered the forest near the aforesaid village and spotted a goatherd pasturing a great flock of goats. They seized him and kept him bound until nightfall, when they released him: but they drove off his flock to a certain town of the Saracens where they sold it . . .

The story comes from a hagiographical work on the life and miracles of Santo Domingo de Silos. Stephen, identified by the goatherd, was soon captured. Rashly swearing his innocence, he was struck blind for perjury, and only a penitential pilgrimage and contrition at the saint's tomb restored his eyesight to him. There must have been other men like Stephen, but who eluded justice.

Another sort of document which sheds light on the economy and society of early medieval Castile is the foundation charter in which pious benefactors recorded their foundation and endowment of a religious community. One such charter was issued by Count García Fernández and his wife, the Countess Ava, in the autumn of 978, when they endowed a religious house for their daughter Urraca at Covarrubias. Happily the original document is still extant and may be inspected in the collegiate church at Covarrubias: and a handsome piece of calligraphy it is too. The count and countess were extremely generous. They provided forty-four separate and widespread estates. They ranged from near Lerma, twenty-five miles south of Burgos, to Salinas, fifty miles to its north-east. They came with various jurisdictional and other privileges, such as freedom from toll throughout Castile for their inhabitants. At one of them there was a market – Améyugo, between Pancorbo and Miranda de Ebro, on a road that was already perhaps conveying pilgrims to Santiago de Compostela. At two of them, possibly more, there were salt-workings. It is of interest to find that some of the estates were under-populated: at two places we hear of holdings *per populare*, 'to be settled'. The founders also gave furniture, musical instruments, large quantities of silver bullion for making church plate, many luxury textiles (most of which probably originated in al-Andalus), and great quantities of livestock: in their own words, '500 cows and 1600 sheep and 150 mares and 30 male and 20 female Moors'. One should note how the human livestock, Moorish slaves, are lumped in with the animal; note too how big the livestock figures are. An additional document drawn up on the same occasion amplifies the information of the principal charter in respect of some of the properties:

> . . . At Salinas de Añana a church called San Quirce de Yesares with its mountain [pasture] and its springs and a smithy in front of the church; and seven plots of arable land and four vineyards by the stream running through their midst; and six salt-pans . . . in Vallejo two salt-pans [with the right to be filled] on the fourth day of the week . . .

Salt-pans of the kind alluded to here may still be seen in Northern Castile.

Documents such as this provide fleeting but all the more precious glimpses of the farming and crafts of Castile a thousand years ago. Arable and vineyard; stud-farms and stock-herding; smithies and salt-works: a modest economy but a busy one, which had already advanced well beyond the exigencies of subsistence agriculture.

Exemption from toll was evidently a privilege worth having. The market at Améyugo may not have been a permanent one, may indeed have been a small-scale affair, but in some places trade, alongside other factors, was bringing permanent and bigger settlements into being. The most important of these towns was Burgos. Burgos was said to have been founded by one of the early counts of Castile, Diego, in 884, though it is likely that there was some sort of defensive site there at an earlier date. In a deed of the year 912 Burgos was described as a *civitas*, a word which is commonly translated 'city' but which is more likely at that date to have meant something such as 'centre of an administrative area'. The use of the term shows that the new settlement was prospering. By the middle years of the tenth century we have the first evidence of distinct names given to different quarters or districts of the town, the *Barrio de Eras* and the *Barrio de San Juan*. The multiplication of *barrios* or quarters is another indication of urban growth: there were at least four of them by about 1050. Settlement was beginning to occur in the flat land or *vega* between the fortress on its rock and the River Arlanzón. In 972 we hear for the first time of a *concejo* or council: a lawsuit was heard 'in the presence of Count García Fernández and all the council of Burgos'. At a later date the term *concejo* would come to mean 'town council': in the 970s it more probably indicated a gathering of prominent landowners from round about; but at least it shows that judicial pleas were being held in Burgos. The counts and their successors the kings of Castile had a favourite residence there. The town was the setting for important ceremonial occasions and affairs of state, such as the marriage in 1032 of Fernando, son of Sancho the Great and later to be the first king of Castile, or the meeting of an important ecclesiastical council in 1080. State prisoners

could be kept in captivity there: it was at Burgos that Sancho II
imprisoned his brothers in 1071–2. Meanwhile, Burgos was developing a flourishing commerce. In 982 the monks of Cardeña thought
it worth their while to acquire from the count 'two shops in the
middle of the town, one to the left and the other to the right of the
public highway which leads everywhere, from the east to the west
and from the south to the north'. The enthusiasm of the count's
notary who drafted this deed seems to have outrun his clarity of
expression: I take his words to mean that the monks acquired property at the crossroads in the town centre; prime urban 'high street'
sites which doubtless proved a tidy investment as the years went by
and the town continued to grow and flourish. Other businessmen
who were attracted to Burgos were the Jews, of whom there was a
small community there by the 1060s.

Burgos formally became the seat of a bishopric in 1074. The
region which was to become known as Castile had first received a
bishopric, it would seem – although the evidence is inferential – in
the fourth century. The seat of the bishopric then and during the
Visigothic period was at Auca or Oca, about twenty miles to the
east of Burgos. After the Islamic conquest the bishops of Oca withdrew to the safety of the Asturias and we lose track of them. They
re-emerge into the half-light of history early in the ninth century
when they established themselves at Valpuesta in the upper valley
of the Ebro about twenty-five miles north-west of Miranda de Ebro.
As the centre of gravity of the county of Castile shifted southward,
so too the seat of the bishopric: by the time of Fernán González the
diocese was governed from Muñó, on the River Arlanzón some
nine miles south-west of Burgos. About the time of Almanzor's
campaigns against the Christian states, in the late tenth century, the
bishops first started to spend much time at Burgos, initially as a
place of refuge; and gradually it became apparent that the town
would be the most suitable site for their see. In 1074 the *infantas*
Elvira and Urraca, sisters of the reigning monarch Alfonso VI, gave
Bishop Simeon a church at Gamonal, a site just outside Burgos, 'in
order to establish a new seat for the bishop there'. The church was
enlarged or rebuilt, and consecrated as the new cathedral four years
later. For some reason the site seems not to have been satisfactory,
for in 1081 we find Alfonso VI granting the bishop a new cathedral
church in Burgos (underlying today's Gothic cathedral) and the
royal residence beside it to serve as an episcopal palace.

The early bishops of Castile, before the eleventh century, are
shadowy figures. We have a few names and dates, but practically
nothing else. Owing to the chance of documentary survival we are
much better informed about the monasteries, the most important of
which, in approximate order of foundation, were Cardeña, Arlanza,
Covarrubias, Berlangas, Silos and Oña. Each of them had close

connections with the ruling dynasty. Cardeña was founded in 899. Situated close to Burgos, its fortunes were bound up with those of the town. In its archive, exceptionally rich in documents of the tenth and eleventh centuries, we can trace its relation with the counts of Castile and see, incidentally, how wealthy this connection made it. The body of Count García Fernández was brought to Cardeña for burial after his death in captivity in Córdoba in 995. Arlanza was founded in about 912, on the site of a former Roman villa as we now know from recent excavations. Fernán González and his wife were notable benefactors and chose to be buried there – she in a magnificent reused Hispano-Roman sarcophagus which is now to be seen at nearby Covarrubias, where some sort of religious community was in existence by 937. The re-foundation of 978 was effected, as we have already seen, by Count García Fernández and his wife for their daughter. She ruled as abbess over a double house for both men and women. We first hear of Berlangas in 942, when it was the recipient of a grant from Fernán González. Silos was founded by Fernán González in or about 954; Oña by Count Sancho in 1011 for his daughter Tigridia, later to be venerated as a saint: he was buried there, and so was his son García Sanchez.

The monasteries of tenth- and eleventh-century Europe were not simply communities of devout men and women living a life given over to corporate prayer and worship. 'Envisaged by monastic teachers as arks of salvation in a flood of worldly perils, they remained an integral part of the society which brought them into being.' This comment, made about the monasteries of Normandy, could fittingly be applied to those of Spain. The Castilian monasteries were repositories of dynastic tradition, mausoleums, power-houses of loyalty to the comital family. Urraca, the daughter of Count García Fernández for whom Covarrubias was re-founded in 978, was still ruling the community in 1024, possibly as late as 1032. There was no danger of the count being forgotten there, any more than at Cardeña where his body rested and where prayers were said regularly for his soul. One wonders how many other abbots or abbesses were founder's kin. Entrants to monasteries were often, perhaps usually, expected to make a substantial donation to the house they joined: this informal property qualification could, in effect, restrict the inmates to the wealthier classes (or those of their dependents whom they chose to favour). Links between the landed aristocracy and the monasteries were thus extremely close. Noblemen looked to the monastic houses of which they were the often very generous patrons for diverse reciprocal services and expressions of gratitude. The provision of hospitality was one of these: a patron would expect to be put up (with all his human and animal retinue), and probably in some style, in 'his' monastery as in some sort of private hotel. The hospitality sought might be permanent. The active career of an aristocratic warrior might be as short as that of a twentieth-century professional footballer, and he had to have somewhere to spend what might be a long retirement. It is probably correct to envisage the monasteries of this period as containing more than a few incapacitated or elderly knights among the community: assured of comfort and security, surrounded by fellows of their social rank to some of whom they might be related, ideally placed to receive news and gossip, they must have spent their declining years in an agreeable way. Historians of medieval literature are steadily more inclined to stress the role of monastic communities in the formation of heroic epic: against this background of old soldiers re-fighting the campaigns and feuds of the past, how right they surely are.

Another service rendered by monasteries was banking. Monasteries were secure places where valuables could be deposited. Rich communities, holders of bullion, they were well placed to make loans. Here is an example. A man named Domingo, from Soto de San Esteban near Osma, was captured by the Saracens. His family could not raise the very considerable sum demanded as his ransom – 500 *solidi* – so they turned to other sources, 'as is customary' comments our witness for the story. Among others they approached Abbot Domingo of Silos, who contributed to their fund by giving them a horse. Though we are not told its value, it could have gone a long way towards meeting their needs. Horses could be very valuable. In 1042 Bishop Gómez of Burgos, recently promoted from the abbacy of Cardeña, gave his king a bay horse and a dun mule, each worth 500 *solidi*. There is a further point of interest here. It is noteworthy that in these and other reported incidents eleventh-century abbots evidently had valuable horses to dispose of. Presumably in Castile as elsewhere horse-breeding for aristocratic patrons was another service rendered by monks. One thinks of the prodigious number of mares given to Covarrubias in 978: presumably Abbess Urraca was expected to run a stud-farm for her father the count.

As it happened, the fund-raisers who turned to the abbot of Silos did not need his worldly generosity. He said a mass for the captive, who was miraculously freed. (And this is why we possess the story: it was committed to writing because it demonstrated the abbot's sanctity.) In an environment so little amenable to control, in a social world so violent and so changeable, intercessory prayer was the most valuable service of all that the monks could render their patrons. They were the experts. Their prayers were the most likely to capture God's attention; for He had to be approached with circumspection like an earthly king, through intermediaries who were familiar with the rituals of pleasing. This explains the veneration accorded to God's courtiers, the saints. They had privileged access to God, and human petitions forwarded, so to say, through the saints had a better chance of success than those without such sponsorship. The most effectual way of approaching the saints was by literally going to them as a suppliant: hence the appeal of pilgrimages, to the tomb of St James at Compostela among many, many other places. This is why competition to possess relics of the saints was so intense, why the bodies of the holy dead were dug up, traded, stolen, fragmented, multiplied. This is why accounts of the movement or 'translation' of relics – for example, of St Cristeta from deserted Avila to Arlanza in 1062 – survive in such abundance from this period, and why they are marked by a tone of triumphant possessiveness. Cristeta had died a martyr, it was believed, many centuries beforehand. But there were living saints in eleventh-century Castile such as Abbot Domingo of Silos (d. 1073), and saints who were venerated if not before at any rate very soon after their deaths such as Iñigo, abbot of Oña (d. 1069), or Sisebut, abbot of Cardeña (d. 1086).

It will be obvious enough that such men and women as these, whether saintly or not, would be among the highest in the land, powers in state as well as church. Neither is it surprising to find churchly office, like secular, running in aristocratic families. Gómez was succeeded in the bishopric of Burgos by his nephew Simeon or Jimeno, while another nephew followed him as abbot of Cardeña. Although the family was a landed one which might have been – for we know nothing of its origins – long established in Castile, it owed its spectacular eleventh-century success to royal favour. In the charter of 1042 recording a royal grant, which provides our earliest evidence for Gómez's tenure of the bishopric, King Fernando I praised him as 'most faithful' and stated that he was rewarding him 'for the good service which you have done me and which you have promised to do' in the future. Identical phraseology occurs in Fernando's first grant to Gómez's nephew Simeon in 1062. Wording of this type, in this sort of royal charter, normally indicated that the faithful servant in question was a trusted counsellor of the king, and it is a reasonable if unprovable assumption that the bishopric was part of his reward.

One may suspect that part of Gómez's services as abbot of Cardeña before 1042 had consisted in winning his community round to full-hearted acceptance of a new ruling dynasty. As we saw in the last chapter, when Sancho the Great of Navarre acquired the county of Castile in 1029 his son Fernando, then aged only about eighteen, was appointed to govern it as his father's deputy. In 1032 Fernando married Sancha, the sister of King Bermudo III of León. When Sancho died in 1035 Castile fell to Fernando in the division of his realms. Two years later Ferando defeated and killed Bermudo III at the battle of Tamarón and incorporated his kingdom of León (with

Galicia) under his sway. He was crowned and anointed at León in June 1038.

The reign of Fernando I, king and emperor of a combined kingdom of León and Castile from 1037 until his death in 1065, is ill-served by the surviving sources and – partly for this reason – has attracted little in the way of modern scholarly attention. Much remains mysterious about it, but that he was regarded in his time as a great king there can be no doubt. Part of his greatness lay in successfully imposing himself first upon Castile and then upon León and Galicia, though the means by which he did this are at present unclear. A fair amount of violence was involved: those who stood in the king's way risked death or exile. The peaceful and constructive side of the coin lay in building up a team of loyal supporters, king's men drawn from the magnate families or raised up to form new such families, vassals on whom the king could rely in the day-to-day running of the kingdom. (The family of that faithful servant Bishop Gómez looks like just such a dynasty.) Fernando I could attract and retain the loyalty of such vassals only for so long as he could reward them with land, plunder, power and opportunity. This he was able to do principally by taking advantage of the vulnerability of his neighbours to the south, the taifa kings of al-Andalus. Fernando profited from their weakness in two ways. One was through territorial gain at their expense. Here Fernando's most famous conquest was the town and surrounding territory of Coimbra, in central Portugal, in 1064. But much the more important way was through the exaction of tribute.

The operation was fairly simple. In essence it was, as a recent historian has put it, 'a protection racket'. Fernando exacted tribute from a dependent taifa ruler in return for his 'protection'. There was nothing original about it, but Fernando I showed himself exceptionally skilful or exceptionally ruthless (or both) in wringing cash out of the luckless kinglets of the Muslim south. By the time of his death in 1065 and almost certainly for several years before that, Fernando was exacting regular tributes from Zaragoza, Toledo and Badajoz, and occasional ones from Seville and Valencia. These tributes, known as *parias*, were such an important feature of life in eleventh-century Spain that we must devote a little attention to them.

The sources for Fernando's reign are so meagre that we can know practically nothing in detail about the workings of the *paria* system. However, two documents of a slightly later date are revealing. The earlier of the two is the text of a treaty between a Muslim ruler and a Christian king. After Fernando I's death al-Muqtadir of Zaragoza threw off the Castilian protectorate and turned instead to the kingdom of Navarre. In 1069 a treaty was negotiated with Sancho IV, and renewed in 1073. On the latter occasion, after swearing peace and friendship, al-Muqtadir undertook to pay Sancho 12,000 gold *mancusos* (one of several Latin terms for the Andalusi *dinar*) every year. In return Sancho promised to provide military aid when required, 'whether against Christians or against Muslims'. Any Navarrese troops sent to serve in the taifa of Zaragoza were to be paid 'for each day what it is customary to give the men of Castile or of Barcelona' – a minor but telling indication of the ease and frequency with which mercenary troops could be hired in eleventh-century Spain. Treaties such as this were probably drawn up and committed to writing in the *paria* agreements negotiated by Fernando I (and later by his son Alfonso VI). The second document consists of information about tribute-paying recorded by the ex-king of Granada, 'Abd Allah, in the memoirs he composed in exile in Morocco in the 1090s. Particularly revealing is his vivid account, too long to be quoted here, of negotiating with Alfonso VI in 1074. The same elements are present. 'An agreement was concluded between us,' wrote 'Abd Allah, stipulating that neither should attack the other and specifying an annual payment of 10,000 *dinars* to the Christian king. Presumably it was committed to writing in a document akin to the treaty of the year before between al-Muqtadir and Sancho IV of Navarre. 'Abd Allah's account suggests the hard bargaining that preceded the agreement, and he also tells us how the payment of cash was accompanied by presents of silk textiles, carpets and plate. This is one factor which makes it difficult to calculate the amount of tribute which flowed towards the Christian rulers: an unknown proportion was made up of goods over and above the stipulated payments of cash. But we can be sure that the aggregate of the sums paid over to the Christian rulers was enormous.

Catalonia's rulers also were busy exacting *parias* from their Muslim neighbours. The documentation surviving from that area is vastly more abundant than that which survives from Castile and with its aid we can gauge something of the socio-political effects of the influx of gold. Between 1048 and 1076 Count Ramón Berenguer I of Barcelona's *recorded* expenditure on the purchase of castles totalled 32,000 *uncias* of gold. This is a unit of account (originally of weight) equivalent to between 224,000 and 320,000 *mancusos* or *dinars*. Money was also used for the payment of troops. Soldiers could be hired for a daily wage, as the 1073 treaty makes clear. Specialists such as Adalbert the engineer (*ingeniator*) whom we find in charge of the count's siege-train – itself a novelty here attested for the first time – in 1058 could presumably command higher rates than ordinary troops. (If his German name is anything to go by, he had been imported from a long way away and foreign military technicians do not usually come cheap.) The institution of what would elsewhere be called a money-fief, i.e. the retaining of a knight on the basis of an annual salary, is first attested in the county of Barcelona in the 1040s. To give but one example from many, a certain Roland Guillem agreed in 1067 to serve the count for a salary of twenty *uncias* a year. A chance documentary survival from 1056 or shortly before, evidently drafted by a comital notary, is a list of names each followed by a sum of money, probably disbursements by the count to members of his household: 'To Guillem Berenguer, 7 *mancusos* . . . To Bremo the seneschal, 5 . . . 3 *uncias* to the three clerks . . .' and so on. The new wealth contributed to the final stages of the process by which the counts of Barcelona pulled ahead of other rivals for power in Catalonia. It also enabled them to do something that no ruler in Western Europe had done for more than three centuries: from 1037 onwards they were striking gold coinage of their own at Barcelona.

In the kingdom of León-Castile, in the same way, money was handed on by the primary recipient of *parias*, the king, to his vassals in the form of wages and donatives. The amount of liquid wealth, ready cash, being pumped about the kingdom by the force of commercial transactions will surprise anybody who thinks that the economy of the eleventh century was sluggish or in some way 'primitive'. Take the case of Count Gómez Díaz, the patron (and perhaps the founder) of the monastery of San Zoil de Carrión in western Castile, a man prominent among the aristocratic supporters of Fernando I. A document drawn up in 1057 records his acquisition of a large amount of land by means of forty-seven separate transactions with different individuals (mostly by purchase, some by exchange). He spent money on what we would call 'developing' the town of Carrión, for example by building a bridge over the river to facilitate and increase traffic. We cannot *prove* that the resources for investment consisted of Moorish gold which came to him from his king, but it looks not improbable. Likewise, we cannot demonstrate that the 1600 Moorish gold pieces which Count Gonzalo Salvadórez left to the monastery of Oña in 1082 came to him directly or indirectly from the king, but once again it seems probable.

Fernando I himself could afford to be a lavish patron of the church. He brought the relics of St Isidore from Seville and deposited them in the splendid religious house which he founded in the saint's honour in León. He it was who commissioned foreign craftsmen to fashion the silver-gilt reliquary which contained them, and the ivory crucifix presented by him and Queen Sancha in 1063 (illustrated in Plate 7). However, his most famous benefaction was made to a church outside Spain – to the monastery of Cluny.

At some point in the latter part of his reign which cannot be exactly determined, perhaps about 1055, Fernando undertook to make an annual payment of 1000 gold pieces (*aurei*, i.e. *dinars*) to the monastery of Cluny. With the possible exception of Montecassino,

Cluny was at this date the wealthiest monastic house in Western Europe. Fernando's annual subvention exceeded Cluny's entire income from her ample patrimonies. It was colossal; 'by far the largest gift Cluny had ever yet received from a king or other lay donor, one which was never to be surpassed' – except by Fernando's son Alfonso VI, who doubled it in 1077. The establishment of the Cluniac *census*, as the grant was called, strengthened the bond linking monastery and dynasty which had first been forged by Sancho the Great. It was followed by the making of other links. Between 1073 and 1077 Alfonso VI entrusted four Spanish monastic houses which were under royal patronage to the monks of Cluny; they were the first of several peninsular communities to enter the far-flung network of Cluniac dependencies. The higher nobility of León-Castile followed the lead of their king: in 1076 the Countess Teresa, widow of Gómez Díaz, made over to Cluny the family monastery of Carrión. In 1079 Alfonso's marriage to Constance of Burgundy, the niece of Abbot Hugh of Cluny, established Cluniac interests at the heart of the royal court. Cluniac churchmen made their way to Spain in ever-increasing numbers during the last quarter of the century to seek careers under royal patronage in the Spanish church. The most famous and influential of these was Bernard, successively abbot of Sahagún and archbishop of newly re-conquered Toledo from 1086, whom we shall meet again.

The Cluniac imprint upon the Spanish church was deep and lasting. But Cluniacs were not the only foreign churchmen to become active in the kingdom of León-Castile. Here is another example. Among Queen Constance's protégés was a French monk named Adelelm from the monastery of La Chaise Dieu at Issoire in Auvergne who came to Spain at her invitation in about 1081 and was subsequently put in charge of a religious community at Burgos devoted to caring for pilgrims on their way to Santiago de Compostela. The queen made it clear that Adelelm's responsibilities were wider than this alone. She looked to him to improve religious observance in Spain. What she almost certainly had in mind were the liturgical changes that were convulsing the life of the church in León-Castile at this time.

During the Visigothic period Spanish churchmen had developed a distinctive liturgy of their own. Subsequently, when the Spanish church was to a large degree isolated from the rest of Western Christendom, it had been unaffected by the pressures for liturgical standardisation which were emanating from Carolingian ecclesiastical reformers and from the papacy. Foreign observers in the eleventh century were therefore confronted by certain liturgical customs which struck them as odd. The ecclesiastical calendar was different in Spain, so that, for example, Lent began not on Ash Wednesday but on the Monday preceding it. Different saints' days were celebrated in Spain: no one beyond the Pyrenees had heard of St Nunilo of Huesca or St Verissimus of Lisbon. The clergy wore different vestments in Spain, and recited different prayers and lections. The laity took communion in both kinds; when they recited the Creed they said *natum non factum* rather than *genitum non factum*, 'born not made' instead of 'begotten not made'; when the Lord's Prayer was recited they said 'Amen' after every clause instead of just once at the end. And this list of differences could be continued.

These deviations from a norm that was being enforced with increasing stridency elsewhere were looked upon with disfavour by the ecclesiastical reformers. Pressures to conform to the general usage of Latin Christendom mounted as the century wore on and became irresistible during the pontificate of Gregory VII (1073–85). He was determined that the ancient and much-loved Spanish liturgy should be replaced by the Roman rite, and pursued this goal obsessively and intemperately in his dealings with Spanish churchmen and monarchs, among the latter especially Alfonso VI. In the end he had his way. At the council of Burgos in 1080 the decision was taken to adopt the Roman liturgy. The replacement of one rite by another seems to have been a gradual process and may have been a troubled one. At all events, it was going forward during the last twenty years of the century. Among the agents of enforcement were another species of newcomer on the Spanish ecclesiastical scene, papal legates. These included such prominent figures as Gerald, cardinal-bishop of Ostia, in 1073; Cardinal Richard of Marseilles, who presided over the council of Burgos in 1080; Abbot Jarenton of Dijon in 1084; and Cardinal Rainerius, later Pope Paschal II (1099–1118), who held a church council at León in 1090.

This, then, was the Castile in which Rodrigo Díaz was born and grew to manhood. Its precarious infancy lay in the past, though the memory of it was cherished. Eleventh-century Castile was steadily prospering. Sparse though they are, the records of its herds and horses, towns and markets, knights and noblemen, bishops and abbots, testify to vitality and bustle. The frontier was still not far away, but its dangers had receded after the disintegration of political power in al-Andalus. For the Castilians the Moorish south now represented not danger but opportunity. Muslim gold whetted appetites, opened perspectives, suggested possibilities. The Eldorado that was opening up could not long remain unexplored. The monks of Cluny were the earliest major beneficiaries of this bonanza. There were plenty of others who would want to join in among the feudal aristocracy of Western Europe, whose religious needs were so nicely gauged and so satisfactorily provided for by Cluniacs and other monks. We must try to grasp the tone and temper of aristocratic life in the eleventh century, for it is as much a part of Rodrigo Díaz's world as his Castilian homeland.

6

✳ *Contemporaries*

While the caliphate of Córdoba was in its death-throes and Fernando I
was learning the art of government in Castile, another struggle was
being played out several hundred miles to the north. In the summer
of 1030 Olaf Haraldson, the recently ousted king of Norway, tried
to win his land back from the regents who were governing it in the
name of the great Canute, ruler of Denmark and England. Olaf was
defeated and killed at the battle of Stiklestad, near Trondheim: from
a date very shortly after his death he was to be venerated as a saint,
St Olave. In the battle he had been aided by his young half-brother
Harald, son of a member of one of Norway's many princely dynasties, a chieftain known as Sigurd Sow. Harald Sigurdson was
wounded in the battle but managed to make his way across the
mountains to safety in Sweden. In the following year he took ship
and crossed the Baltic to enter the service of King Jaroslav of Russia.
There is record of his fighting on a Russian campaign against the
Poles. A few years later he moved southwards, making his way to
Constantinople where he took service in the army of the emperor,
Michael IV. The recounted saga of his life, which took on its final
form in thirteenth-century Iceland, has much that is legendary to
report of his exploits in Byzantine service: how he conquered eighty
cities; how he fired a besieged town by capturing and setting light
to the swallows who nested under the eaves of the thatched roofs
of the houses within it; how the Empress Zoe had him imprisoned
out of sexual jealousy; how he miraculously escaped, gouging out
the sleeping emperor's eyes and abducting his niece Maria before he
sailed away. There is plenty more of this sort of thing, and very
valuable it must have been in the smoky longhouses of medieval
Iceland in alleviating the crushing boredom of the winter nights.

But it is not all fanciful. In the late 1070s an elderly Byzantine general, Cecaumenos, living in retirement on his estates near Larissa in Thessaly, composed a work known as the *Strategicon*, a book of advice for his descendants. Cecaumenos was not given to flights of fancy: a cautious, prosaic man, suspicious of dash and artifice, reliable in his information. He has something to say of 'Araltes' and his brother 'Julavos' – Harald and Olaf. According to Cecaumenos, Harald saw service against the Muslims of Sicily under the greatest Byzantine commander of the day, George Maniaces, between 1038 and 1041. On another occasion he accompanied an army led by the emperor in person to suppress a rebellion in Bulgaria; Cecaumenos himself served on this campaign. Harald may perhaps also have seen service in Asia Minor and northern Syria, and made a pilgrimage to Jerusalem. Whatever the precise details of his exploits, it was later recalled that they made him rich. The saga grows monotonous in its repetitions about the treasure that Harald acquired:

> Harald garnered an immense hoard of money, gold and treasure of all kinds. All the booty he did not require for expenses he used to send by his own reliable messengers to Novgorod into the safe keeping of King Jaroslav.

The source may be late, but its tales about the riches accumulated by Harald must be true. The sequel proves them so. In about 1044 Harald left Byzantine service and made his way via Russia back to Scandinavia. Able to attract warriors – the proof of his wealth – he managed to compel his nephew Magnus, who had succeeded to the kingship of Norway, to share power with him. When Magnus died in 1047 Harald became sole ruler of Norway. He governed Norway violently and successfully for nineteen years before embarking on his last adventure, the invasion of England in 1066. There he met his end, on the field of Stamford Bridge, at the hands of his namesake Harold II of England. 'The thunderbolt of the north', as the contemporary German chronicler Adam of Bremen called him, would strike no more.

The Varangian guard retained by the emperors in Constantinople was recruited principally from Scandinavia and Russia but also, especially after 1066 when the Norman conquest forced many into exile, from England too. It played an important part in the military establishment of the empire from its inception in the tenth century until the fall of Constantinople to the armies of the Fourth Crusade in 1204. Glamourised by modern writers – the initiative seems to have been Scott's in *Count Robert of Paris* – the Varangian guard is in no danger of being forgotten. What can easily be overlooked is that the Varangians were but one foreign contingent among many in the Byzantine military and naval forces. Like the Roman predecessors to whom they constantly looked back as exemplars, the emperors of the eleventh century recruited mercenaries from outside the imperial frontiers into their armies in a steady stream: Georgians and Turks from the East, Petchenegs and Cumans from beyond the Danube, Varangians from the North and Normans from the West.

Among the latter, one in particular achieved special notoriety in the Byzantine empire about a generation after the Sicilian exploits of Harald Sigurdson. Roussel of Bailleul was a Norman of whose origins nothing is known save that he is presumed to have been a native of Bailleul near Argentan in southern Normandy. One near-contemporary writer tells us that he played a part in the conquest of Sicily by his fellow Norman Roger Guiscard. In the surviving Byzantine sources he suddenly emerges as a prominent mercenary captain in the late 1060s, commanding a force of Franco-Norman cavalry. His troops accompanied the Emperor Romanus Diogenes on his ill-fated expedition against the Seljuk Turks in eastern Asia Minor in 1071. The Byzantine army was defeated, and its emperor captured, at the battle of Manzikert. Roussel's troops stood aloof and played no part in the fighting; perhaps, it was rumoured, bribed into inactivity by the Turks. Whatever the truth about the campaign of 1071, Roussel maintained his following and his employment in imperial service. During the years following the defeat at Manzikert the authority of the central government crumbled away and Asia Minor drifted into anarchy. Ordered power shrank into the cities and their immediately surrounding territories. Turkish invaders first plundered and then began to settle the countryside. Refugees blundered about. Rival governmental factions in Constantinople undertook various hesitant initiatives to restore order and collect taxes.

Opportunities were there in plenty to be grasped by the enterprising freelance. In 1073 Roussel of Bailleul was sent against the marauding Turks with a Byzantine army under Isaac Comnenus, nephew of a former emperor. Roussel deserted his commander (who was captured by the Turks) and set off with his own following of troops into the northern parts of Anatolia where he established himself at Amasya, inland from the Black Sea coast in central northern Turkey. There he established what was in effect an independent principality. He defeated armies sent against him. He 'ran' a pretender to the imperial throne, in whose support he could send a raiding party as far as the Bosphorus. When captured he was ransomed by his wife. He succeeded in winning the respect of the citizens of Amasya, presumably by defending them effectively – a local boss who could provide a modicum of peace for a troubled community. Eventually Alexius Comnenus, brother of Isaac and later to be emperor between 1081 and 1118, was sent against him. Alexius managed to bribe a Turkish chieftain to capture Roussel and had him sent back to Constantinople 'like a lion in a cage'. We learn no more of Roussel, and may suspect that his fate was a grim one: but for a short time he had had a good run for his money.

The exploits of Roussel of Bailleul did not deter the Byzantine authorities from employing foreign troops. Indeed they could not have done so, for two reasons. Such recruitment was in accordance with traditional imperial policy stretching back for the better part of a millennium; and the parlous state of the empire in the eleventh century, attacked by new enemies on every side, absolutely necessitated reliance upon foreign contingents. So, despite his experiences with Roussel, Alexius I continued the policy after he became emperor. Here is one example of it. On his way back from a pilgrimage to Jerusalem, probably in 1089, Count Robert of Flanders, one of the greatest magnates of France, had a meeting with Alexius and agreed to supply him with troops. The details of the arrangement are not known. However, it is likely that its terms were not dissimilar to those which were agreed between Robert's son and King Henry I of England in 1101 and again in 1110: one thousand Flemish knights to serve in England and Normandy for an overall fee of £500 to the count who provided them, the knights themselves to be paid and compensated for losses 'as is customary'. The Flemish troops were certainly sent to the Byzantine empire, where they were employed against the Petchenegs in 1091. The employment of the Flemish mercenaries had been so successful that Alexius was emboldened to try again. In 1095 his ambassadors appeared at a church council presided over by Pope Urban II at Piacenza in northern Italy and appealed to the West for military aid. It is fairly certain that what Alexius wanted was a small, manageable force of well-armed and well-trained soldiers such as the count of Flanders had furnished. What in the event he got was a huge disorderly rabble which historians call – though contemporaries did not – the armies of the First Crusade. But that is another story.

The Byzantine empire, despite its difficulties in the eleventh century, was resilient, as its history in the twelfth was to show. It retained its reputation in Western Europe as a source of limitless wealth, offering good pay and prospects for soldiers. But it was not alone in this. Consider another Norman family, the Tosnys. Strictly speaking, the Tosnys were French rather than Norman in origin: the temptation to interpret them as living out some atavistic Viking wanderlust should be resisted. The earliest member of the family of whom we can form any impression was a certain Ralph of Tosny, a vassal of Duke Richard II of Normandy in the early eleventh century. For reasons of which we know nothing he fell out with his lord and was sent into exile. He next turns up in southern Italy where he was taken into the service of some Apulian rebels against the authority of the Byzantine emperor (which still embraced Apulia and Calabria at that date). That is the last we hear of him. His son,

Roger, seems to have been involved in his father's fall from ducal favour, for at much the same time as Ralph was fighting in Italy (c. 1020) Roger may be traced to Spain where he entered the service of the Countess Ermesenda of Barcelona, recently widowed and governing the county as regent for her young son. Roger was employed in defending her principality against its Muslim neighbours, especially Mujahid of the taifa kingdom of Denia, and acquitted himself well. Legends about his exploits there quickly grew up. Within at most fifteen years it was said that he had hastened the submission of his enemies by perpetrating acts of cannibalism upon his Muslim prisoners of war. Whatever the truth behind this fantastic story – as a twelfth-century annotator observed, it seems to owe something to the legend of Atreus and Thyestes – Roger became notorious for his Spanish adventures: he was known in Normandy as 'Roger the Spaniard'. Reconciled with the ducal family, he returned to Normandy early in the 1030s. His foundation of the abbey of Conches in about 1035 was made possible at least in part by the wealth he had accumulated in Spain. Roger did not long survive his return. He was killed in 1040 in the course of a feud with a neighbouring family, the Beaumonts. Roger's son Ralph succeeded to his father's rank and estates. He too fell foul of his lord, Duke William, and was sent into exile in about 1060. Recalled in 1063 when William's invasion of Maine made expedient a reconciliation with the barons of southern Normandy, Ralph thereafter served his duke faithfully. He fought at Hastings in 1066 and though he did not personally acquire any lands in England, other members of the family did: Domesday Book reveals Tosnys holding estates in Nottinghamshire, Lincolnshire, and Yorkshire. Like his father Roger, Ralph visited Spain (between 1066 and 1076): we do not know whether this was in quest of military adventure or as a pilgrim to Santiago de Compostela. Ralph lived to a considerable age. Before his death in 1102 he saw his son-in-law Baldwin of Boulogne, one of the leaders of the First Crusade, established in the east first as count of Edessa (1098–1100) and then as king of Jerusalem (1100–18).

The world of the Tosnys and their connections was a big one: Normandy, Apulia, Catalonia, England, Syria. It was even bigger than this. A kinsman of Roger de Tosny named Ansgot, a warrior like him under the dukes of Normandy, abandoned secular life to become a monk. He became prior of the pilgrim hospital at Melk, on the Danube between Linz and Vienna. Our source for this, as for much of the foregoing, is Orderic Vitalis, Anglo-French monk of Saint-Evroul in southern Normandy, most observant of contemporary chroniclers, who has left us an incomparably rich account of the Norman aristocracy of his day. His informant was Goisbert,

1. Wood and ivory casket carved at Cuenca in 1049–50 for a member of the ruling dynasty of the taifa principality of Toledo.

2. Ivory panel from a casket carved at about the same time and in the same workshop as the casket featured *above*: at a much later date it was 'christianised' by the insertion of the angel.

3. Fragment of eleventh-century Andalusian silk found in the tomb of Pedro, bishop of the Castilian see of Osma, a contemporary of th Cid.

7. Ivory crucifix commissioned by Fernando I of León-Castile and his wife Queen Sancha (whose names may be seen at the foot) for presentation to their most cherished religious community, San Isidoro in the city of León, in about the year 1063.

5. The foremost item of eleventh-century scientific technology: an astrolabe, made at Toledo in 1067.

6. Coinage issued by the taifa rulers of eleventh-century Spain.

4. An archway from the palace in Zaragoza constructed by the ruler al-Muqtadir in the third quarter of the eleventh century. The Cid was in exile at the court of Zaragoza between 1081 and 1086 and will have known this building well.

8. The tomb of Alfonso Ansúrez, who died young in 1093. (The youth is represented at the lower left-hand corner of the slab.) His father count Pedro was prominent among the magnates of Alfonso VI and a friend of the Cid.

TOP 9. The opening words of a charter recording the grant of landed property by the Cid and his wife to the Castilian monastery of Silos in 1076. The donors' names – 'ego Rodric Didaz et uxor mea Scemena' – may be read near the beginning of line 3. Note the open-ended letter a, whose significance is discussed in chapter 7.

BOTTOM 10. Part of a charter issued by Pedro I of Aragon in 1100, showing the king's signature in Arabic. Pedro's alliance with the Cid was an important factor in the latter's defence of Valencia between 1094 and 1099.

11. King Alfonso VI of León-Castile, rendered by an artist at Compostela in about 1130.

12. Hell, as pictured by an artist in the Castilian monastery of Silos in 1109: Avarice is represented by the figure of Dives, clutching his money-bags in the centre while being tormented by demons.

13. The castle of Atienza in Castile, which is mentioned in the *Poema de Mio Cid*: the existing fifteenth-century structure rests upon much earlier foundations.

14. The ruins of the fortress of Murviedro (now Sagunto) which the Cid captured in 1098.

15. Equestrian statue of the Cid by Anna Hyatt Huntington which stands in the grounds of the Hispanic Society of America.

16. A still from the film *El Cid* showing Charlton Heston in the title role. Ramón Menéndez Pidal acted as historical adviser during the making of the film.

17. Part of a leaf (folio 89 *recto*) from the earliest surviving manuscript of the *Historia Roderici*. The passage describes the Cid's devastation of the Rioja in 1092.

Ralph of Tosny's doctor and then a fellow monk of Orderic's for about thirty years. Orderic knew what he was talking about.

It is notable that the travels of the Tosnys were often involuntary, the compulsion of exile. The dukes of Normandy, like other eleventh-century rulers, used exile frequently as a form of punishment. It was cheaper than keeping a troublemaker in prison and brought profit to the ruler through the confiscation of the exile's property. There was a general expectation that exile would not normally last all that long. Its length would depend upon a number of variables: the nature of the misdeed, the standing and connections of the misdoer, the ruler's relative poverty or need for warriors, the amount the exile could pay to regain his lord's goodwill, and so forth; but except in very special cases it was unlikely to last for more than a few years. For the aristocratic warriors of the eleventh century a spell or two of exile was as common a hazard of life as doing time in the Gulag archipelago is for Russian dissidents of the twentieth; but nothing like so nasty. A more cheerful comparison might be with the British expatriates (sometimes a euphemistic term) who settled in Kenya's Happy Valley in the 1920s and 1930s.

Feud is another feature of the Tosny family history. As we saw, Roger of Tosny was killed in the course of a feud in 1040; we do not know exactly how it arose. It seems to have sprung from a contest for power between two rival noble families. Roger of Tosny is said to have levied war on Humphrey of Vieilles. Humphrey's son Roger of Beaumont killed Roger and two of his sons. In retaliation a vassal of the Tosnys then killed a brother of Roger of Beaumont. Peace seems afterwards to have been mediated between the feuding families, or imposed by the duke, for we hear no more of this vendetta.

There are several other comparable feuds among the Norman aristocracy reported by Orderic Vitalis, but lest the impression be given that the Normans were particularly feud-prone let our next example come from England. In 1016 Earl Uhtred of Northumbria was murdered at the instigation of his brother-in-law by another Northumbrian nobleman named Thurbrand. Ealdred, the son of Uhtred, avenged his father's murder by slaying the killer. Carl, the son of Thurbrand, inherited the feud. At this point friends intervened to attempt a reconciliation. Peace was made between the two families, and Carl and Ealdred even made plans to go on a pilgrimage to Rome together in token of friendship. But for some reason strife flared up again: Carl killed Ealdred in about 1038. Ealdred left no son, but one of his daughters was married to Earl Siward of Northumbria, who in his turn inherited the duty of vengeance and passed it on to his son Waltheof. Waltheof managed to corner all Carl's sons and grandsons while they were feasting at a family gathering at Settrington, near Malton in Yorkshire, and massacred all but two of them. The vendetta ended only with Waltheof's own execution at the hands of William I (for reasons unconnected with it) in 1076. This feud had endured for sixty years, had involved four generations of two leading aristocratic clans in the north of England, had drawn in their kinsmen and neighbours and must have gravely threatened social order and stability.

The most famous aristocratic adventurers of the eleventh century were the leaders of the Norman conquest of southern Italy and Sicily. This conquest is a convenient shorthand phrase with which to label a long-drawn-out and muddled process. Like all labels, it can mislead. The 'Norman' conquest was only partly Norman; it was emphatically not a planned conquest as was Duke William's conquest of England; and the invaders who operated in Italy can have had no conception whatever that in the following century a unified state would come into being, still less that historians would call it the Norman kingdom of southern Italy and Sicily. Italy south of Rome invited exploitation in the eleventh century in the same sort of way as did al-Andalus under the taifa kings, or Asia Minor after Manzikert. It was a tangle of rival claims and failed initiatives where centralised government had long ago fragmented (if indeed it had ever existed). Byzantine outposts in Apulia and Calabria, the so-called 'Lombard duchies' of Benevento, Capua and Salerno, city-states that were effectively independent such as Naples and Amalfi, the Muslim amirates of Sicily – all lived in uneasy co-existence, their intermittent hostilities sporadically joined by outsiders, German or papal armies, or the expedition from Constantinople led by George Maniaces in which Harald Sigurdson served.

Mercenaries drifted into this area, from France, from Normandy, from northern Italy. All sorts of factors brought them – chance, desperation, boredom, exclusion from inheritance, piety in the form of pilgrimage to the shrine of St Michael, patron of warriors, at Monte Gargano, the goad of exile, the prospect of easy pickings in loot and land. The more enterprising among them were not slow to grasp at opportunities. A Norman named Rainulf acquired the town of Aversa, near Naples, in about 1029; his nephew Richard extended this dominion by taking Capua after a long siege in 1058; their dynasty ruled the principality of Capua until the 1130s. On the other side of the Italian peninsula another Norman, Robert, the son of Tancred of Hauteville, nicknamed Guiscard 'the Crafty', gradually assembled a principality for himself in Apulia: the last outpost of Byzantine authority, the city of Bari fell to him in 1071, the year of Manzikert. His younger brother Roger invaded Sicily in 1061: Messina fell to him in that year, Palermo in 1072 and Syracuse in 1085. In the last years of his life Robert Guiscard, accompanied by his son Bohemond, took his struggle against the Byzantine empire across the Adriatic: he took Corfu in 1081, Durazzo (the modern Dürres on the coast of Albania) in 1082, and invaded Thessaly in 1083, only to be badly defeated there. At the time of his death in 1085 Robert was planning another invasion of the Balkans. His son Bohemond inherited these ambitions as a man might inherit a feud.

War as a means of livelihood; the amassing of retainers, treasure and land; the pursuit of feud and the experience of exile: these activities are central to the quality of aristocratic life in eleventh-century Europe. Common to all of them was *movement*. This was a world of people constantly on the move. It is a commonplace that kings of this period governed by itineration. It is less often remembered that their subjects were intensely mobile as well. And not just secular men. Consider for example the origins of the ten popes who occupied the see of St Peter during the lifetime of the Cid, from Clement II (1046–7) to Urban II (1088–99): one Swabian, two Bavarians, three Rhinelanders, a native of Champagne, a Lombard, a Campanian and only one Roman. 'Because I have loved justice and hated iniquity', said – in the words of the Psalmist – the only Roman among them, Gregory VII, on his deathbed in Salerno, 'therefore I die in exile.' His successor Urban II undertook his great tour of France in 1095–6, in the course of which he launched the First Crusade, in part at least because he was exiled from Rome. This was the age in which two successive archbishops of Canterbury, Lanfranc and Anselm, were natives of northern Italy. Archbishop Adalbert of Bremen (d. 1072) sent German clergy to Iceland and Greenland. English missionaries worked in Sweden. A Burgundian became bishop of Santiago de Compostela in 1094 and the Norman Arnulf of Chocques became patriarch of Jerusalem in 1099. The quest for a purer religious life could lead men to distant places. Ansgot of Melk was far from being unique. St Bruno, founder of the Carthusian order, was born in the Rhineland, taught at Rheims, founded his first monastic house near Grenoble and his next in Calabria. Anastasius, a native of Venice, became a monk of Cluny, transferred to Mont-Saint-Michel on the coast of Brittany, went to Spain to preach unsuccessfully to the Muslims and ended his life as a hermit in the French Pyrenees.

And not only those of exalted rank or wealth were on the move. The overpopulated Low Countries sent out settlers to places as diverse as Saxony, Pembrokeshire and Palestine. The Anglo-Portuguese commercial connection goes back to the twelfth century. Already a century earlier English merchants travelling to Italy were sufficiently influential with their government for Canute to negotiate privileges for them in the course of his pilgrimage to Rome in 1027. Italian businessmen were to be found in Constantinople and Alexandria by the second half of the eleventh century (if not before). Slavs could end up in the slave-markets of Fustat or Córdoba. Pisan soldiers campaigned in Tunisia in 1087. Four German bishops led a vast party of pilgrims to the Holy Land in 1064. Craftsmen from Constantinople worked at Montecassino; German moneyers were employed in English mints; Salernitan doctors were in demand in Galicia; French architects practised in Navarre; German Jews fled from persecution to England.

The list could be extended and it would contain surprises and puzzles. What first-hand traveller's tales must have ceased in County Wexford in 1060 when 'Domnall Déisech, chief of the Gaedil in piety and charity, he who travelled all the journeys which Christ travelled on earth, rested in the Lord at Tech Munnu.' What, on the other hand, had a Greek bishop been doing in the north-west of Spain in the year 1012? We have not the remotest idea, but his name – *Andreas episcopus de Grecia* – is among the witnesses to a charter for the church of Oviedo. Did the Lincolnshire squire Ulf and his wife Madselin ever reach Jerusalem, for which they were just about to set out when Ulf made his will in about 1067? We shall never know. Did the Jewish boy from Przemysl in south-eastern Poland, captured in war, sold into slavery at Prague, redeemed by a fellow Jew from Constantinople, ever see his home again? Strangest career of all, perhaps, was that of Guynemer: a pirate from Boulogne preying upon shipping in the Channel and the North Sea, he ended up as governor of Tarsus, in Cilicia, in 1097.

These patterns repeat themselves in Spain. This is not surprising, but it has received less emphasis than it deserves. It is essential to take account of it if we are to understand the social context of the Cid's career. We have already seen professional soldiers from the Christian north enlisting in Andalusian armies, and we shall encounter further examples of the phenomenon in due course. Here for the moment is one: when al-Muqtadir of Zaragoza attempted to murder his brother Yusuf of Lérida in 1058 he used as the assassin a Navarrese knight in his service. By the same token, Christian employers might recruit Muslim troops. Ramón IV, count of Pallars in the Pyrenees, called in Muslim ravagers, presumably from Zaragoza, and unleashed them upon his domestic enemies. He must have feared that rebels against his authority would try to pay him in the same coin, for he had his barons swear not to. The Castilian epic of *Los Siete Infantes de Lara* – possible the earliest epic poem to survive from medieval Spain – centres upon a family feud, betrayal and revenge in a setting of the late tenth century: it would have made no sense to an audience which was not intimately familiar with the aristocratic vendetta. Exile was as frequent in Spain as elsewhere. The *infante* Ramón who murdered his brother, King Sancho IV of Navarre, in 1076 by pushing him over a cliff spent the rest of his life in exile in the taifa kingdom of Zaragoza. Alfonso VI of León-Castile – who himself had lived in exile in Toledo for some months in 1072 – sent the rebel Count Rodrigo Ovéquiz into exile in 1088. The count's associate in rebellion, Bishop Diego Peláez of Compostela, was forced to resign his see and exiled to the kingdom of Aragon. Count Pedro Ansúrez was exiled by Alfonso VI between 1103 and 1109.

Count Pedro spent his exile in the Catalan county of Urgel. He had a family connection with the area, through his daughter who had married the count of Urgel. Thus marriage could link widely distant aristocratic clans. It could also, of course, link the Spanish kingdoms to other parts of Europe. Alfonso VI's first wife was the daughter of Count William VIII of Aquitaine, his second, Constance, was the sister of the duke of Burgundy and his third belonged to an unidentified noble dynasty of northern Italy. King Sancho Ramírez of Aragon (1903–94) married Felicia de Roucy in 1071. Her father, Hilduin de Roucy, a prominent baron of very distinguished family in northern France, had fought alongside the Aragonese at the capture of Barbastro, in the Pyrenees, in 1064. Her brother Ebles de Roucy was planning a campaign in Spain in 1073 with the encouragement of Gregory VII. One of her nephews, Rotrou of Perche, fought in the armies of her son Alfonso *el Batallador*, 'the Battler', king of Aragon from 1104 to 1134, the conqueror of Zaragoza in 1118. Another nephew, Bishop Bartholomew of Laon, was present at the consecration of Zaragoza Cathedral in 1119: his benedictional contains blessings for the weapons of those who were going off to fight in Spain. A great-nephew of Felicia's, Bertrand, met his death on the battlefield of Fraga, Alfonso *el Batallador*'s last fight and only defeat, in 1134: his obit was celebrated back home in his uncle's cathedral of Laon.

The campaign against Barbastro had involved other lordly warriors from France besides Hilduin de Roucy: William VIII of Aquitaine, Robert Crispin and possibly William of Montreuil. Robert Crispin afterwards moved on to fight in the Byzantine empire, like Roussel of Bailleul. William of Montreuil, a Norman – he belonged to the Giroie family who had been among the founders of Orderic's monastery of Saint-Evroul – had gone to Italy in about 1050 and taken service under Richard of Capua; later he transferred to the service of Pope Alexander II whose troops he commanded in Campania.

Pilgrimage to the shrine of St James brought hundreds, perhaps thousands of people to Spain every year. French settlers were coming to re-populate Spanish towns and villages. Commercial interest almost certainly lay behind the participation of fleets from Genoa and Pisa in the siege of Tortosa in 1092. Merchants from southern France were crossing the Pyrenees to trade in Catalonia, Aragon and Navarre, and English merchants are attested in north-western Spain in the early years of the twelfth century.

The traffic was not all in one direction. Alfonso VI sent relics to Countess Ida of Boulogne, the mother of the crusader Baldwin. The king's daughter Elvira married Count Raymond IV of Toulouse, the most distinguished of the leaders of the First Crusade. At least three bishops from his dominions attended Pope Urban II's council of Clermont at which the crusade was launched in 1095. Spanish knights participated in the crusade – somewhat to King Alfonso's dismay: he subsequently got the pope to issue orders to them to stay in Spain; there were plenty of infidels to be fought at home.

Pilgrims, craftsmen, brides, bearers of letters or presents, ecclesiastics, refugees, businessmen, slaves, settlers, scholars: people travelled in huge numbers and for diverse reasons in the eleventh century, as in any other. The widespread notion that medieval people were less mobile than their descendants is seriously misleading. In the present context what needs special emphasis is that the aristocratic warrior-adventurers travelled principally if not exclusively for profit.

'Stand fast, trusting wholeheartedly in the faith of Christ and the victory of the Holy Cross, because today you will all (God willing) be made rich men.' This was the watchword passed along the crusaders' lines before they charged the Turks at the battle of Dorylaeum in 1097. The account from which the quoted sentence comes was composed by a participant in the battle within at most four years of it. One could not ask for a more candid statement of the mixed motives which sustained the crusading armies. Another example of the appeal to cupidity is to be found in a piece of crude propaganda masquerading as a letter from the Emperor Alexius to Count Robert of Flanders which is a scarcely disguised invitation to the knighthood of Western Europe to lay hands on the riches of Constantinople. While it would be idle to deny that many participants in the First Crusade were fired by motives of the most exalted idealism, or that such motives could co-exist with self-interested ones, it is undoubtedly the case that large numbers of the crusaders were out for what they could get. Among the leaders this was especially true of Robert Guiscard's son Bohemond.

The emperor Alexius Comnenus was apprehensive when he heard that Bohemond had joined the crusade in 1096. As we have seen, Bohemond had accompanied his father in the invasion of the Balkan provinces of the empire in 1081–4. Bohemond had been promised that he could hold any lands conquered there as his own principality. He was unshakeably hostile to the empire and had perhaps convinced himself that he had some sort of claim upon a part of its territory. His reception in Constantinople in the spring of 1097 was of the most guarded kind, while Bohemond for his part feared that the emperor might try to poison him. 'He not only refused to taste any of the food, but would not even touch it with his finger-tips,' recalled the emperor's daughter Anna in her memoir of her father. Alexius's apprehensions were fully justified. After the crusading armies had crossed Asia Minor they settled down to besiege Antioch in October 1097. The city was betrayed to them in June 1098. The leaders of the crusade had sworn to Alexius that they would restore any formerly Roman territories which they might re-conquer to his control. But when early in the new year of 1099 they moved on towards Jerusalem under the leadership of Raymond of Toulouse, Bohemond did not accompany them. He stayed put as – in a title he took for himself soon afterwards – 'Prince of Antioch'.

Bohemond devoted the rest of his life to an attempt to consolidate his hold on Antioch and its surrounding territories, and to fight off his Byzantine Christian and Syrian Muslim enemies. He expelled the Greek clergy from Antioch and replaced them with Latins. He granted commercial privileges to the Genoese in return for naval assistance. He sought recruits and settlers from his Apulian estates. But he was not lucky. In the summer of 1100 he was captured by one of the Anatolian Turkish amirs and spent three years in captivity. During this period his nephew Tancred governed the principality of Antioch as his regent. Released on payment of a colossal ransom in 1103, Bohemond returned to Antioch. Military reverses in 1104 convinced him that it was vital to raise larger forces than were available to him in the East, so he returned to Western Europe – again deputing the regency to Tancred – and spent the years 1105 and 1106 in Italy and France raising men and money. In 1107 he opened hostilities with the Byzantine empire by laying siege to Durazzo. The Emperor Alexius was by this date in a far stronger position than he had been a quarter century earlier when Bohemond and his father had first campaigned in the Balkans. Outmanoeuvred by the Byzantine troops, Bohemond was compelled to make a humiliating peace in 1108. After this he retired to Apulia where he died in 1111, and was buried in the exquisite little mausoleum which still stands at Canossa di Puglia.

Bohemond may have died desolate, but his descendants ruled the principality of Antioch which he had founded until 1268. His career furnishes a notable example of the possibilities that unfolded before the aristocratic adventurers of the eleventh century. The Cid's exploits were cast in the same mould as those of Bohemond. Valencia was a lesser city than Antioch, lacking the numinous grandeur of Antioch's imperial and Christian past. Rodrigo left no male heirs to inherit the principality which he founded in 1094, and it lasted a mere eight years. Yet the Cid's fame has far outlasted Bohemond's. How can we know what we think we know about him?

❋ *Intermission*

7

✹ The Sources

The surviving written sources which bear upon the life of Rodrigo Díaz may be comfortably read in the space of a day. As such, they are reasonably abundant by present standards of survival from the eleventh century. A fully critical scrutiny of them would take much longer, for their interpretation is notoriously difficult. The sketch which follows is an attempt to provide an introduction to their nature and shortcomings.

Early medieval historical writing in Christian Spain was meagre and undistinguished. This poverty of Spanish historiography has often been remarked upon but never satisfactorily explained. Perhaps the principal reason is simply that in Spain there never had been any masters of the art of historical composition who might have inspired a living tradition of study and writing; nor was there much familiarity with the work of such masters elsewhere. The greatest masterpiece of early medieval historical writing, the *Ecclesiastical History of the English People* by the Northumbrian monk Bede, completed in 731, had far-reaching effects upon the writing of history, not just in Bede's native land but also throughout the kingdom of the Franks where it became widely known. But the *Ecclesiastical History* did not circulate in Spain; neither did Spain produce a Bede of her own. It is true that Latin learning was cultivated very seriously in Visigothic Spain, and in the seventh century the most learned scholars and the best-stocked libraries in Western Europe were to be found there. However, the writing of history seems to have been found unattractive. The most distinguished scholar of the age, Isidore of Seville (d. 636), did indeed write some history, among much else, but it was spare, thin, to our eyes disappointing stuff. Isidore's most influential legacy to later historians was a series of brief notes on the

89

reigns of the Visigothic kings known as the *History of the Goths*. This tradition of historical composition was taken up again in the Asturian kingdom in the ninth century, perhaps stimulated by the import of Isidore's works through the agency of Mozarabic immigrants from al-Andalus. Under the sponsorship of the royal court in the time of Alfonso III, chronicles in continuation of Isidore's – and sharing its scanty nature – were composed which carried the story of the kings from the seventh century to the middle of the ninth. These in turn were later continued by Bishop Sampiro of Astorga (d. 1042) and Bishop Pelayo of Oviedo (d. 1153): Sampiro's chronicle embraces the period from 866 to 982, Pelayo's that from 982 to 1109.

Pelayo's chronicle does at least provide us with an outline of public events in the kingdom of León-Castile during Rodrigo's lifetime. But it must be stressed that this outline is a very basic one. By comparison with the far more elaborate chronicles which were being produced in other parts of Latin Christendom, Pelayo's work was extremely sketchy. Here, for example, is a translation of his account of the reign of King Alfonso V of León who reigned from 999 to 1028:

> On the death [of Bermudo II] his son Alfonso, aged five, succeeded to the kingdom in the Era 1037 [AD 999]; and he was brought up by Count Menendo González and his wife the Countess Mayor in Galicia. They gave him their daughter Elvira in marriage, from whom he bore two children, Bermudo and Sancha. In those days King Fernando, the son of King Sancho [of Navarre], married Sancha, daughter of the aforesaid King Alfonso. Then the said King Alfonso came to León and held a council there with his bishops and counts and magnates, and re-populated the city of León which had been laid waste by the Muslim King Almanzor: and at León he issued ordinances and laws which are to be observed until this world shall end; and they are written at the end of the history of the kings of the Goths and of the Aragonese. He reigned for twenty-six [sic] years and was killed by an arrow at the town of Viseu in Portugal. He is buried at León with his aforesaid wife Elvira.

This is all that our principal source has to tell us about a reign of nearly thirty years. It is not much to go on.

Annalistic chronicles, whether pegged to the passing years or, as here, to the succession of kings, were one of the main genres of early medieval historical composition. Another was what may loosely be called Christian biography. The principal constituent here was hagiography, writing concerned with men and women who were regarded as holy, the saints. The prime purpose of the hagiographer was not simply to record information but to celebrate his subject and in doing so to teach. Examples of godly living and holy dying, of temptations overcome and miracles wrought, were designed to uplift the devout and spur them to veneration and emulation. Works of this sort are easy to mock, but they constitute one of the modern historian's most important sources of information about the early medieval period. Sensitively handled, the lives of the saints have much to tell us about beliefs, assumptions and expectations which can be gleaned from no other source, as well as a great deal of information about the mundane business of everyday life. For example, the anecdote about San Juan de Ortega and the pilferers of his building materials, quoted in an earlier chapter, is drawn from a twelfth-century life of the saint. Yet here once more the Spanish literary tradition was very weak. Only three works of hagiography survive from the Visigothic period, in contrast to the dozens composed in Francia, Italy and the British Isles during the seventh and eighth centuries. As with chronicles, so with hagiography the paucity of early models in Spain seems to have inhibited later development. The only saint's life that survives from eleventh-century Spain is the *Life of Sto. Domingo de Silos* (d. 1073), and that was the work of an immigrant from France.

Hagiography combined with elements of a rediscovered classical tradition – especially the *Lives of the Caesars* by Suetonius – gave rise to another type of Christian biography, the life of a king. Pioneered by Einhard's *Life of Charlemagne* in the ninth century, this was a well-established literary genre by the eleventh, from which period there have come down to us lives of three German emperors, two English kings and one French king. Not a single such royal biography was composed in Spain. The author of the chronicle known as the *Historia Silense* – which despite its name ('Silos History') was composed at León in about 1120 – did, it is true, plan to write a life of Alfonso VI (1065–1109), because he tells us so. If the work were ever composed, it has been lost; but it is more likely that it never got written.

Chronicle and ecclesiastical history, saint's life and royal biography – these were the principal types of Latin prose historical writing which were current in eleventh-century Western Christendom. The contribution of Spain was either meagre or non-existent.

Poetry could also be a vehicle for historical writing. Lives of saints or histories of religious communities could be rendered in verse, as for example in Alcuin's eighth-century poem on the history of the church of York. A rediscovery of classical panegyric poetry and a readiness to extend the potential of the hymn prompted the celebration of public events in Latin verse – the delivery of Paris from Viking attack, the deeds of Otto I of Germany, the expedition of the Pisans against the Tunisian city of Mahdia or the triumphs of the First Crusade. Here again the Spanish contribution was undistinguished, though something of an exception must be made for Catalonia where certain centres of learning, notably the monastery of Ripoll, cultivated a tradition of public poetry.

The earliest literary composition devoted to the exploits of Rodrigo Díaz is a poem of this type. Now in the Bibliothèque Nationale in Paris, it has come down to us in a manuscript which was brought from Catalonia to France in the seventeenth century. The manuscript had been copied at Ripoll about the year 1200, certainly before 1218. It contains three poems of the celebratory type discussed above. The first deals with the crusaders' conquest of Jerusalem in 1099 and the third is in praise of Count Ramón Berenguer IV of Barcelona (d. 1162). It is the second which is our concern. It is a set of Latin verses celebrating the early military exploits of Rodrigo Díaz, who is referred to several times in the course of it by the title *campi doctor* (of which more later). This feature has furnished scholars with the title by which the poem, untitled in the manuscript, is usually known: *Carmen Campi Doctoris* or 'Song of the Campeador'. In the manuscript copy the poem is incomplete, consisting of 129 lines divisible into thirty-two four-line stanzas and the first line of a thirty-third. There is no indication of authorship.

The poem opens with some conventional stanzas in which the anonymous author bewails his unworthiness to sing of the hero Rodrigo. After this he turns to examine Rodrigo's background, his youthful triumph over a champion from Navarre and his service in the royal households successively of Sancho II of Castile and of Alfonso VI. He goes on to relate how Rodrigo's enemies at court poison the king's mind against him so that he is sent into exile. Rodrigo defeats an army sent against him by King Alfonso under the command of the Castilian Count García Ordóñez. The author then turns to a third military exploit, Rodrigo's victory over the count of Barcelona at Almenar, near Lérida. This is approached by an elaborate description of the hero arming himself, but the poem as we have it breaks off before battle is joined. (The missing part of the text has been deliberately erased from the manuscript for reasons at which we can only guess. It approximated to ten further stanzas.)

Here is a sample of the verse, followed by an English prose translation (Stanzas 6 and 7, Lines 25–32):

> *Hoc fuit primum singulare bellum*
> *cum adolescens devicit Navarrum;*
> *hinc campi doctor dictus est maiorum*
> *ore virorum.*
>
> *Iam portendebat quid esset facturus,*
> *comitum lites nam superatus,*
> *regias opes pede calcaturus*
> *ense capturus.*

This was his first single combat, when as a young man he defeated the

Navarrese champion; for this reason he was called *campi doctor* by his elders.

Already he was foreshadowing what he was (later) to perform: for he would defeat the strivings of counts, trample beneath his feet and capture with his sword the wealth of kings.

Of course, the verve of the original is lost in a prose translation. The poem is composed in a rhythm and metre – technically known as rhythmic sapphics with homoteleutic rhyme – often though not exclusively used for hymns and clearly intended for recitation aloud.

The author was evidently a learned man, capable of writing accomplished verse in good Latin. He knew his Bible and he knew his Virgil. Furthermore, he must have written for an equally learned audience, to whom not only his diction but also his allusions to Homer, Aeneas and the Trojan War would have been intelligible. Most scholars regard it as very probable that the *Carmen* was composed at the monastery of Ripoll. There has been much discussion about the likely date of composition. A strong case has recently been made for a date very shortly after the latest event mentioned in the poem, that is the battle of Almenar which took place in 1082. Although the arguments put forward in support of this date have not commended themselves to all, they seem to me to be sufficiently cogent to permit the working hypothesis that the *Carmen* was composed in about 1083. There will be more to be said about the circumstances in which it was composed in a later chapter.

The second Latin literary work devoted to Rodrigo Díaz is of a markedly different character; more important to us than the *Carmen*, and very much more puzzling. It is a prose account of the deeds of Rodrigo, conventionally known to scholars as the *Historia Roderici*. This is not the original title but a modern one. In the earliest surviving copy, now preserved in the library of the Real Academia de la Historia in Madrid, the work is headed simply *Hic incipiunt gesta Roderici Campi Docti*, 'Here begin the deeds of Rodrigo the Campeador'. There is no indication of authorship and no dedication.

Modern editors have divided the work into seventy-seven chapters: though these divisions are not found in the manuscripts, the convention is a useful one which will be followed here. The first six chapters narrate very summarily the first thirty-odd years of Rodrigo's life, until his marriage: the author evidently knew little about his subject's early career. The next section of the text, Chapters 7–24, relates in considerably more detail the events leading up to Rodrigo's exile from Castile in 1081 and the course of his exile in Zaragoza between 1081 and 1086. Chapters 25–7 pass sketchily over his return to the favour of Alfonso VI and to his homeland in the years 1086–8. The author then provides a much more detailed narrative (Chapters 28–64) of Rodrigo's activities between 1089 and

1094, culminating in his siege and capture of Valencia. The years 1095 and 1096 are passed over, and the final chapters (65–75) chronicle the course of the last two years of Rodrigo's life, 1097–9. An epilogue in Chapters 76–7 rounds off the story with an account of the evacuation of Valencia in 1102.

Coverage of Rodrigo's career is thus uneven: the anonymous author seems to have known a good deal more about certain phases of it than about others. Indeed, he admits as much himself in the single sentence which constitutes Chapter 27:

> Not all the wars and warlike exploits which Rodrigo accomplished with his knights and companions are written in this book.

It is a curious disclaimer: honest, artless, unsophisticated. These are qualities of the author and his work, indeed, which strike the reader on his every page. He was a plain man who wrote in simple Latin. There is one clear reminiscence of biblical phraseology in Chapter 28 but no indication that the author had received any deeper literary cultivation. He communicates directly and economically. There are no frills. His style is unadorned to the point of bleakness; in the entire work the only figure of speech is a single simile, used twice: 'Rodrigo remained as still as a stone'. The *Historia* will be freely quoted in the next four chapters, but just to give the reader a first taste of the work's flavour, here is a short passage translated from Chapter 15, which deals with the campaigning of the year 1082:

> Now Rodrigo was based at that time at the castle of Escarp, between the rivers Segre and Cinca, which he had boldly taken earlier on and made all its inhabitants captive. From there he sent a messenger to al-Mu'tamin to tell him of the sufferings of and the threat to the castle of Almenar and to let him know that all those who were in the castle were worn out and starving and almost at the end of their tether. Again Rodrigo, gravely anxious, sent other messengers bearing his letters to al-Mu'tamin imploring him to come and relieve the castle which he had built. Al-Mu'tamin came at once to Rodrigo and found him at the castle of Tamarite. There they took counsel together . . .

The author maintains this even level of stylistic sobriety, this utter absence of dash, throughout the work.

The earliest surviving text of the *Historia Roderici* occurs in a manuscript copied in the first half of the thirteenth century. When it was first brought to the attention of scholars, towards the end of the eighteenth century, it was housed in the monastery of San Isidoro in León. However, it is likely that it had originally been copied further east, perhaps in Castile or the Rioja area. It has been suggested that the surviving manuscript may be identified with one referred to in a document of 1239 as having been copied for the priory of Carrión in 1232 or 1233 from an exemplar in the monastery of Nájera; an identification which is plausible but unprovable. The manuscript contains a large collection of other early Spanish historical writings. Isidore is there, and the seventh-century narrative by Julian of Toledo of the rebellion of Count Paul against the Visigothic King Wamba, the chronicles of the reign of Alfonso III, the twelfth-century compilation known as the *Crónica Nájerense* ('Chronicle of Nájera') and various miscellaneous documents such as royal genealogies. Among these the *Historia Roderici* is included without comment.

It is clear that the editor or scribe of the extant manuscript was not the author of the *Historia*. The text contains a number of mistakes in transcription which show that the scribe was copying from an exemplar in front of him (or dictated to him). So our earliest surviving manuscript is at least one remove, conceivably more, from a lost original. The problem is to discover when before c. 1230, putative date of the surviving copy, the anonymous author composed his work. This is a question that has been keenly, and inconclusively, debated. The latest datable event referred to in the text is the evacuation of Valencia by Rodrigo's widow Jimena in 1102, three years after her husband's death. This provides us with a *terminus post quem*: the work can have taken on its final form only after 1102. But how long after?

Two considerations incline me to opt cautiously for a date fairly soon afterwards. The first arises from what might appear to be no more than a trivial slip of the pen in the rendering of the patronymic 'Sánchez' (son of Sancho) in the early manuscript, at Chapter 23: the letter 'a' is replaced by the letter 'u'. It is a trivial slip, but there is more to it than meets the eye. During the latter part of the eleventh century and the early part of the twelfth the traditional script used in Spain, known as Visigothic script, was gradually being replaced by the script known in Spain as *francesa*, 'French' writing. The change was part of the body of ecclesiastical and cultural changes which were transforming Spanish life at this period, touched on in an earlier chapter. The new script owed its name to its origins in the Frankish kingdom in the time of Charlemagne, the age of the so-called Carolingian renaissance: hence it is often known as Caroline or Carolingian script. Its letter-forms were in all essentials those that we still use today. Although the older Visigothic script hung on in the most conservative parts of northern and western Spain, the Asturias and Galicia, until the second half of the twelfth century, in Aragon, Castile and León its employment was rare by about 1125 and almost unknown by the 1140s. One point of difference between the Visigothic and *francesa* scripts lay in the rendering of the first letter of the alphabet: in Visigothic script the letter 'a' was open at the top and looked remarkably like the letter 'u' as written by a scribe working in *francesa*. Where scribal error occurs in which the open-topped 'a' is rendered as 'u' there is a reasonable presumption that the manuscript from which the scribe was copying was in Visigothic script. It is a common error in Spanish manuscripts of this period. It would therefore seem likely that the lost original text of the *Historia Roderici* had been written in Visigothic script. While this does not of course prove that the original had been committed to writing before about 1125, it renders it likely.

The second consideration is of a different order and concerns not the form in which the work has been transmitted but its content. The anonymous author was so well informed about some passages in the Cid's career that it is difficult to believe that he had not himself been present to witness the events he described (or at any rate had talked to those who had). Consider, for instance, this account of Rodrigo's activities on the eastern coast of Spain in the early months of the year 1090 which occurs in Chapter 36:

> After the king returned to Toledo, Rodrigo encamped at Elche; there he celebrated Christmas Day. After the feast he departed thence and made his way along the coast until he reached Polop where there was a great cave full of treasure. He laid siege to it and invested it closely; after a few days he defeated its defenders and boldly entered it. He found, inside it much gold and silver and silk and innumerable precious stuffs. Loaded thus with the riches he needed from what he had found he left Polop and moved on until he came to *Portum Tarvani* [unidentified], and outside the city of Denia, at Ondara, he restored and strengthened a castle. He fasted there for the holy season of Lent and celebrated at the same place the Easter of the Resurrection of Jesus Christ our Lord . . .

The abundant detail of dates and places – one of the latter so obscure as to be unidentifiable today – in the relation of these fairly insignificant events suggests that the testimony of an eye-witness lies behind it. There are other immediacies in the *Historia*. The author quotes documents whose relevance would not long have outlasted the circumstances which gave rise to them (e.g. the letters in Chapters 38 and 39). He can list the prisoners taken by Rodrigo in some of his engagements (e.g. Chapter 23). He is *au fait* with the bewildering shifts of political fortune among the taifa rulers with whom Rodrigo had dealings. Time and again he shows himself familiar with the topography of the different regions of eastern Spain where Rodrigo campaigned. He can describe how Rodrigo rebuilt the castle of Benicadell (Chapter 46); he provides the best account available of the succession to the throne of Aragon in 1094 (Chapter 64); he knows the value of the chalice which Rodrigo gave to the cathedral of Valencia in 1098 (Chapter 73). These features of the work do not of course prove that it was composed at an early date, but they are the more readily explicable if the work was composed within, say, twenty years of Rodrigo's death than they would be if it were composed about 1145 or about 1170 (the two other most favoured dates).

Two further features of the *Historia Roderici* may support this view. In the first place, several critics have been struck by the author's failure to mention certain events which were germane to his subject: for instance, the death of King Alfonso VI (1109), the Almoravide capture of Zaragoza (1110), the death of the Cid's widow Doña Jimena (about 1116?), or the siege and capture of Zaragoza by Alfonso I of Aragon (1118). The great Spanish critic and historian Ramón Menéndez Pidal was so impressed by this series of omissions that it became the main plank in his argument for a date of composition before 1110. But negative evidence of this sort is nearly always slippery. It is the scholar's interpretation of the unknown author's intentions that gives significance to his omissions. So I am inclined to give less weight to this argument than Menéndez Pidal chose to do. But I would not neglect it altogether.

The other feature of the work which may be held to support an early date of composition is the author's general neutrality of tone. The work is avowedly an account of the *gesta Roderici*, 'the deeds of Rodrigo'; the author evidently admired him and we shall see in due course that he did his best to present Rodrigo's doings in a good light. Nevertheless, the hero is not consistently treated heroically. In one remarkable passage, indeed, the author is sharply critical of him. It occurs in Chapter 50 and is worth quoting:

> At length Rodrigo left Zaragoza with a very great and innumerable army, and entered the regions of Calahorra and Nájera which were in the dominions of King Alfonso and subject to his authority. Stoutly fighting, he took both Alberite and Logroño. Most savagely and mercilessly through all those regions did he lay waste with relentless, destructive, irreligious fire. He took huge booty, yet it was saddening even to tears. With harsh and impious devastation did he lay waste and destroy all the land aforesaid. He altogether stripped it of all its goods and wealth and riches, and took these for himself. Then he left the region behind him and went to the castle of Alfaro . . .

For once, perhaps significantly, the author's stylistic discipline breaks down: the Latin of the passage quoted is convoluted and my rendering is a paraphrase rather than a translation. But there can be no doubt that the author was shocked by Rodrigo's savage wasting of the Rioja in 1092 and did not mind saying so. Later treatments of Rodrigo were to be unfailingly laudatory. Again, observe the author's treatment of his subject's burial. In the final chapter he tells us that Doña Jimena had Rodrigo's body buried at the monastery of Cardeña. But nothing more is made of this. At a later period, as we shall see, the monks of Cardeña were to make as much as they possibly could of their possession of the bodies not only of Rodrigo and his wife but even of his horse. The failure of the author of the *Historia* to linger on the matter of the Cid's last resting-place would seem to support the case for an early date of composition.

Biographies of laymen who were neither kings nor saints were exceedingly rare in the early Middle Ages. The *Historia Roderici* has a claim to be regarded as one of the earliest ever composed. This very rarity has understandably caused critics to be sceptical. But, supposing that it is early, it is not absolutely without parallel. The deeds of Richard of Capua, the Norman adventurer who made himself prince of Capua and died in 1078, were celebrated by Amatus of Montecassino in his *Historia Normannorum*, which was probably composed before 1080. Geoffrey Malaterra celebrated the deeds of Count Roger of Sicily in a work composed during its subject's lifetime. Another parallel exists in the work known as the *Gesta Tancredi* ('The Deeds of Tancred'). As we saw in the preceding chapter, Tancred was the nephew of Bohemond, son of Robert Guiscard. He accompanied his uncle on the First Crusade and assisted him in the capture of Antioch. During Bohemond's absences from Antioch, first in captivity (1100–03) and then in the West (1104–06), Tancred acted as regent. After Bohemond's death in 1111 Tancred succeeded him as prince of Antioch until his own early death in 1112. Shortly after his death the Norman priest Ralph of Caen, an immigrant to the principality of Antioch, composed his *Gesta Tancredi*. There was a certain similarity between the near-contemporary careers of Rodrigo and Tancred. Ralph's *Gesta* is a work of very different character from the *Historia Roderici*: it is a good deal longer, and more self-consciously literary. I find it highly unlikely that the author of the *Historia Roderici* knew of Ralph's work or vice versa. My point is simply that not-dissimilar military-political contexts at different ends of the Mediterranean could give rise to celebrations of famous deeds in Latin prose not long after they had taken place. (It is quite likely that at least the existence of literary works devoted to the Norman leaders in Italy had reached the ears of some Spaniards: Amatus of Montecassino's *Historia* celebrated Robert Guiscard as well as Richard of Capua, and Robert's daughter was married to Count Ramón Berenguer II of Barcelona. There was at least one Spanish monk in the community of Montecassino at this period.)

This has been a long discussion and an inconclusive one. In summary, a case can be made for the composition of the *Historia Roderici* reasonably soon after its subject's death. This fact combines with certain other features of the work, such as its general sobriety of tone and treatment, to inspire confidence in the tale it tells. Of course, the anonymous author must not be read uncritically, and will not be in what follows. His work remains, however, our most authoritative source for the interpretation of Rodrigo's career.

Muslim inhabitants of al-Andalus who composed works of history in Arabic belonged, it need hardly be said, to a literary tradition very different from that which flourished in Latin Christendom. Three works, in distinct literary genres but which may all be loosely termed historical, have importance for our study of the life of the Cid. Ibn 'Alqama – or to give him his full name Abu 'Abd Allah Muhammad ibn al-Khalaf ibn 'Alqama – was a native of Valencia born in 1036–7 (AH 428) who spent most of his life as a bureaucrat in one of the taifa kingdoms of eastern Spain, possibly Denia, where he died in 1116. He composed a work of local history devoted to his native city – a popular genre in Arabic literature – which focused upon the Cid's capture of it and his subsequent rule there. It was called 'The clear exposition of the disastrous tragedy' and it appears to have been composed before Rodrigo's death in 1099. The original text of Ibn 'Alqama's work has been lost, but large parts of it were reproduced word for word by the later historian Ibn 'Idhari who was writing in Morocco about 1300 and who is generally considered a reliable transmitter of the texts he used. The title of Ibn 'Alqama's work is a candid revelation of his point of view. Hostile to Rodrigo though he may understandably have been, his work has the great value of giving an Islamic reaction to the Cid's rule as prince of Valencia between 1094 and 1099. It also furnishes information about the character of his government there which is to be found in no other source.

Another contemporary Arabic writer was Ibn Bassam (Abu l'Hassan Ali ibn Bassam). He was a native of Santarem in Portugal who can be traced at Lisbon in 1084–5, at Córdoba in 1101 and at Seville in 1109. While living in Seville he composed the third book of his 'Treasury of the excellencies of the Spaniards', a biographical dictionary of the notable inhabitants of al-Andalus – another very common Arabic literary genre. In the course of the third book he had an entry for Ibn Tahir, ruler of the taifa kingdom of Murcia from 1063 to 1078 when he was deposed, after which he settled in Valencia. As we shall see, he survived the Cid's rule in Valencia with some difficulty. Ibn Bassam has a few pages devoted to the Cid appended to his account of Ibn Tahir. Like Ibn 'Alqama, Ibn Bassam was hostile to Rodrigo; but again, it is this very hostility which gives the work its value.

One other Arabic work deserves mention, though it has nothing to say about the Cid. This is the autobiography of 'Abd Allah ibn Buluggin, the last ruler of the taifa state of Granada, deposed by the Almoravides in 1090 and exiled to Morocco where he composed his memoirs apparently in the years 1094 and 1095. The work was referred to by a number of Arabic authors of the later Middle Ages, but the text seemed to have been lost until its dramatic rediscovery by the French orientalist Lévi-Provençal in the library of the Garawiyyin mosque in Fez in 1932. 'Abd Allah's memoirs have freshness and immediacy and engaging candour. They cast a flood of light not just on the details of the dealings between the author and King Alfonso VI, the author and the Almoravide leader Yusuf, and so forth, but on the whole tone and style of public life in the age of the taifa rulers.

The four works discussed above – the *Carmen* and the *Historia*, the writings of Ibn 'Alqama and Ibn Bassam – are the only surviving treatments of the Cid's career composed either in or shortly after his own lifetime. There are several later accounts of his deeds in prose and verse, Latin and Spanish. But all of them have been infected by the growth of legend about him. Some enquirers, eloquently led by Ramón Menéndez Pidal, have believed and forcefully argued that these later works do contain some reliable historical information which can be sifted out from the legendary material and used for the reconstruction of Rodrigo Díaz's career. There are two particularly famous, or notorious, examples. One is the epic poem known as the *Poema* (or *Cantar*) *de Mio Cid*. Menéndez Pidal argued that the poem contains trustworthy information about such matters as Rodrigo's activities during his exile between 1081 and 1086, his dealings with the count of Barcelona and the names of several members of his military retinue. He founded this opinion on his views about the process and the date by which the poem was composed, since in his judgement it drew on oral traditions current in the Cid's own lifetime and had been committed to writing in the form in which it has come down to us by about 1140. Nearly all critics are now agreed that the epic was composed in a rather different manner and at a considerably later date. These are matters to which I shall return in Chapter 12. For the present, let it suffice that though the *Poema* will occasionally be quoted in the chapters which follow, no substantive historical argument will be supported by the 'evidence' which some critics have persuaded themselves that it furnishes.

The other work is the thirteenth-century vernacular chronicle known as the *Primera Crónica General*. The title is something of a misnomer. The chronicle edited under that name by Menéndez Pidal (published in 1906) has subsequently been shown to be only one skein in a more complex web of vernacular chronicles composed initially under the sponsorship of Alfonso X of Castile (1252–84) – justly called Alfonso *el Sabio*, Alfonso the Learned – in the late thirteenth and early fourteenth centuries. The tangle of different versions in different manuscripts, their chronological order, their borrowings and inter-relationships, has not yet been satisfactorily unravelled, though important recent work has gone a long way towards sorting the muddle out. The Alfonsine compilers – there seems to have been an editorial team – of this cycle of chronicles devoted a great deal of space to the exploits of the Cid. Their method was skilfully to stitch together very full extracts from all the earlier authorities on which they could lay their hands. Now it may be that the texts used for this purpose were available to the thirteenth-century compilers in fuller or more accurate versions than those in which they have come down to us in the twentieth century. To give an example: might it not be that the extracts from Ibn 'Alqama in the Alfonsine chronicles preserve better and fuller information about the Cid's rule in Valencia than is to be found in the text of Ibn 'Alqama as transmitted to us by Ibn 'Idhari? Menéndez Pidal's answer to this question was vigorously affirmative. Accordingly, he set about 'restoring' earlier texts with the help of the *Primera Crónica General* and thereby enlarging the corpus of information about the Cid with what he took to be reliable, near-contemporary materials embedded like fossils in the strata of the much later chronicles. The temptation to indulge in this approach to the texts is strong, but it should be resisted. Its drawbacks are grave and obvious. Today's scholars are much more cautious. The chronicles of the Alfonsine cycle have at best an uncertain status as historical witnesses, and no recourse will be had to their aid in what follows.

The *Carmen Campi Doctoris*, the *Historia Roderici*, the writings of Ibn 'Alqama and Ibn Bassam, widely though they differ from one another, have this in common: they are literary compositions. A different class of evidence altogether is furnished by legal documents in which the Cid's name features in some capacity or other in the course of his adult life. This is strictly contemporary evidence and, it might seem, reliable in the sense that official documents are less prejudiced than poets or biographers: there is less potential for mendacity in a title-deed than in a memoir. Here is one example. In 1098 Rodrigo granted endowments to the cathedral church of Valencia and to its bishop Jerónimo, and his donation was committed to writing on parchment, in Latin, in the form of a document technically known by the Latin term *diploma*. After the evacuation of Valencia in 1102 Jerónimo was transferred to the see of Salamanca, whose bishop he remained until his death in 1120. He took with him for safekeeping the muniments of the church of Valencia, which is why Rodrigo's diploma is still preserved at Salamanca. The document seems to be authentic, it bears what appears to be the autograph signature of Rodrigo himself and, as we shall see later on, it is of considerable historical interest. So far, so straightforward.

Matters are rarely quite so simple. One complicating factor is that most of the documents that survive from this period do so not in their original form but as copies; and their texts might have been corrupted in the course of transmission, whether by accident or by design. Again, the overwhelming majority of surviving documents are in one form or another what we would call title-deeds: they are the record of individual or corporate title to possession of lands, goods, rights or exemptions. They were kept and have come down to us because they were of value to the possessors as a means of proof of title, if challenged, in court of law. Like all such deeds from any period, they must be scrutinised attentively before they can be accepted for what they claim to be. Where eleventh-century Spain is concerned, this is more easily said than done. *Diplomatic* – the word is derived from the Latin *diploma* and has nothing to do with diplomacy – is the name that was given to the science of the study of documents by its originator, the great seventeenth-century French Benedictine scholar Jean Mabillon, in his work *De Re Diplomatica*, published in 1681. It was Mabillon's concern to demonstrate, in this the first and greatest work on its subject, that authentic documents might be distinguished from spurious ones by painstaking scrutiny of such features as their script, their phraseology, their means of authentication, and so forth. Little keys can open big doors. The science of *diplomatic* was carried to new levels of sophistication by German scholars of the nineteenth century and their example has been followed by medievalists elsewhere. The elaboration of this science was a major advance in historical method. It is disheartening to have to record that it has made little progress in Spain. With the honourable exception of a very small number of scholars who have done distinguished work, it has generally been the case that Spanish editing and criticism of medieval documents have been deplorably unsystematic and unsophisticated. It follows that there is scope for considerable disagreement about the credibility of individual documents.

Here are two examples. In the spring of 1075 a law-suit between Bishop Arias of Oviedo and Count Vela Ovéquiz was heard at Oviedo. One of the judges appointed by Alfonso VI to hear the case was 'Rodrigo Díaz the Castilian', generally assumed to have been the Cid. The document recording the hearing survives in a copy made about fifty years later. Can we trust it? In answer to this we may show, first, that the verbal formulae employed are consistent with those used in similar documents of the period; and secondly, that a certain amount is known from independent sources about the background to the dispute which provides a credible context for it. There is no good reason for doubting the fundamental reliability of this document.

My second example is much more tricky. A diploma of King Sancho II of Castile, dated 26 August 1070, survives among the archives of the monastery of Oña. By it the king promised that the final resting-place of his body would be at Oña, granted to the community the right to resettle and build churches on all its lands then held or to be acquired in the future, and favoured these landed possessions with exemption from all royal or episcopal taxes or dues for ever. Rodrigo Díaz's name features among the witnesses to the grant. If the document may be trusted, it might be held to bear out what the *Carmen Campi Doctoris* and the *Historia Roderici* tell us about Rodrigo's association with Sancho II, that he occupied a prominent place at the king's court. But can it be trusted? It is true that Oña was closely connected with the royal dynasty and that Sancho II was indeed buried there after his murder in 1072. Royal undertakings to be buried at a certain cathedral church or monastic house were not uncommon in early medieval Europe and were of keen concern to the beneficiaries because of the gifts that were likely to be made to the community in whose care the mausoleum was. So there is nothing inherently implausible about this clause – even though one can imagine circumstances after Sancho's death in which the monks of Oña might wish to establish that their possession of the king's body was in accordance with the king's wish as unambiguously expressed in writing. But the other provisions of the diploma are more fishy. Such a blanket concession to resettle land and build churches would be extremely unusual in a genuine diploma of 1070, and the grant of fiscal exemptions is so suspicious as to be frankly incredible. Furthermore, the verbal formulae in which these concessions are couched are more akin to the legal language of the late twelfth century than to that of Sancho II's reign. Now it so happens that the script of the surviving copy of the diploma is the script of about 1200 clumsily trying to imitate the Visigothic script that would have been current in 1070: the diploma is what is called a pseudo-original. The argument is clinched by a further consideration. In the course of the period between about 1185 and 1210 the monks of Oña were engaged in prolonged dispute with their diocesan, the bishop of Burgos. One matter at issue was the extent of his episcopal rights over the parish churches on the monastic estates. Therefore the diploma of Sancho II was very probably concocted in its present form – along with several other eleventh- and twelfth-century royal diplomas – in order to defend what the monks believed to be their rights against the claims of the bishop. Finally, we should note that this forgery was perpetrated at about the time that Rodrigo Díaz, El Cid, was undergoing transformation into a great Castilian hero. The force of King Sancho's grant would have been strengthened by the subscription, as a witness, of his most famous subject.

All this may be said, and it casts the severest doubts upon the claims to authenticity of Sancho's diploma in the form in which it has come down to us. But what we cannot do is to *prove* that there did not exist some perfectly genuine diploma of that date which the monks decided to improve later on. Had such a document existed, it might have borne the subscription of Rodrigo Díaz. Or it might not.

Although this has been a laborious discussion, its justification is that it is most important to grasp that the official documents of this period are difficult for the historian to handle. When the reader encounters (as he will) phrases such as 'charter evidence tells us', he should bear in mind how fragile that evidence sometimes is. Each document has to be considered on its own merits. Decisions about the trustworthiness of any individual document made by one enquirer will not always command the support of others.

With these admonitory cautions uttered, the preliminaries are over; and the reader may – at long last! – confront the subject of this book, so to say, face to face.

✳ Part Two

8

❋ The Campeador

The birthplace of Rodrigo Díaz has traditionally been placed at Vivar, a village about six miles north of Burgos. In modern times the place has been renamed Vivar del Cid in order to stress the association. The earliest evidence for the connection is to be found in the *Poema de Mio Cid* in which Rodrigo is repeatedly referred to as '*el de Bivar*', 'the man from Vivar'. The poet may have preserved an authentic tradition: we cannot tell. Vivar at any rate is a fair enough guess. Rodrigo's family held land thereabouts and he himself owned land there by the time of his marriage. The date of his birth is as uncertain as its place. Since he was active as a warrior by 1063 he must have been born about the middle of the 1040s: 1043 is the most favoured date, though it could have been as late as 1046 or even 1047.

In the *Poema* Rodrigo was insulted by the drunken Assur González:

> Ah knights! whoever has seen such evil?
> Since when might we receive honour from my Cid of Vivar?
> Let him be off to the River Ubierna to dress his millstones
> And take his miller's tolls in flour, as he used to do!

Here the historian can be more positive, and rebut this slur on Rodrigo's origins. His family was aristocratic. It is important to stress this point, for there has been a tendency in the century of the Common Man to 'democratise' the Cid and to provide him with the glamour of a 'rags-to-riches' story. It is indeed true that he did remarkably well for himself, but the home-base from which he set out was not a humble one.

The earliest piece of writing about Rodrigo, the Latin poem known as the *Carmen Campi Doctoris*, says of his ancestry:

> Nobiliori de genere ortus,
> Quod in Castella non est illo maius,

which may be literally translated: 'He is sprung from a more noble family, there is none older than it in Castile.' The phrasing is curious. In an age when distinguished ancestry was rated highly, this would seem to be a polite way of indicating that Rodrigo did not belong to the topmost ranks of the aristocracy. To be 'more noble' than some implies being 'less noble' than others. The anonymous author of the *Historia Roderici* reports Rodrigo's ancestry with a slight note of caution – 'This then is said to be the origin of his stock' – and furnishes a genealogy tracing his descent from Laín Calvo, one of the possibly legendary 'judges' of Castile in the ninth century. The more distant branches of this family tree are frankly incredible, but this need not discredit what it has to tell us of Rodrigo's more recent forebears. We can learn a little about some of them from contemporary documents. His paternal grandfather, Laín Núñez, may be traced between the mid-1040s and the early 1060s: he was a man of sufficient standing to witness charters issued by King Fernando I during Rodrigo's boyhood. His son, Rodrigo's father Diego Laínez, was a distinguished soldier who defeated the Navarrese in battle and recovered from them a number of places ceded by Fernando I to his brother García of Navarre in 1037–8: Ubierna, just north of Vivar in the valley of the river of the same name, Urbel and La Piedra a few miles away to the north-west. These exploits, hard to date, may have occurred during the late 1050s.

Nothing at all is known of Rodrigo's mother. The fact that he was given a name that was current in her family but not in his father's might perhaps indicate that her family was rather grander than his. His maternal grandfather, Rodrigo Alvarez, was certainly a man of note. He and his brother Nuño had been early and firm supporters of Fernando I. Rodrigo attended his coronation in León in 1038 and frequently witnessed his charters. Nuño held the important fortress of Amaya, north of Burgos, on the king's behalf and Rodrigo the castle of Luna, north of Miranda de Ebro. Rodrigo also administered the regions depending on Mormojón, Moradillo, Cellorigo and Curiel, the last three of them being sensitive areas contiguous to Castile's eastern and southern marches.

Relatives so well-connected and so loyal to the ruling dynasty could afford to do well by the younger members of the family. The young Rodrigo was placed in the household of King Fernando's eldest son Sancho, the heir to the throne of Castile. This would have occurred when he was about fourteen. We have just a very few hints about his upbringing before this. He was literate – there survives indeed a specimen of his handwriting – and it is reasonable to suppose that he acquired his literacy at an early age. His slightly older contemporary Domingo, later abbot of Silos, 'neglected the study of letters' while he was a boy – which at least implies that he was offered it. It is likely that tuition was to be had in nearby Burgos: perhaps Rodrigo was sent to school there, or a tutor hired to come out to his parents' home in the Ubierna valley. As an adult Rodrigo would be appointed to hear law-suits by the king on at least two occasions: the implication that he had been taught some law is inescapable. Whether he had had to sweat over the whole corpus of Visigothic law in its archaic seventh-century Latin we have no means of telling. A fine surviving manuscript, now in the Biblioteca Nacional in Madrid, was copied at León for a layman, a judge named Froila, in 1058. Such people may have existed at Burgos too. Alternatively, perhaps all that was needed was famili-arity with those parts of the corpus which touched the day-to-day concerns of a Castilian landowner.

Rodrigo, then, was not wholly lacking in intellectual cultivation. A most surprising glimpse of him towards the end of his life, credible because it comes from a hostile source, is afforded by Ibn Bassam:

> It is said that books were studied in his presence: the warlike deeds of the old heroes of Arabia were read to him, and when the story of *Mohallab* was reached he was seized with delight and expressed himself full of admiration for this hero.

It is an intriguing sidelight on the leisure hours of the conqueror of Valencia. (One wonders if they were read to him in Arabic. Rodrigo must have acquired at least the rudiments of the language during his exile in Zaragoza. Hugh Bunel, who was exiled from Normandy after hacking off the head of Mabel of Bellême as she lay in bed, lived for twenty years among the Saracens, studying their customs and language: as a result he was able to offer useful services to the armies of the First Crusade.) Rodrigo's taste for heroic deeds must have been implanted at an early age through Bible stories, legends of the saints, tales of the Spanish past and pride in the exploits of ancestors. Martial virtue tempered by a certain crude Christian morality was what eleventh-century noblemen sought to inculcate in their sons.

Horsemanship was the first prerequisite for a military career. Rodrigo would have had his first riding lessons almost as soon as he could walk. Under the strict gaze of his father's grooms he would have progressed from donkey to pony, from pony to horse, learning by practice how to keep his seat, how to govern a fractious beast or calm a nervous one, how to ride for long hours over rough country without tiring, and all the other skills that would go to preserve his life in the mêlée of combat. Hunting and hawking, the nobleman's pastimes, developed further skills: an eye for country – surface and slope, vantage point and dead ground; the habit of moving on horseback in company, if necessary swiftly and silently; the difficult art of shooting from horseback with bow and arrow at a moving quarry; the courage needed to dismount and face the charge of a boar with only a spear to protect the hunter from its tusks; endurance of heat and cold, hunger and thirst; care of weapons and tack, where a loose knife-haft or a girth worn to breaking could cost limb or even life.

Military training proper succeeded the grounding in horseman-ship, and in the eleventh century it seems to have started at about the age of twelve. It was a matter of learning how to manage the shield of defence and the weapons of offence while on the back of one of the war-horses for which Spain was renowned. (Robert of Bellême, son of the luckless Mabel and one of the foremost barons of the Anglo-Norman realm, imported his horses from Spain.) These were difficult skills – difficult for the horse as well as the rider – which took long to perfect and which needed to be kept in trim by regular practice. Rodrigo will have continued to learn them after his move to the court of the young Prince Sancho. We are told that Sancho 'girded him with the belt of knighthood' and this probably marked the end of Rodrigo's apprenticeship. The ceremonial involved was rudimentary in this age, compared to what it was to become with the development of chivalrous ideas in and after the twelfth century. The best illustration of what contemporaries did is to be found in the scene in the Bayeux Tapestry where Duke William 'gave arms' to Earl Harold in about 1064. The two men stood facing each other and William, holding Harold's upper right arm with his right hand, placed a helmet on Harold's head with his left; in his left hand Harold held a pennanted spear, presumably presented to him a moment before by William. Customs varied throughout Europe, but some such ceremony as this took place between Sancho and Rodrigo, perhaps in about 1062.

In that year of 1062 a certain Pedro Rúiz, of whom we know little save that he was a courtier of Fernando I and a friend of Rodrigo's grandfather (and therefore very likely known to Rodrigo too), granted some land to the Castilian monastery of Arlanza, and threw in with it

> my equipment, that is my gold-embossed saddle with its bridle, my sword and sword-belt, my spurs, my shield with its spear, my other decorated swords, my coats of mail and my helmets, the other swords

which are not decorated, and my shields and horses and mules, and my clothes, and my other spurs, and the other bridle chased with silver.

This is as good a description as any of the equipment of an aristo-cratic soldier in the middle years of the eleventh century. Pedro Rúiz was approaching the end of a successful career and had amassed great riches. In 1062 Rodrigo would not have owned anything like the quantity of this gear, or the value – for knightly equipment was extremely expensive. Still, it must have been what he hoped to possess one day.

The armour was made up of mail-coat, helmet and shield. The *lorica* or mail-coat was a long-sleeved, knee-length garment, suf-ficiently loose to be worn over a padded tunic beneath; horsemen and sometimes footsoldiers too had it slashed below the waist before and behind for greater ease of movement; sometimes the lower half took the form of knee-breeches. The more expensive mail-coats were made of thousands of tiny steel rings riveted together, giving the effect of coarse knitting; cheaper versions consisted simply of overlapping steel rings sewn on to leather. Plate armour was still a good two-and-a-half centuries away. The helmet was a conical iron or steel cap with a projecting piece, the nasal, to give some pro-tection to the nose, and sometimes with ear-flaps or cheek-guards, or a curtain of mail at the back to protect the neck. It was padded within to soften the shock of a blow to the head. Shields were either kite-shaped or round. They were made of wood, or boiled leather stretched on a wooden frame, and strengthened with metal hubs or spokes or studs (or all of these). The sword was the weapon *par excellence*, a long, double-edged blade designed for cutting and slash-ing, ideally suited to use from horseback against an enemy on foot. Swords were often richly decorated about the hilt and pommel, and this is presumably the meaning of the word 'decorated' (*labratas*) in Pedro Rúiz's list; though it could alternatively indicate that the swords in question were damascene, a technique originating in Damascus by which the metal was worked into wavy patterns. Sword-belts too were often decorated.

It is a little surprising that Pedro Rúiz should mention only one spear. The spear or lance was a much cheaper weapon than the sword. It could be used in various ways, as we may see on the Bayeux Tapestry (the best illustration of troops in combat that survives from the eleventh century) – hurled as a projectile, held over- or under-arm to deliver a thrust, or couched firmly under the armpit. The last-named method of handling a spear seems to have been developed about the middle years of the eleventh century. Here is a good description of it: the spear

is tucked tightly under the right armpit, so that it remains steady, and gripped further back, with the left arm free to handle reins and shield. Horse, rider and lance are thus gathered together into what has been called 'a human projectile'. A body of horsemen thus armed can deliver at a massed enemy a hammer blow, whose effect depends on the momentum of the charge and the shock of impact . . . To make the manoeuvre effective, a heavier lance was needed: a light one would simply shatter on impact. It was also found that the rider who fought in this way could grip his lance somewhat further back from the natural point of balance and still hold it steady, and he could therefore use a longer lance, which was an obvious advantage.

Pedro Rúiz's rather curious reference to 'my shield with its spear' suggests that spear and shield went together and that there was something special about this spear in particular. Could it perhaps have been one of the heavy lances needed for the new tactic of the charge with couched lance?

A knight would look to have a string of horses: a palfrey for everyday travel, a war-horse for combat (not yet the immensely heavy horses of later medieval warriors), mounts for servants and baggage which in Spain would often be mules rather than horses because they consume less water. Saddle, bridle and spurs offered further opportunities for display. With the development of the charge saddles were tending to become heavier and to develop prominent pommels and saddle-bows to help to fix the rider more firmly in his seat and lessen the risk of his being hurled off on impact.

The first significant military campaign in which Rodrigo served was that directed against the Pyrenean town of Graus by the *infante* Sancho of Castile in 1063. In the spring of that year King Ramiro I of Aragon – brother of Fernando I, uncle therefore of Sancho – had attacked the ruler of the taifa principality of Zaragoza, al-Muqtadir. The background to this seems to have been a fair amount of fishing in the turbulent waters of Zaragozan politics by the Aragonese, which was regarded with apprehension by the Castilians. As seen from the Castilian royal court the balance of power in the Peninsula required that Zaragoza be protected from the hostility of her neighbours lest their territorial pickings render them over-mighty. This possibility came closer to reality when the Aragonese captured Graus. The town was in itself not particularly important, but it stands in the foothills of the Pyrenees, and its capture indicated Aragonese designs on bigger towns such as Barbastro and Huesca, and ultimately upon the rich valley of the River Ebro and its capital Zaragoza itself.

The king of Castile sent his son Sancho to assist al-Muqtadir to recover Graus. The Aragonese were successfully dislodged after defeat in a battle. What made the campaign memorable was the death of the Aragonese King Ramiro in the battle (8 May 1063). He was killed, so it was alleged by a Muslim chronicler who was living in Zaragoza in the 1070s, by a skilled frontiersman named Sa'dada whose command of the Romance language of the Aragonese troops enabled him to enter their lines in disguise and get near enough to the king to strike him down with a lance-blow to the eye. The author of the *Historia Roderici* is laconic:

> When King Sancho went to Zaragoza and fought with the Aragonese King Ramiro at Graus, whom he defeated and killed there, he took Rodrigo Díaz with him: Rodrigo was a part of the army which fought in the victorious battle.

The Graus campaign is a fine example of the complexities which arose in the age of the taifa kings: a Castilian prince defeats and kills his Aragonese uncle in order to preserve the territorial integrity of a Muslim ally. Rodrigo was being initiated into diplomacy as well as war. The lessons he learned and the contacts that he made – for the young knights of Sancho's household must have met their opposite numbers at the court of Zaragoza – would be of service to him later on.

Little else is known about Rodrigo's activities in these early years before the accession to the throne of his patron Sancho. A victory in single combat with a Navarrese warrior named Jimeno Garcés was later remembered. We cannot date the episode, let alone reconstruct the circumstances which gave rise to it. It is a fair guess that his father's skirmishings with the Navarrese had left behind a web of vendetta in which Rodrigo found himself caught up: perhaps the explanation lies here. Also to be remembered and recorded was a combat with a Saracen of Medinaceli whom Rodrigo defeated and killed. Here too the date and circumstances elude us: the fight with the Navarrese is attested in the *Carmen Campi Doctoris* and the *Historia Roderici*, that with the champion from Medinaceli only in the *Historia*. We need not reject them, as some scholars have, simply because they have no corroboration in other sources. They are exactly what we should expect to learn of a young warrior of the eleventh century with his way to make in the world. These exploits brought Rodrigo fame, no doubt, in a modest way, as an up-and-coming man. They must also have brought him wealth: the ransom of Jimeno Garcés, the battle-gear of the man from Medinaceli.

In the autumn of 1065 Fernando I led his last campaign. It was directed against the city of Valencia on the Mediterranean coast. A chronicler in León, perhaps contemporary, tells us that he would have conquered it had he not been stricken there with his last illness. The ailing king-emperor was carried back to León and there prepared for death. On Christmas Eve he was brought into the basilica of St Isidore, newly built under royal patronage to house the relics of the saint which the king had had brought from Seville two years before. Fernando participated in the Matins of the Nativity in the early hours of Christmas Day and attended mass later on. On the following day he renounced his royal office, symbolically divesting himself of royal robes and crown, and entered the state of a penitent. He lingered in the penitential state for two further days and on the third, 29 December 1065, he died at noon.

Two years previously Fernando I had made provision for the partition of his realms, on his death, between his three grown sons. To Sancho the eldest, he left Castile; to Alfonso, his favourite, León; and to García, the youngest, Galicia. He also divided among his sons the annual revenues from tributes paid by the taifa kings. Sancho got the tribute from Zaragoza, Alfonso that from Toledo, and García those from Badajoz and Seville.

Rodrigo's patron was now a king in his own right. The status of the members of his household would have risen accordingly. Rodrigo witnessed a number of Sancho II's charters between 1066 and 1071, which indicates his continued prominence at the royal court. The author of the *Historia Roderici* tells us that Sancho made him 'commander of his whole military following (*militiam*)'. That is to say, Rodrigo was given the office in the royal household of *armiger* (in Latin) or *alférez* (in Romance), the position commonly known in feudal France or England as *constable*. The king's *armiger* was originally just what the Latin word literally means, the bearer of the king's arms. On ceremonial occasions in the eleventh and later centuries the *armiger* continued to be the royal servant whose duty and privilege it was to carry the king's sword, lance and shield. But by Sancho II's day the responsibilities of this officer were far wider than the merely domestic or ceremonial. The *armiger* was responsible for overseeing the king's household militia, the body of troops who formed the king's escort and were the nucleus of the royal army. While we do not possess any contemporary description of the duties of the *armiger*, it is likely that he was responsible for recruiting, training and keeping order among these often unruly young men; perhaps for supervising the arrangements for their payment too. He had to have an eye for potential talent, to be demanding in his appraisal of mounts and equipment, to be firm and tactful in sorting out the scrapes his subordinates landed themselves in. He was also one of the king's principal military advisers. Thus the *armiger* had to be at once staff-officer, adjutant, regimental sergeant-major – and something of a counsellor. It was a demanding job. Usually held by fairly young men, it equipped them for independent command.

Rodrigo's tenure of the office of *armiger* has been doubted. It is indeed true that Sancho II's charters never give him the title, but they are unusually sparing in their indication of *any* lay office-holders of the royal household, so this silence cannot be taken to prove a negative. It is also true that the *Carmen Campi Doctoris* says of King Sancho that 'he wanted to give [Rodrigo] command of his main troops', rather than that he actually did; but this wording could have been dictated by the demands of the metre of the poem, and the implications of the phraseology should not be pressed too far. There is no insurmountable difficulty in believing that Rodrigo was indeed what his biographer says that he was.

It could have been during his period in the household of Sancho II that Rodrigo came to be known by another title: *campi doctor, campi doctus,* or in its Romance and more familiar form, *campeador.* The term is found in Late Latin writers of the fourth and fifth centuries, and occurs on a handful of inscriptions of the same sort of date. After this it ceased to be current, though it occasionally surfaces in the writings of the more learned authors of the Middle Ages. It was known, for example, to John of Salisbury (d. 1180), whose knowledge of the Latin literature of antiquity was very wide. The literal meaning of the term *campi doctor* is 'teacher of the (military) field', and in the late Roman army it seems to have indicated just this – a regimental drill-instructor. It is curious to find the term resurfacing in eleventh-century Spain and its appearance there has never convincingly been explained. Interestingly enough it does characterise the duties of a royal *armiger*. However, it need not – though it could – have been used at the court of Sancho II. It might have been discovered and put into circulation by the author of the *Carmen Campi Doctoris*, who had probably been educated at the Catalan monastery of Ripoll. There was an excellent library at Ripoll and the author could have come across the term in the course of his reading there. What is certain is that it did achieve currency during Rodrigo's lifetime. It was applied to him by a member of his entourage in an official document given in his name in 1098.

Rodrigo had a busy time of it as *armiger* to Sancho II. The annual tribute from Zaragoza had to be exacted by the threat, possibly the employment, of force. In the late summer of 1067 the so-called 'war of the three Sanchos' took place, a conflict between Sancho II of Castile on the one side and on the other the forces of his cousins Sancho IV of Navarre and Sancho Ramírez of Aragon. Details about the campaign are furnished only by late and unreliable chroniclers. It seems to have been occasioned by bickerings over the frontier between Castile and Navarre, rivalries over the protectorate of Zaragoza, and the king of Aragon's desire to avenge the death of his father at Graus.

Shortly afterwards, on 7 November 1067, the Dowager-Empress Sancha, the widow of Fernando I, died at León. If, as seems likely, her authority had imposed restraint upon her children, her death precipitated the fratricidal strife which Fernando's partition of his kingdom had made almost inevitable. It had not been an equitable division: Alfonso had received, in León, a better deal than either of his brothers. Hostilities between Castile and León broke out in 1068. In a battle fought at Llantada, Alfonso of León was defeated by Sancho of Castile, though probably not decisively since his kingdom remained intact. Peace between the brothers was patched up. Three years later they turned upon the third brother, García of Galicia. He was defeated in May 1071. Sancho and Alfonso seem to have ruled Galicia jointly. The experiment must have been almost unworkable, and it quickly broke down. Hostilities broke out between the brothers and early in January 1072 Alfonso was defeated and captured by Sancho at Golpejera, near Carrión. Sancho was crowned king at León on 12 January. Alfonso, briefly imprisoned and then released, went into exile at the court of al-Ma'mun of Toledo. García went into exile at Seville. Sancho had reunited the dominions which his father had governed: his sway extended from the Montes de Oca east of Burgos to the Atlantic coast west of Santiago de Compostela. The responsibilities and rewards of his *armiger* increased correspondingly. As the author of the *Historia Roderici* put it succinctly:

> In every battle which King Sancho fought with King Alfonso, at Llantada and Golpejera, and defeated him, Rodrigo bore the king's royal standard, and distinguished himself among the soldiers, and bettered himself thereby.

Sancho II's rule over Castile, León and Galicia lasted only nine months. On 7 October 1072 he was killed outside the Leónese town of Zamora. The circumstances of Sancho's death generated much legend, rendering it difficult to get at the historical truth. Two things seem reasonably certain: first, that Sancho was at Zamora in order to put down an insurrection against him; and second, that his murder involved treachery.

Zamora lies on the north bank of the River Duero about twenty-five miles east of the present frontier between Spain and Portugal. At the time of Sancho's death it was the southernmost settlement of any significance in the Leónese part of his kingdom. Beyond it lay the Tierras Despobladas, the no-man's-land of the trans-Duero frontier zone which would not come securely under Christian control until another decade or so had passed. This in itself suggests that the trouble which took Sancho to Zamora was an attempt to invade his kingdom from the south, that is to say from the taifas of either Badajoz or Toledo. That the king himself should have gone to Zamora suggests that the threat was serious. There is one further point about Zamora. It lies on the main road, Roman in origin, leading from south to north across easy, level country which can be quickly traversed, up to the imperial city of León. An invasion from the south by way of Zamora is likely to have been directed at León. All these considerations lead one to suppose that the thrust was planned by the deposed Alfonso VI of León, exiled in Toledo. Was it even led by him? One of our sources, possibly the earliest, tells us that Alfonso was in Zamora at the time of his brother's death. Another, composed about fifty years later, and favourable to Alfonso, claims that he remained in Toledo, assisting the revolt from a distance. We cannot decide between them. One may observe that in eleventh-century conditions it would have been most unusual for an invasion of this kind not to have been led by the claimant in person. It should also be borne in mind that the later of the two authors was concerned to exonerate Alfonso from any direct complicity in Sancho's murder. A third source, composed in about 1130, informs us that the rising at Zamora was led by the Princess Urraca, sister of Alfonso and Sancho, and by 'a certain count called Pedro Ansúrez'. Urraca is implicated in other, much later and less reliable sources, which cannot be used to provide corroboration. She may at this date, as she did later, have owned estates in the Duero valley towards Zamora. If she were known to favour the claims of Alfonso, this could have helped to decide the route of the invasion. Pedro Ansúrez belonged to a very important family of Leónese magnates. He was a man of about the same age as Rodrigo Díaz, perhaps a few years older, and as closely associated with Alfonso VI as Rodrigo was with Sancho II. In 1067 he held one of the great court offices, that of *mayordomo*, and by 1071 he had been promoted to the dignity of count. His fortunes fell with his king's and he accompanied Alfonso into his Toledan exile. He had everything to gain by supporting the attempted comeback. It is worth noting that he too held lands near Zamora.

All surviving sources save one agree that Sancho met his death through treachery. (The one exception is, perhaps surprisingly, the *Historia Roderici*, whose author records the death of Sancho II neutrally and in passing.) The earlier among them report the fact briefly, and no more. King Sancho was killed *fraudulenter, dolose, machinatione*, all of them words signifying that foul play was involved. Later and less reliable sources furnish more detail: by the middle of the thirteenth century a whole vernacular epic devoted to Sancho's siege of Zamora had been composed; but the historian need not concern himself with these legendary materials. The point we should most like guidance on but where we are least likely to receive it concerns the extent of Alfonso's guilt in his brother's death. One early and hostile source implicates him; the other early sources are, as we have just seen, discreet. Alfonso profited from Sancho's death, but that does not make him guilty of it, any more than Henry I's accession to the English throne in 1100 proves that he was guilty of the death of his brother William Rufus in the New Forest. Specu-lation is fruitless. All that we may reasonably surmise is that in some quarters Alfonso would have come under suspicion. Suspicion would presumably have been liveliest among the Castilian henchmen of the murdered king.

Rodrigo, as the king's *armiger*, was in Sancho's army at Zamora. His biographer told of his exploits there; possibly they had grown a little in the telling:

> When King Sancho besieged Zamora it happened that Rodrigo Díaz fought alone with fifteen enemy knights . . . one of them he killed, two he wounded and unhorsed, and the remainder he put to flight by his spirited courage.

Sancho was buried, as he had wished, at the Castilian monastery of Oña. We may presume that Rodrigo was among the cortège of the dead king's household retainers who would have accompanied their lord's body home to Castile for burial. Alfonso meanwhile – whether or not he was at Zamora when Sancho was killed – made his way to the royal city of León from which he had been expelled nine months earlier: two of his charters dated 17 and 19 November 1072 were almost certainly issued at León. A third charter, dated 8 December 1072, is the earliest surviving charter of Alfonso VI granted to a Castilian beneficiary, the monastery of Cardeña outside Burgos, and it was subscribed by several prominent Castilians, among them Rodrigo Díaz. He had transferred his loyalties to Alfonso and had been accepted among the king's vassals. The author of the *Historia Roderici* stressed the point:

> After the death of his lord King Sancho, who had maintained and loved him well, King Alfonso received him with honour as his vassal and kept him in his entourage with very respectful affection.

These words deserve emphasis as an early and authoritative state-ment about the nature of the relations between Rodrigo and King Alfonso. For here too the myth-makers were to become busy. In the thirteenth century there was to be recorded the story that Rodrigo exacted an oath from the king, in the church of St Gadea in Burgos, to the effect that he had no part in bringing about his brother's murder. The story is fantastic, though it has found its modern defenders. Ramón Menéndez Pidal, most influential of modern historians of El Cid, urged its truth. Central to his interpret-ation of Rodrigo's career was the notion of deep-seated mistrust between Alfonso and Rodrigo. Because the hero had to be blameless, this meant that the king must have been at fault. Menéndez Pidal expended great ingenuity in unravelling the recesses of Alfonso VI's

character. He portrayed the king as an egoist, the spoilt favourite
child of his parents, a man who lacked confidence in himself and
could not bear to contemplate success in others, a victim of morbid
jealousy. He compared Alfonso to Saul, Rodrigo to David.

Such an interpretation of the character of Alfonso VI is untenable
for the simple reason that the sources do not support it. The trouble
is that they do not permit any view at all of his character beyond
what may be inferred from the record of his public acts as king of
León-Castile. As we saw in the preceding chapter, the author of the
Historia Silense intended to compose a biography of the king but
probably never did so. This is certainly a loss, but one whose
magnitude we should not exaggerate. Surviving eleventh-century
royal biographies, for example of the German emperor Conrad II
or of William the Conqueror, do not tell us much of their subjects'
personality. Authors tended to deal in stereotypes. Kings are just,
pious, brave, prudent, or whatever other quality. Such comments
as we have about Alfonso VI are of this type. For example, the
cathedral community of Santiago de Compostela, looking back from
the strife-torn reign of his daughter Urraca (1109–26), remembered
him as 'most noble, . . . most pious . . . glorious . . . most illustrious . . . of happy memory', and so forth. This is hardly surprising;
neither is it particularly helpful. In consequence we cannot penetrate
the secrets of Alfonso VI's personality.

The public record establishes Alfonso VI as one of the greatest
rulers of his age. A crowned monarch for nearly forty-four years,
for almost thirty-seven of them he governed successfully a large and
expanding kingdom. He fulfilled every expectation of an eleventh-
century monarch with conspicuous success, saving only one; but it
was a genetic accident, not the royal fault, that he failed to leave a
male heir. (Neither was it for want of trying: five wives, at least
two concubines.) The art of being a successful king in the eleventh
century, as at other times, largely resolved itself into the business
of patronage or man-management. Rodrigo Díaz was one of many
men, and by no means the most important among them, whom
Alfonso had to manage. How were they going to fare?

Rodrigo's standing at the court of Alfonso VI could not have
been what it had been in Sancho's. The new king had Leónese
followers to reward. Prudence might suggest a conciliatory attitude
towards Sancho's men but would also counsel against entrusting the
more important offices to them. The king's *armiger* in the years
1072–3 was the Leónese Gonzalo Díaz. Rodrigo was never again to
hold this office. He had been displaced from the supreme military
command that he had held under Sancho.

And yet he was a trusted servant of the king. The earliest surviving
indication of this is the record of a law-suit heard in April 1073. It
was occasioned by a dispute over grazing rights between the monas-

tery of Cardeña and the landowners of the valley of Orbaneja, a little to the north. The document which is our sole evidence of this has been garbled in transmission and is not wholly intelligible. But what is clear is that the dispute, apparently after smouldering for some time, had erupted into violence: 104 oxen belonging to the monks had been seized. The matter came before the king's court. Two prominent local notables represented the abbot of Cardeña: one of them was a certain Ciprián, who was *merino* (or governor) of Burgos, and the other was Rodrigo Díaz. After lengthy argument they won their case, and the record of it was duly preserved among the abbey's muniments.

Two years later the hearing of another suit, in a different part of the country, was delegated to Rodrigo by the king. We know something of the background to this one. Early in the century Count Gondemar Piniólez and his wife Mumadona had founded a monastery at Tol, to the west of Oviedo near the estuary of the River Eo which divides the Asturias from Galicia. After Gondemar's death his widow had given the monastery to Guntroda, the count's daughter by an earlier marriage. Guntroda's was to be a life-interest only: after her death Tol was to pass into the possession of the cathedral church of Oviedo. Guntroda had lived out her life as a nun, and died in February 1075. The bishop of Oviedo's claims to Tol were then contested by Count Vela Ovéquiz and his brother, who were great-nephews of Count Gondemar. The case came before the king when he was in the Asturias in the early part of 1075. He appointed four judges to hear it: Bernard, bishop of Palencia, Sisnando Davídez, lord of Coimbra; Rodrigo Díaz; and a *grammaticus*, a teacher and scholar, named Tuxmarus. (The last name, a very odd one, might have been corrupted in transmission.) After hearing the claims of both sides, examining the documents the parties brought forward, and referring to the Visigothic law-code, the judges found in favour of Bishop Arias and the church of Oviedo.

The royal court had made its way to the Asturias for an occasion of the utmost solemnity. The most precious possession of the cathedral church of Oviedo was a chest of great antiquity which was believed to contain relics of the saints. The story went that these had been assembled from various places at Toledo at the time of the Islamic invasion and transferred for safe-keeping to Oviedo. As the years went by, people forgot exactly what the chest contained. An early eleventh-century bishop of Oviedo, Ponce, had ventured to open it. But as soon as the lid was prised open a little a blinding light shone forth, so that the bishop and his assistants were unable to see what lay inside. So matters remained until the days of 'the most serene worshipper of God', King Alfonso VI. It was on his initiative that the decision to attempt another investigation was taken. The royal court made its way to Oviedo for the beginning of Lent (18

February 1075) and embarked upon a stricter than usual observance of the Lenten fast. In the middle of Lent, on Friday, 13 March, the chest was opened and found to contain, in the words of a witness who wrote on the following day, 'an unbelievable treasure' of relics – fragments of the True Cross and of the bread of the Last Supper, phials of the blood of Jesus and of the Virgin Mary's milk, relics of St John the Baptist and several apostles and St Stephen the Protomartyr, and of at least sixty other saints ranging from those venerated throughout Western Christendom such as St Martin of Tours, to those whose cults were limited to Spain such as St Emilian the deacon and St Eulalia of Barcelona. The king commissioned a sumptuous silver reliquary to contain the remains, which is still to be seen in the cathedral treasury of Oviedo.

Rodrigo subscribed the royal diploma drawn up on the following day which is our main record of the occasion, so we may take it as reasonably certain that he himself witnessed the rediscovery of the relics. In addition to his duty of attendance at court, there may have been a further, domestic reason for his journey to the Asturias in the early months of 1075. We encounter here the difficult problems presented by the evidence relating to Rodrigo's marriage. The author of the *Historia Roderici* tells us in his usual straightforward fashion that

the king gave him one of his relatives to wife, the lady Jimena, daughter of Count Diego of Oviedo.

Difficulties begin when we try to probe a little further into Jimena's background. Menéndez Pidal reconstructed her genealogy on the side of her mother, Cristina, a grand-daughter of King Alfonso V (d. 1028) and Queen Elvira, her other grandparents being none other than Count Gondemar Piniólez and Mumadona, the founders of the monastery of Tol. But the documents on which he relied to establish this genealogy are less trustworthy than he believed. Jimena's father Diego is even more elusive. We cannot demonstrate with certainty that a Count Diego ever existed in the middle years of the eleventh century. On the other hand, it must also be said that we cannot show that he did *not*. We are simply very poorly informed about the succession of the counts who administered the Asturian region during this period. Two men with the patronymic Díaz, i.e. son of Diego, were just embarking on distinguished public careers which would make them successive counts of Oviedo. Their father must have been a man of high rank, presumably in that region. Were they Jimena's brothers? It is widely assumed that they were. Although considerable difficulties remain, I am inclined to think that Rodrigo did marry into an Asturian family of noble rank, even though we cannot confidently identify it. The marriage was arranged by the king. From Alfonso's point of view it bound together two prominent families from different parts of the kingdom, and thus might be hoped to contribute to his realm's coherence. From Rodrigo's, it may have brought, all other things that marriage brings apart, connection with a clan somewhat grander than his own family. For Jimena, she was marrying an up-and-coming man with good connections and prospects.

By an astonishing chance the document recording the settlement that Rodrigo made on his bride has survived among the archives of the church of Burgos. It is technically known as a *carta de arras*, a charter of *arras*, the *arras* being a settlement of property by a husband upon a wife at the time of the wedding. The *arras* remained the wife's portion throughout married life and widowhood, and was then passed on to the children; if she were to remarry, the *arras* from the first marriage was to go to the children of that marriage at the time of the second. The *arras* granted by Rodrigo to Jimena was determined 'according to the custom of León'. This meant that he settled up to half of his property on her. (There was no precise stipulation in existing law. Under Castilian custom it was usual to settle one-third of property on the wife. According to Leónese custom this proportion might be exceeded up to the limit of one-half.) The estates listed in the charter of *arras* should therefore indicate the approximate extent of between a third and a half of Rodrigo's landed wealth at the time of his marriage. Unfortunately for us the document does not specify the size or value of the individual properties. They were for the most part recorded in the form, for example, *in Gragera et in Iudeco meas porciones*, 'my lands in Grajera and Yudego'; and we cannot always tell whether the 'lands' in question were, at one extreme, a plot of vineyard or garden or, at the other, a whole village with its surrounding arable and pasture and other appurtenances such as mills. So the record cannot tell us how rich Rodrigo was. What it can and does do is indicate how very widely scattered his estates were.

There is another way in which the charter of *arras* is revealing. Rodrigo named two men as *fidei jusores*, guarantors of the settlement. They were Pedro Ansúrez, the companion of King Alfonso's exile and now count of Zamora, and García Ordóñez, lord of Pancorvo in north-eastern Castile, like Rodrigo a former associate of Sancho II and lately *armiger* to Alfonso VI. The charter was witnessed by the king and his two sisters and by a bevy of distinguished courtiers. Rodrigo was moving in high circles and we may suspect that the wedding was one of the smartest social occasions of its year.

It is difficult to be sure when that year was. The charter is dated 19 July 1074. Though widely regarded as an original, the document is in fact a somewhat later copy and the dating clause could have been inaccurately transcribed by the copyist. Independent evidence shows that Rodrigo and Jimena were married by May 1076. But one of the witnesses is recorded as holding an office which – so far as we know – he did not hold until 1078. There is no way of resolving these difficulties. The *arras* charter remains problematic in certain respects, though basically reliable as to its content. It seems to me likely that Rodrigo and Jimena were married in the summer of either 1074 or 1075.

This impression of close association with the great ones of the land is confirmed by other evidence from these years. In May 1076 Rodrigo and his wife granted some land to the monastery of Silos: the deed was confirmed in the presence of the king when the court was staying at the monastery of Cardeña. Rodrigo's name continued to feature among the witnesses of royal charters. In 1079 we find him in the company of the bishop of Burgos. In 1080 he attended the important council held at Burgos at which Alfonso VI and his leading churchmen, following the bidding of the papal legate, Cardinal Richard of Marseilles, formally accepted sweeping liturgical changes in the Spanish church by abandoning the ancient 'Mozarabic' liturgy in favour of the 'Roman' one.

These were prosperous and expansive years for Alfonso's kingdom. In the summer of 1076 Alfonso invaded Navarre following the assassination of its king, and annexed the Rioja and much of the (present-day) Basque provinces of Alava, Vizcaya and Guipúzcoa: perhaps Rodrigo accompanied the king on this campaign. From about the same time the king was recommencing the task of resettling the lands to the south of the Duero across which he had returned to the kingdom in 1072 – towns such as Medina del Campo and Olmedo with their dependent territories in what is now the southern fringe of the province of Valladolid. Further to the south his tribute-levying hand lay heavy on the taifa kings. He felt so sure of his income from this quarter that in 1077 he doubled the annual payment of gold that he made to the monastery of Cluny.

The royal entourage must have shared in the general buoyancy. We may well believe that Rodrigo Díaz did too. In the wake of King Sancho's murder his future had looked uncertain. Now it was rosy again. He had shown himself willing to serve, and the king to use his services. He was prominent at court. His knowledge of the law was respected. He had married advantageously. Well connected, successful and rich, he could look to the future with confidence.

But all optimistic expectations were to be shattered.

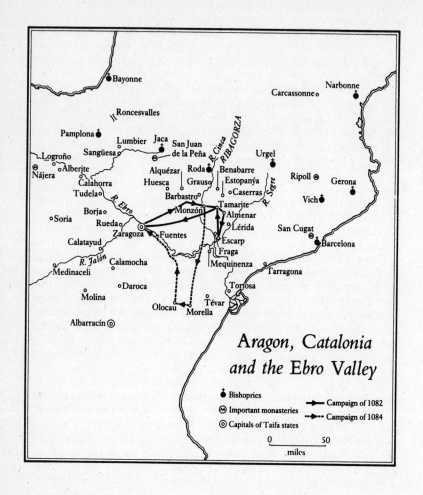

Bayonne

Carcassonne   Narbonne

Roncesvalles

Pamplona   Lumbier   Jaca   San Juan
Sangüesa   de la Peña   Urgel

Logroño   Alberite
Nájera   Ripoll   Gerona
Calahorra   Alquézar   Roda   Benabarre
Tudela   Huesca   Grauso   Estopanya   Vich
Barbastro   Caserras

Borja   Monzón   Tamarite   San Cugat
Rueda   Almenar
Zaragoza   Fuentes   Lérida   Barcelona
Soria   Escarp
Calatayud   Fraga

R. Jalón   Calamocha   Mequinenza   Tarragona
Medinaceli   Tortosa
Molina   Daroca
Olocau   Tévar
Albarracín   Morella

Aragon, Catalonia
and the Ebro Valley

Bishoprics
Important monasteries
Capitals of Taifa states

Campaign of 1082
Campaign of 1084

0   50
miles

9

❖ Exile in Zaragoza

What went wrong in Rodrigo Díaz's career is soon told. He made enemies at the court of Alfonso VI. Partly through their agency, partly through ill-judged actions of his own, he incurred the king's displeasure and was exiled in the summer of 1081. He spent the next five years as a mercenary soldier in the service of the Muslim ruler of Zaragoza. In the course of them he continued to amass fortune and renown. At the end of this period he was reconciled with the king and returned to Castile. This bald recital summarises a series of events of great complexity. The skein must be unravelled patiently, strand by strand.

Alfonso VI's dealings with the taifa kingdom of Toledo form one such strand. As we have already seen, his father Fernando I had been exacting annual tributes, or *parias*, from Toledo which he bequeathed to Alfonso in the division of his kingdom and revenues upon his death in 1065. In the period of confusion which ensued the ruler of Toledo, al-Ma'mun, emancipated himself from this Christian protectorate and halted payment of the tribute. Al-Ma'mun was an able man who had already governed the taifa of Toledo for over twenty years. His ambition was to enlarge the scope of his authority at the expense of the neighbouring taifa rulers. Immediately upon Fernando's death he invaded the kingdom of Valencia – weakened by its recent struggle against the king of Castile – dethroned its ruler 'Abd al-Malik (who happened also to be his son-in-law) and incorporated it under his sway. It was perhaps to celebrate this conquest that the panegyric poem in al-Ma'mun's honour, quoted in Chapter 2, was composed: the phrase translated 'Possessor of dual glory' is likely to have referred to al-Ma'mun's position as ruler of both Toledo and Valencia. 'Abd al-Malik was packed off into exile in the kingdom of Toledo where he died shortly afterwards and al-Ma'mun ruled Valencia in his stead.

Al-Ma'mun then turned his attention southwards. In 1067 we find him fishing in the troubled waters of Granadan politics and managing to land the town and territory of Baza. But his real ambition was fixed on Córdoba. So, unfortunately, was that of a formidable rival, al-Mu'tamid of Seville. In 1070 al-Ma'mun attempted to seize Córdoba but was narrowly forestalled by al-Mu'tamid. However, he bided his time and engaged the help of a prominent Córdoban exile, Ibn 'Ukasha, who captured the city early in 1075 and handed it over to his patron. Al-Ma'mun entered Córdoba on 25 February 1075. Ruler of Toledo, Valencia and the former caliphal capital of Córdoba, he was at the zenith of his power.

Alfonso VI, as we have already seen, spent about nine months in exile in Toledo in 1072 before returning to León-Castile at the time of his brother Sancho's murder. A good deal of anecdote later attached itself to this stay. A chronicler writing in León about ten years after Alfonso's death believed that in his exile could be seen the workings of God's providence, for as he strolled about the city of Toledo he pondered how it might one day be conquered. The theme was embroidered by later writers. A chronicler writing in the last quarter of the twelfth century reported a curious tale of how on one occasion during Alfonso's exile the hair of his head had stood upright for an hour, to the consternation of al-Ma'mun's courtiers who took it for a dangerous omen. They had urged al-Ma'mun to have him killed, but al-Ma'mun had honourably refused to violate the code of hospitality. By the middle of the thirteenth century a story was circulating that while dozing under a tree Alfonso had overheard al-Ma'mun and his courtiers discussing the weak points in Toledo's defences. These and other stories were committed to writing long after Alfonso's conquest of Toledo in 1085, with the advantage of hindsight. If Alfonso *did* have designs on Toledo in or shortly after 1072 – which is anyone's guess - he was in no position to prosecute them. Gratitude to al-Ma'mun, it has been suggested, may have restrained him. It is more likely that he was too busy trying to consolidate his shaky hold over his kingdom to have time for foreign adventures.

Al-Ma'mun's triumph did not last long. He died only four months after entering Córdoba, on 28 June 1075, allegedly poisoned, and his death precipitated a sharp change in the fortunes of his kingdom. He was succeeded by his grandson al-Qadir, a young man of feeble character who was quite unfitted to rule. His *laqab* or honorific name could not have been less suitable: al-Qadir means 'the powerful'. Valencia at once threw off Toledan lordship. Abu Bakr, the son of 'Abd al-'Aziz (d. 1061) and brother of 'Abd al-Malik who had been deposed in 1065, re-established Valencian independence. Al-

Mu'tamid, ruler of Seville, renewed his designs on Córdoba. But much more serious for Toledo in the longer term than the crumbling of these always fragile hegemonies was an act of criminal irresponsibility perpetrated by al-Qadir. Two months after his succession he had his grandfather's much-respected first minister, Ibn al-Hadidi, murdered (25 August 1075). The assassination plunged the city of Toledo into a state of near civil war. Feud and faction, never far beneath the surface of public life, broke out. Al-Qadir panicked and turned for assistance to Alfonso VI, who eagerly grasped the opportunity of renewing his father's protectorate over Toledo in return for the payment of tribute. The formal written treaty which might have recorded this agreement – as in the case of Sancho IV's treaties with al-Muqtadir in 1069 and 1073 – has not survived, so we cannot date it accurately. Presumably it belonged to the year 1076: it must surely have occurred before Alfonso doubled the annual *census* paid to the monastery of Cluny in July 1077. (Possibly the king's adoption of the title of 'emperor of all Spain' [*imperator totius Hispaniae*], first recorded in a charter of October 1077, is to be connected with the renewal of the Toledo protectorate.)

Al-Qadir's submission to the king of León-Castile did not solve his problems. The unrest precipitated by Ibn al-Hadidi's murder continued. His financial exactions to pay the tributes demanded by Alfonso further increased his unpopularity. Voices began to be raised protesting that his levies were contrary to Islamic law: this was a cry which was to have unlooked-for consequences at a later date. As his situation steadily worsened, al-Qadir found that he could no longer live safely in his capital city. In the spring of 1079 he retreated north-eastwards to Cuenca, where his family's estates lay. From there he launched an appeal for help to the Christian king, Alfonso.

In Toledo the factions opposed to al-Qadir cast about for a new ruler. In the summer of 1079 they offered the kingdom to the ruler of the taifa of Badajoz. 'Umar al-Mutawakkil, who governed Badajoz from 1068 to 1094, was an easy-going man, given to the pleasures of the table, a poet and a patron of poets. He is said to have devised an ingenious means of serving food at his banquets by diverting a stream through his palace so that dishes could be deposited on its surface in the kitchens to come bobbing and dancing before his guests where they reclined to dine. His best-known poem was the impromptu invitation, said to have been scribbled on a cabbage leaf, which he sent to his friend Abu Talib:

> O Abu Talib, rise
> And hasten to our view,
> Then fall like morning's dew
> Upon our weary eyes.

The necklace that we are
Its middle gem still wants
To crown its brilliance,
While you remain afar.

Al-Mutawakkil was apprehensive of the designs of Alfonso VI upon Estremadura which were indeed to bear fruit in his conquest of Coria in September 1079. The chance to enlarge his dominion and simultaneously to discomfort King Alfonso was too good to be missed. He accepted the invitation and established himself in Toledo in June 1079. But he was too idle to take precautions against the Christian king, whose duty and interest lay in a proper observance of his role as protector of the feeble ruler of Toledo. In the summer of 1080 Alfonso invaded Toledo, chased al-Mutawakkil back to Badajoz and re-established al-Qadir in his capital. It was probably at this time that he exacted some fortresses in the northern marches of the Toledan kingdom from al-Qadir, as the price of his assistance: these included Zorita, Brihuega and Canales.

Alfonso's dealings with the taifa kingdoms were not of course confined to Toledo. As already indicated, he nursed territorial ambitions over the northern parts of the kingdom of Badajoz. To the east, he was eager to restore his father's protectorate over Zaragoza: at some point between 1076 and 1080 he despatched Sisnando Davídez – a very prominent royal servant whom we shall meet yet again – on an embassy to Zaragoza, possibly to discuss the renewal of earlier arrangements. Looking still further to the east, Alfonso would not have been unmindful of his father's last campaign, against Valencia. And then there was the south. 'Abd Allah of Granada has left us a graphic account, in his memoirs, of how Alfonso bullied him into paying tribute in the winter of 1074–5. Another of the Christian king's ambitions was to revive the protectorate which Fernando I had exercised over Seville. And in this Alfonso seems to have succeeded (though the circumstances are very obscure), perhaps partly in consequence of his ascendancy over Toledo established in 1076. At all events, by the late 1070s Alfonso was receiving *parias* at least intermittently from Seville. It was this that brought Rodrigo into unwelcome limelight.

In the autumn of 1079 – probably: the date cannot be established with certainty – Rodrigo was sent by King Alfonso as his envoy to Seville to collect the tribute due to him. (The *Historia Roderici* implies that he was sent to two separate rulers of Seville and Córdoba. They were of course, since 1076, one and the same person, al-Mutamid of Seville. Critics have made needlessly heavy weather of this minor inaccuracy.) At the same time, and for the same purpose, an embassy had been sent to Granada. 'Abd Allah of Granada seized the opportunity of using this contingent of Christian notables, each with his retinue of knights, as the spearhead of his troops in a campaign against his inveterate enemy the king of Seville. Rodrigo sent a letter from Seville to 'Abd Allah and his Christian allies beseeching them 'for the love of their lord King Alfonso' to desist. But they paid no attention and continued their advance, laying waste the countryside as they came on. Rodrigo went out to confront them. The armies met at Cabra, and after a hard-fought battle the Granadans were defeated.

This at least is the story as told by Rodrigo's biographer. It is legitimate to wonder what he does *not* tell us. For example, it is unlikely that Rodrigo was the only Castilian magnate sent on the embassy to Seville: such delegations usually consisted of several prominent men; four such persons led the party which went to Granada. Again, it is unlikely that al-Mutamid did not send his own troops to defend his kingdom alongside the Castilian contingent. In other words, the author of the *Historia Roderici* has probably exaggerated Rodrigo's role. There is nothing surprising, nor especially reprehensible, in this. It is slightly more disturbing to find that Cabra, where the encounter took place, was probably in the kingdom of Granada rather than in that of Seville. That 'probably' should alert the reader to patches of uncertainty in the argument. We do not know *exactly* where the frontier ran in 1079: given the state of endemic bickering among the taifa kings we can be reasonably confident that strongpoints would have changed hands frequently. However, such information as we do possess suggests that Cabra was a Granadan possession. In other words, Rodrigo may have been invading Granada rather than defending Seville.

Doubtless the military situation was a good deal more fluid than we shall ever be able to know: military situations usually are. The engagement at Cabra itself was of little military significance. It was not even mentioned by 'Abd Allah in his memoirs (though one can think of other reasons for his reticence). Viewed from the royal court of Castile it was no doubt embarrassing and unedifying that the king's men were getting involved in a scrap far away in al-Andalus. However, this was the sort of thing that tended to happen under the *paria* régime, as Alfonso well knew. He could not have been seriously displeased for very long.

But some people were. In the course of the skirmish Rodrigo managed to take some distinguished captives. In the words of the *Historia*:

There were captured in that battle Count García Ordóñez and Lope Sánchez and Diego Pérez and many others of their knights. After his victory Rodrigo Díaz kept them captive for three days: then he deprived them of their baggage and all their weaponry and set them free to go their way.

These were important people. The most important among them was García Ordóñez. He was a contemporary of Rodrigo, and like him a Castilian of aristocratic background. He first appears in surviving records in the 1060s. Like Rodrigo he subscribed several of the charters of Sancho II and successfully transferred his loyalties to Alfonso VI, whom he served as *alférez* or *armiger* in 1074. He and Rodrigo obviously knew each other well: we have already met him as one of the guarantors of Rodrigo's marriage settlement. In the competitive society of the royal court, friendships could easily turn sour. After he had conquered the Riojan provinces of the kingdom of Navarre following the murder of King Sancho IV, Alfonso made García count of Nájera and married him to Urraca, the sister of the murdered king. García was thus promoted to an office more responsible – and lucrative – than any that Rodrigo held or was to hold, and made a marriage more exalted than his own. Was Rodrigo envious? It would be surprising if he were not. What we can say is that Rodrigo's capture of García at Cabra inflicted humiliation on him, and the ransom no small pecuniary loss. It would also seem, if we press the evidence a little further, that Rodrigo took care to render García's humiliation as public as possible. Rodrigo's exploit in dishonouring him was dwelt on by contemporaries as widely different as the Catalan author of the *Carmen Campi Doctoris* and the Muslim chronicler Ibn Bassam. Since men tend not to advertise their own humiliations we may take it that Rodrigo was responsible for orchestrating the ridicule. He had made an enemy. It was to cost him dear.

Rodrigo was not simply taking on an individual. Another of the known Castilian ambassadors to Granada was a certain Fortún Sánchez, a native of the Basque country, *alférez* and later *mayordomo* at the court of Sancho IV, who transferred into the service of Alfonso VI after 1076. Now Fortún was married to Ermesinda, another sister of Sancho IV, so that he was the brother-in-law of García Ordóñez. Fortún was not captured at Cabra, but his brother Lope was. (Of the third leader captured, Diego Pérez, nothing is known.)

After the Cabra campaign Rodrigo returned to Seville, collected the tribute and returned to King Alfonso's court. However, goes on his biographer darkly, 'many men became jealous and accused him before the king of many false and untrue things'. Among them, it is assumed, was García Ordóñez. It is Ibn Bassam who tells us that the count was nicknamed 'Crooked Mouth'. We do not know how the name arose. It could have referred to some physical defect such as a hare lip. But there is always the possibility that it referred to moral rather than physical defects. Count García's calumnies might have smeared others besides Rodrigo.

Rodrigo was rash enough to give his enemies a means of exercising leverage. In the early summer of (probably) 1081 a raiding party entered Castile, surprised the castle of Gormaz on the River Duero and carried off much plunder. The invaders must have come from the kingdom of Toledo, though they were not in any sense officially sponsored. They were simply bandits – the very word (*latrunculi*) which the author of the *Historia* puts into Rodrigo's mouth. Such raids to and fro were, as another contemporary observed, 'extremely frequent'. No doubt the progressive enfeeblement of al-Qadir's government had had the effect of making turbulent elements in the frontier zone even less amenable to control than they usually were. So there is nothing surprising about the episode. What is rather puzzling is Rodrigo's reaction. In the words of his biographer,

> He gathered together his army and all his well-armed knights, and pillaged and laid waste the land of the Saracens in the kingdom of Toledo.

What pretext Rodrigo had for this we do not know. We are told that he had been unable because of illness to undertake a punitive raid under royal direction into Saracen territory earlier in the year. Possibly the bandits knew of this and correctly deduced a weak point in Castile's southern flank. Another possibility is that Rodrigo had some personal interest in the area attacked. The lands which he is known to have owned, listed in such documents as Doña Jimena's *carta de arras*, all lie considerably to the north-west of Gormaz. But the records that happen to have survived are emphatically not a complete guide to his properties and he may well have come to possess estates further south in the valley of the Duero. Alfonso VI was actively resettling the trans-Duero region at this date, which provides a plausible context for acquisitions on Rodrigo's part.

Whatever the background, Rodrigo's reprisals were effective. It is noteworthy that he now had at his disposal a private army to carry them out. The *Historia* tells us that he rounded up 7000 captives, 'ruthlessly laying hold of all their wealth and possessions, and brought them back home with him'. The figure should be taken with a generous pinch of salt. Where the captives came from we do not know. For a force coming from the Gormaz district the natural crossing point from Old Castile into New occurs between Medinaceli and Sigüenza; and the richest pickings were to be found in the plain opening out thence to the south-west, along the valley of the Henares towards Guadalajara, Alcalá and Madrid. If this is the route that Rodrigo took, he would have been operating in an area close to the castles recently ceded by al-Qadir to the king of León-Castile.

The king and his advisers were 'very gravely displeased'. It may be significant that in June or early July 1081 the office of royal *armiger* was bestowed on Rodrigo Ordóñez, the brother of Count

García. This advancement of his enemy's family cannot have made the royal court more well disposed to our Rodrigo. His 'maverick' action was unauthorised and irresponsible. It occurred shortly after Alfonso had re-established his client al-Qadir in Toledo. It threatened the fragile equilibrium of the Christian king's protectorate. It set a dangerous example to other turbulent frontier lords among Alfonso's subjects. It invited counter-reprisals against the vulnerable garrisons of the fortresses recently acquired by Alfonso deep in Toledan territory. The king had to demonstrate his good faith towards al-Qadir and show that he could keep order on his marches. It hardly needed the prompting of Rodrigo's enemies at court to persuade Alfonso that a public example must be made. He banished Rodrigo from the kingdom.

By a fortunate chance we can catch a glimpse of a similar episode a few years later. Grimaldus, a native of northern France who became a monk of Silos, composed a work on the life and posthumous miracles of St Domingo, abbot of Silos (d. 1073), between 1088 and 1109. One of his stories concerned some Castilian knights who attacked a Muslim castle which was under King Alfonso's protection. The king was furious. He arrested the men who had been guilty of perpetrating the outrage and flung them into prison. One of them was miraculously freed through the agency of the saint. This was of course the point of the story as far as Grimaldus was concerned. What concerns us is the tone of the comments that he made about the behaviour of the people involved. The knights who carried out the attack were 'wicked and foolish'; their action was 'utterly irresponsible'; the king's anger was 'fully in accordance with justice'. We have hints here of how Rodrigo's escapade might have been viewed in some quarters. His anonymous biographer asks us to see only a good man brought low by the malice of his enemies. Responsible opinion in Castile might rather have seen a fitting punishment meted out to a law-breaker.

'So Rodrigo, leaving his sorrowing friends behind him, departed from Castile.' He may have left Jimena and the children behind him as well. The only information we have about her whereabouts during his exile comes from a document, not altogether trustworthy, of 1083 which shows her in the Asturias (perhaps with her family). The *Poema de Mio Cid*, whose action starts (at least in the form in which it has come down to us) with the beginning of the exile, has Rodrigo leaving his wife and children in the care of the abbot of Cardeña. The parting of husband and wife inspired the poet to one of his most vivid, indeed savage images: they parted from one another *como la uña de la carne*, 'as the nail from the flesh'. The family's sojourn at Cardeña cannot be documented from historical sources, but it is plausible. It was not unknown for knights departing on campaign or into exile to leave their womenfolk in the safety and comfort of a monastic house.

An aristocratic exile of Rodrigo's type had to find employment in the only calling for which he was fitted: as a soldier. His first destination was Catalonia, where he apparently tried and failed to find asylum and a paymaster with the count of Barcelona. Then he turned to Zaragoza where al-Muqtadir, whom Rodrigo had met in 1063 (and perhaps on other unrecorded occasions subsequently), was still reigning. Rodrigo entered the services of the ruler of Zaragoza and remained in it for the next five years.

Al-Muqtadir had been ruling the taifa of Zaragoza since 1046. Like his contemporary al-Ma'mun of Toledo, he reached the summit of his power towards the end of his life. Just as al-Ma'mun had profited from the confusions of León-Castile between 1065 and 1075, so al-Muqtadir exploited the situation created by the murder of Sancho IV of Navarre in 1076. The Navarrese protectorate of the years 1069–76 came abruptly to an end. Castile and Aragon squabbled over the corpse of Navarre. During the following years al-Muqtadir, an old hand at diplomacy, could play off those who had designs over his realm – Castile, Aragon, Barcelona – against one another. When al-Ma'mun's death signalled the end of the Toledo-Valencia combination, al-Muqtadir's ambitions over the Levante revived. In 1076 he conquered the kingdom of Denia and acquired some sort of lordship over Abu Bakr of Valencia, buying Alfonso VI's acquiescence, it was rumoured, with 100,000 *dinars*. In 1078 or shortly afterwards he managed to capture his brother Yusuf of Lérida, long a thorn in his side, and imprison him in the castle of Rueda near Zaragoza. Al-Muqtadir was a cultivated man – 'a real prodigy of nature in astrology, geometry and natural philosophy' – and a patron of the arts. He built two famous palaces at Zaragoza. One of them, called the Qasr Dar al-Surur or 'abode of pleasure', contained within it 'a golden hall of exquisite design and admirable workmanship'. Entering it upon its completion al-Muqtadir is said to have extemporised the couplet:

> O House of Pleasure and Golden Room,
> thanks to you I have attained
> the summit of my desires.
> If my kingdom contained only you two,
> that would be for me all that I
> could ask!

The other palace, the al-Ya'fariyya or Aljafería, still stands: although it has been much modified and restored over the centuries, enough remains to conjure up the architectural setting of the court at which Rodrigo Díaz found himself between 1081 and 1086.

At the time of Rodrigo's arrival in Zaragoza, probably in the late summer of 1081, the elderly al-Muqtadir was in poor health. In the autumn of that year he delegated power to his two sons, though he remained nominal ruler until his death which seems to have occurred in about July of 1082. The kingdom was partitioned between the sons. Yusuf al-Mu'tamin received the western half based on the capital at Zaragoza; Mundhir al-Hayib, who had been governing Denia under his father, was allotted the eastern half based on Lérida, Tortosa and Denia. 'Abd Allah of Granada described al-Hayib as 'impetuous' and implies that from an early stage there was hostility between the brothers. Strife between them overshadowed the short reign of al-Mu'tamin until his death in 1085.

This was Rodrigo's opportunity. The new ruler of Zaragoza could make use of a distinguished soldier in exile.

> Al-Mu'tamin was very fond of Rodrigo and set him over and exalted him above all his kingdom and all his land, relying upon his counsel in all things.

So the author of the *Historia Roderici*. Once again we may suspect him of some harmless exaggeration. There is no evidence that al-Mu'tamin looked upon Rodrigo as more than a field commander and military adviser. There were certainly other Christian soldiers in his service, and some of them could have been as distinguished as Rodrigo. The military operations upon which he was employed were of a routine kind. Chance and his own skill enabled him to turn his opportunities to advantage.

The most sensitive zone of al-Mu'tamin's dominions in the early 1080s was his eastern and northern march. It was there that his brother al-Hayib would strike. Furthermore, al-Hayib had entered into alliance with Sancho Ramírez, king of Aragon, and Count Berenguer Ramón II of Barcelona. (It may be recalled that the young Rodrigo Díaz had taken part in the battle of Graus in 1063 in which King Sancho's father Ramiro had been killed; also that the count of Barcelona had refused to take him on in the summer of 1081.) The Aragonese had long harboured designs on the valley of the Ebro. As for the Catalans, it should be borne in mind that the ruling princely dynasty had been acquiring land in the southern reaches of the county of Ribagorza, just next to Aragon, in the recent past. For example, in 1067 Ramón Berenguer I had bought the *castellania*, i.e. castle plus dependent territory, of Caserras from Arnal Mir de Tost for the sum of a thousand gold pieces. There were several other such acquisitions (see map p. 124). In addition, therefore, to his treaty with al-Hayib the count of Barcelona had a direct personal interest in this sensitive marchland.

We are particularly well informed about the military operations in this area in the summer of 1082. Rodrigo seems to have been charged with supervising its defence. He headed off a threat from the armies of King Sancho and al-Hayib against the strategically important town of Monzón. From there he turned east to Tamarite where he defeated a detachment of the Aragonese army. Al-Mu'tamin and he then decided to refortify the old castle of Almenar, further still to the east. This done, Rodrigo pushed off to the south and captured, apparently on his own account, the castle of Escarp. It was while he was there that he heard that al-Hayib, the count of Barcelona and other Pyrenean lords had laid siege to Almenar. He sent word to al-Mu'tamin and hurried back to Tamarite. Al-Mu'tamin was all for attacking the besiegers. Rodrigo, aware how big their army was, advised caution and suggested trying to buy them off instead. But al-Hayib was confident and turned the proposal down. Rodrigo, 'greatly worried' as his biographer confessed, prepared for battle. The encounter took place, it seems somewhere between Tamarite and Almenar. To everyone's surprise, it would appear, Rodrigo won a decisive victory. He captured the baggage-train of his opponents. Greatest prize of all, he captured the count of Barcelona himself and his retinue of knights.

Little as we know of the battle, we can hardly doubt that its successful outcome – for Rodrigo – had been a matter of luck. The ever-fortunate Cid, 'he who girded on his sword in a lucky hour' as the poet was to call him, had triumphed again. He observed the proprieties. He handed his captives over to al-Mu'tamin who released them five days later, presumably after ransoms had been agreed. Rodrigo's share must have been considerable. His biographer tells us that al-Mu'tamin 'showered him with innumerable rich presents and many gifts of gold and silver'. So the battle of Almenar replenished Rodrigo's treasure-chests. It ensured his continuing employment by al-Mu'tamin. It also brought him fame.

It is likely that the Latin poem known as the *Carmen Campi Doctoris*, discussed in a preceding chapter, was composed shortly after the Almenar campaign. To understand why a monk of Ripoll should have celebrated the discomfiture of his count in Latin verse we must digress briefly into Catalan politics. Count Ramón Berenguer I of Barcelona died in 1076, leaving two sons, Ramón Berenguer II, known as 'Tow-head', and Berenguer Ramón II. (The comital dynasty of Barcelona was peculiarly unenterprising in the matter of names, which renders study of it tiresome to the historian.) Under the late count's will the two brothers were to rule the dynastic territories jointly. From the start they quarrelled. Within two years these quarrels had become sufficiently serious to engage the attention of the Pope. On 2 January 1079 Gregory VII wrote to the bishop of Gerona urging him to try to bring about a reconciliation. Perhaps as a result of his efforts the brothers agreed in May 1079 to partition their authority, not simply as to place but also as to time: their agreement provided for alternative residence of six-month stretches in the comital palace in Barcelona. It sounds unworkable, and so it evidently proved. A second agreement was necessary, a sure sign that the first had failed, in December 1080, but this pact also proved a failure. Meanwhile, factions formed and re-formed among the aristocracy and the higher clergy in readiness for the violence that was anticipated.

This is the context of the *Carmen Campi Doctoris*. Ripoll lay in the territory allotted to Ramón Berenguer II in the partitions of 1079 and 1080. The diocesan of Ripoll, the bishop of Vich, was one of the leading partisans of Count Ramón. It is not surprising to find that the community should have been opposed to his brother Count Berenguer. The Almenar campaign offered them a handle which they could not fail to grasp. Gleefully they celebrated Berenguer's humiliation in the *Carmen*.

The expected violence came not long after that campaign, quite possibly at the very time the author of the *Carmen* was bending over his rhymes, and it took an extreme form. On 5 December 1082 Ramón Berenguer II was murdered. It was assumed at the time that his brother was guilty; probably correctly. It was the third actual or suspected fratricidal murder among the Christian dynasties of Spain within ten years. The immediate consequence was to precipitate what was in effect a civil war in Catalonia. The trans-Pyrenean counties of Carcassonne and Razés threw off the authority of Barcelona in 1083. In May 1084 two leading Catalan noblemen put into writing an agreement to make war on those who had been guilty of the murder. Others may have done so whose charters have not survived. In 1085 an assembly of magnates presided over by the bishop of Vich engaged the count of Cerdanya to avenge by war the 'unjust and iniquitous murder' of Count Ramón and discussed offering the overlordship of Catalonia to Alfonso VI of León-Castile.

A moderate party seems to have emerged. After what must have been frantic negotiations of which we know nothing, a compromise was reached. At another assembly, in June 1086, it was agreed that Count Berenguer Ramón be permitted to rule for eleven years from Christmas 1086, in effect as regent for his four-year-old nephew (later to be known as Ramón Berenguer III) until he came of age. This Berenguer duly did. But he never lived down the crime, and after his resignation in 1097 he joined the First Crusade as an act of penance and died before the walls of Jerusalem in 1099.

Rodrigo was to have further dealings with Count Berenguer Ramón II later on, in 1090, but in the immediate aftermath of the Almenar campaign Rodrigo's attention was drawn westwards. Intrigues at the court of Zaragoza set in train a series of tragic events in the autumn and winter months of 1082–3. The trouble seems to have started with a certain Ibn al-Royolo, who had formerly been prominent in the service of the last independent king of Denia. He had defected to al-Muqtadir in 1076 and helped him to take possession of Denia. After the death of al-Muqtadir, al-Mu'tamin discovered or at any rate suspected that Ibn al-Royolo was intriguing against him with Alfonso VI, so he had him executed. At about the same time a man referred to in the *Historia Roderici* as Albofalac, who cannot otherwise be identified, rebelled against al-Mu'tamin. Albofalac was governor of Rueda, the castle on the River Jalón about twenty miles due west of Zaragoza where al-Muqtadir had imprisoned his brother Yusuf. Albofalac's revolt took the form of a *pronunciamiento* – as later generations of Spaniards would come to call it – in favour of Yusuf. The rebels immediately appealed to Alfonso VI for help.

It is likely, though we cannot prove it, that the intrigues of Ibn al-Royolo and the rebellion at Rueda were connected. King Alfonso saw in the embarrassment of al-Mu'tamin a means of exerting pressure on Zaragoza which would be more effective than the embassy of Sisnando Davídez had been a few years earlier. He sent an army to Rueda under the command of the *infante* Ramiro of Navarre and Count Gonzalo Salvadórez. Ramiro was the brother of Sancho IV of Navarre, brother-in-law therefore of García Ordóñez and Fortún Sánchez whom the Cid had defeated and captured in 1079. Ramiro had entered the service of Alfonso VI after his brother's murder and had held the lordship of Calahorra between 1076 and 1082; he was a prominent figure at the royal court and a notable benefactor of the Cluniac monastery of Nájera which had been founded by his father. Gonzalo Salvadórez is first traceable as a courtier of Fernando I, then of Sancho II, subsequently transferring his loyalties to Alfonso VI. He had been promoted to the office of count in 1074. He was one of the most powerful and respected noblemen of eastern Castile. Just before he set out for Rueda he made a grant to the monastery with which his family was most closely associated, Oña.

. . . I Count Gonzalo, in readiness for battle against the Moors with my lord, grant and concede to God and to the monastery of Oña where my forebears rest, in order that I may be remembered there for evermore . . . [there follows a list of properties and churches] . . . If I should meet with death among the Moors, may my soul be with Christ; and let my body be borne to Oña and buried there with my kinsfolk, together with [the gifts of] 1600 gold pieces, and three of my noble horses and two mules, and from my wardrobe two silken robes and three of shot-silk taffeta, and two vessels of silver . . . And if my vassals and retainers do not so bear me [to Oña] in the event of my death, they are nothing worth, like the traitor who kills his lord, because I made them rich and powerful.

One could not ask for a more vivid statement of the aristocratic piety of the eleventh century.

When Gonzalo and Ramiro reached Rueda they held discussions with Yusuf and, perhaps at the latter's insistence, summoned the king himself. Alfonso came for a few days, and after discussions of which we know nothing returned to Castile. Evidently he believed that Gonzalo and Ramiro were capable of handling matters on their own. And then Yusuf suddenly and unexpectedly died. Albofalac found himself in the unenviable position of one who, running a pretender, finds himself with only a corpse. He implored Alfonso to come to Rueda at once to take over the castle. Arrangements were made for Gonzalo and Ramiro to take possession of Rueda in Alfonso's name before the king himself arrived. At this point Albofalac seems to have panicked. When Gonzalo and Ramiro entered the castle under safe-conduct on 6 January 1083 the garrison pelted them with stones: the count and the *infante* and many of their noble companions were killed.

The treachery of Rueda was long to be remembered with horror in Christian circles. One person who seems to have been eager to exculpate himself was Rodrigo Díaz. The *Historia* tells us that Rodrigo was in Tudela at the time of the massacre. Tudela is on the Ebro, upstream from Zaragoza, about thirty-seven miles (as the crow flies) from Rueda. It looks as though the threat to al-Mu'tamin presented by the *pronunciamiento* at Rueda must have led him to despatch Rodrigo at once to guard his north-western marches against the king of Castile. When Rodrigo heard of the events at Rueda he hurried to Alfonso's court, which seems to have been nearby at the time. The author of the *Historia* would have us believe that Alfonso sought a reconciliation and that Rodrigo rejoined his service, but that he found the king's professions of friendship insincere and left him to return to Zaragoza. The story is not very plausible. It would seem more likely that Rodrigo hastened to the royal court in order to assure the king that he had had no part in the treacherous murder of his enemy's brother-in-law.

We know nothing of Rodrigo's doings during the remainder of 1083; rather more about them in the following year. In the *Historia* the story runs as follows. Al-Mu'tamin and Rodrigo jointly ravaged southern Aragon in a five-day raid from Monzón. King Sancho of Aragon did not dare to resist them. After this Rodrigo was sent off to treat al-Hayib's territory in the same way. The zone chosen for attention lay far to the south-east in the hinterland of the taifa principality of Tortosa, the area now forming the extreme north-western section of the province of Castellón. Rodrigo ravaged the country round Morella and refortified the castle of Olocau. Sancho Ramírez of Aragon and al-Hayib agreed on joint action against Zaragoza and invaded the kingdom. They joined forces and camped at a place only vaguely described as 'beside the river Ebro'. Rodrigo had returned from his southern *chevauchée* and was not far away. After some preliminaries – which included a contemptuous message from Rodrigo to the Aragonese king – a battle took place and Rodrigo was victorious. The date was probably 14 August 1084. As to the site, all one may say is that the encounter took place somewhere in the lower valley of the Ebro.

This battle was, in the words of Rodrigo's biographer, 'an overwhelming victory'. It was even more than that. When the enemy troops broke and fled, Rodrigo pursued them and took many captives. The author of the *Historia* gives the names of sixteen of the most important of them from the Aragonese army. It is a most interesting list. The two grandest figures were Ramón Dalmacio, bishop of Roda from 1077 to 1094, and Count Sancho Sánchez of Pamplona: the latter was the son of a bastard brother of Sancho IV of Navarre and was later to marry a daughter of García Ordóñez; he was one of the most powerful barons in Aragon until his death in about 1116. Then there was one of the principal officials of the royal household, Blasco Garcés, the king's *mayordomo*. Seven were *tenentes* in the kingdom of Aragon, that is men charged with the administration and defence of a given region as the king's deputy. Two examples may stand for all. Pepino Aznar had held court office under Sancho Ramírez and is traceable as a *tenente* between 1075 and 1093. In 1084 he was *tenente* of Alquézar. He was one of those to whom Pedro I entrusted the resettlement of Barbastro in 1100. His brother García, also captured in 1084, may be traced as a *tenente* in Aragon between 1063 and 1086. He was banished for the murder of the count of Bigorre in 1088 and ended his days in exile among the Saracens. Finally, and most interestingly, there were five men from the dominions of Alfonso VI: Count Nuño of Portugal, Anaya Suárez of Galicia, Gudesteo González, Nuño Suárez of León and García Díaz of Castile. It is likely that these were other exiles, like Rodrigo, from the kingdom of León-Castile, who had entered Aragonese service.

Ibn Bassam wrote of the Cid that 'the Banu Hud' – the family name of the rulers of Zaragoza – 'brought him out of obscurity'. He may have been thinking of Rodrigo's exploits during his exile in the 1080s. If Rodrigo's capture of the count of Barcelona in 1082 had been a lucky fluke which acquired resonance for reasons connected more with Catalan than with Zaragozan politics, his doings in 1083 and 1084 had been successful in a more considered way. At the time of the Rueda crisis he had stood loyally by his lord al-Mu'tamin. He had showed tenacity and patience in the routine campaigning of the eastern frontier. He had won a formidable victory over the combined forces of Aragon and Lérida and had taken captive a string of famous people. He had made himself indispensable. By the end of 1084 Rodrigo must have cut a considerable figure at the court of Zaragoza. He would surely have been present, for example, at such great state occasions as the marriage, in January 1085, of al-Mu'tamin's son Ahmad al-Musta'in to a daughter of Abu Bakr of Valencia, splendidly organised by the Jewish vizir Abu al-Fadl Hasday ibn Hasday, himself one of the luminaries of the court culture of Zaragoza. Everyone of any consequence in Islamic Spain was there.

At some point in the autumn of that year al-Mu'tamin died and was succeeded by al-Musta'in, who continued his father's patronage of Rodrigo. 'Rodrigo remained with him at Zaragoza in the greatest honour and respect for nine months.' What his biographer does not tell us is that towards the end of those nine months Rodrigo found himself resisting King Alfonso, who had come with his army to besiege Zaragoza. Very shortly afterwards Rodrigo and the king were reconciled, his sentence of banishment was lifted and he returned to his native land high in the royal favour. Yet another kaleidoscopic twist of events had shifted and regrouped the distribution of power in the Iberian peninsula.

In order to understand it we must retrace our steps to the year 1080, when Alfonso VI had re-established al-Qadir as ruler of the taifa of Toledo. Al-Qadir returned in vengeful mood and instituted a reign of terror as he hunted down those who had conspired against him in the previous two years. Ibn Bassam, writing in 1109, was to say of this period that the citizens of Toledo 'went in fear of their own shadows'. In order to satisfy Alfonso's insatiable demands for money, al-Qadir squeezed his subjects dry by the familiar techniques of extortion. Another revolt against him erupted in May 1082 and the whole region dissolved into chaos. Again the king of León-Castile intervened to support his puppet; further fortresses were ceded; additional demands for tribute were made. It was from this time that Alfonso's troops, ostensibly upholding al-Qadir, became a permanent presence in the taifa of Toledo, their random depredations an additional burden upon its unfortunate inhabitants.

At the risk of over-simplification one might characterise the various factions in the city of Toledo at this time somewhat as follows. There was first of all the princely establishment itself, ranging from al-Qadir at the top, down to the grubby crowd of informers and torturers who sustained his régime at the bottom: a government, if such it may be called, hated and feared by its subjects, destitute of policy, drifting from expedient to expedient. Its Muslim opponents may be divided into two groups. The moderates had lost all hope in al-Qadir; al-Mutawakkil of Badajoz had failed them; no other taifa ruler could come to their aid. They were gradually coming to the view that it would be prudent to accept a *fait accompli*. Alfonso VI was now effectively in charge of the kingdom: would it not be wise to make terms with him while good terms could still be made? The extremists were opposed to any compromise with a Christian king. The corruption of al-Qadir's régime must be purged by a return to the sternest Islamic rectitude; and there were those, not far away across the Straits in North Africa, who might help them to translate this vision into reality.

Toledo also contained large communities of Jews and Mozarabic Christians. They suffered from al-Qadir's rule in common with their Muslim fellow citizens. It is inaccurate to regard the Christians of Toledo as some sort of 'fifth column' working for Alfonso VI. Nevertheless it was bound to have been the case that to be ruled by a Christian was perceived as preferable to being ruled by a Muslim. As for the Jews of Toledo, they were probably encouraged to look favourably upon the Christian king by an episode that occurred in 1082. Alfonso had sent a Jewish ambassador to Seville to collect the tribute. A dispute took place: the Castilian delegation complained that the tribute was being paid in debased coin and accompanied their complaint with insults. Al-Mu'tamid had the Jewish ambassador crucified. Alfonso VI was livid with rage and mounted a punitive raid to avenge his envoy's death. He may also have wanted to warn Seville of the likely consequences of any interference in the affairs of Toledo. (It may have been in the course of this campaign, in which the royal army ravaged down the valley of the Guadalquivir and along the Atlantic coastline south of Cadiz, that Alfonso rode his charger into the sea exclaiming, 'Here I am at the uttermost limit of al-Andalus, and I have trampled it beneath my feet!' So at any rate the story later went.) The incident perhaps encouraged the Toledan Jews to believe that in Alfonso VI they would find a strong and trustworthy protector.

It seems finally to have dawned on al-Qadir that his position was untenable: the game was up. Casting about for an escape-route, he recalled his grandfather al-Ma'mun's rule over Valencia between 1066 and 1075. At some point in the summer of 1084 he proposed a deal with Alfonso. If the Christian king would help to instal him in the principality of Valencia he would surrender Toledo to him. Having taken this initiative al-Qadir shut himself up in his palace in Toledo and waited upon events. It was left to Alfonso to make the next move. The existence of the extremist faction in the city determined what that move had to be. In the autumn of 1084 he laid siege to Toledo. The city occupies a position of great natural strength, standing on a precipitous outcrop of rock surrounded on three sides by the waters of the Tagus. It was not to be taken by assault. It would have to be starved into surrender.

The winter of 1084–5 was severe. There was much rain, and heavy falls of snow in the Sierra de Guadarrama threatened Alfonso's supply-lines. But he persisted. As the spring of 1085 crept in, famine and disease became widespread in the beleaguered city. By April the end was in sight. Terms of surrender were discussed in the first week of May and on the 6th a formal capitulation took place. On Sunday, 25 May 1085 – by coincidence the same day on which Pope Gregory VII died in exile at Salerno – Alfonso VI, emperor of León and Castile, made his ceremonial entry into the city. Toledo, ancient capital of the Visigothic kingdom, had passed once more into Christian hands after some three hundred and seventy years of Islamic rule.

The consequences of the fall of Toledo were manifold. One of them was to inspire Alfonso VI to a hawkish mood of militant expansionism. In the spring of 1086 he sent an army under Alvar Fáñez to instal his puppet al-Qadir as ruler of Valencia. He called upon al-Mu'tamid of Seville to surrender his kingdom. He despatched a Christian raiding party into the principality of Granada which reached as far as Nivar, only six miles north of the capital. Another task force was sent to capture the castle of Aledo, between Murcia and Lorca. And in the early summer of 1086 he led an army to Zaragoza and laid siege to it. Among its defenders would have been, presumably, al-Musta'in's trusted lieutenant Rodrigo Díaz. It looked as though Zaragoza would go the way of Toledo.

But this was not to be. It was while he was supervising the siege operations at Zaragoza that disturbing news was brought to Alfonso. An enormous army from North Africa had landed in southern Spain. The invaders were heading northwards, apparently intent on the re-conquest of Toledo. They had to be headed off. The king mustered his forces and moved south-westwards. The armies met at Sagrajas or Zallaqa, near Badajoz, on 23 October 1086. There Alfonso VI, the conqueror of Toledo, was resoundingly defeated.

As a result of this shattering blow Rodrigo and Alfonso VI would presently be reconciled. This was one minor consequence of the invasion of the Almoravides. Their arrival on the scene caused a seismic upheaval in Spanish life. Who were these people?

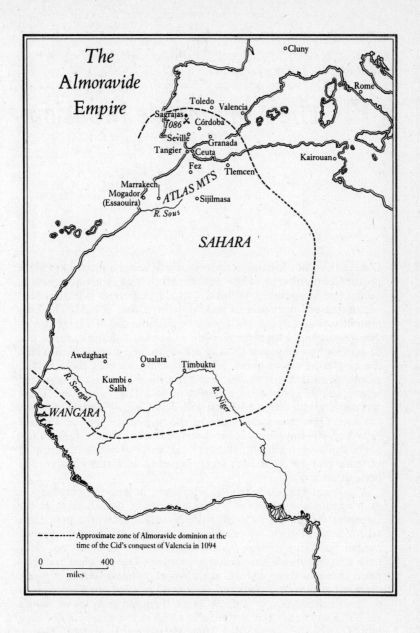

The
Almoravide
Empire

Cluny

Rome

Toledo Valencia

Sagrajas
1086   Córdoba

Seville   Granada
Tangier Ceuta

Kairouan

Fez
Tlemcen

Marrakech
Mogador   ATLAS MTS
(Essaouira)   Sijilmasa

R. Sous

SAHARA

Awdaghast   Oualata   Timbuktu

Kumbi
Salih

R. Senegal

WANGARA

R. Niger

------- Approximate zone of Almoravide dominion at the
time of the Cid's conquest of Valencia in 1094

0   400
     miles

IO

🌟 The Almoravide Invasion

During the Cid's lifetime stories circulated about a distant kingdom on the southern side of the Sahara which was fabulously rich in gold. The geographer al-Bakri (d.1094) reported that the dogs which guarded the palace of its king wore collars of gold. The king himself was said to possess 'a piece of gold the size of a large stone'. This prodigious nugget grew in the telling: in al-Idrisi's great work of geography completed in 1154 it had become a boulder to which the king tethered his horse; in the fourteenth century Ibn Khaldun would claim that it weighed a ton. But these later and exaggerated reports should not blind us to the value of al-Bakri's account. There was such a kingdom. Al-Bakri called it Gana – mistakenly as it happens: *Gana* was actually one of the titles of its king and means 'war-leader' – and gives a sober description of it. Some Arab geographers had even visited it. Ibn Hawkal, parts of whose description of tenth-century al-Andalus were quoted in an earlier chapter, had been there in 951.

A party of English botanists, witnessing in June 1871 in the port of Mogador the lading of a consignment of ostrich feathers for shipment to Europe, reflected that the sufferings of the merchants who conveyed them across the Sahara 'must reach the verge of human endurance'. Many Islamic merchants of the tenth and eleventh centuries made that arduous journey. The principal starting-point at the northern end was the town of Sijilmasa, which was just outside the modern settlement of Rissani in southern Morocco, in the fertile depression of Tafilelt. From there the caravans of camels set out southwards across the Sahara. After some 1400 miles they would strike the Niger valley somewhere near Timbuktu. Thence their route lay west-south-west for another 300 miles or so, after which they found themselves in the kingdom they called Gana. Ibn Hawkal also tells of a western route from Sijilmasa through the Sous valley of today's southern Morocco and round the edge of the Sahara, but it seems that this was less frequented than the Sijilmasa-Timbuktu route. (It is curious that the sea-route along the Atlantic coast was not used.) The Gana's suzerainty – constantly shifting, a sphere of influence over tribal groups, in no sense a territorial dominion – was felt in the region roughly delimited by the River Senegal to the west, the River Niger to the east and to the north the southernmost zone of the modern state of Mauretania. The most active trading centres were in the northern sector of this area: Kumbi Salih, hazardously identified by French archaeologists to the north of Nara in Mali; Oualata, in Mauretania, due west of Timbuktu; Awdaghast, near Tamchaket, also in Mauretania. Here the salt, textiles, metals and beads brought from the north were exchanged, for gold principally, but also for ivory, ebony and slaves. The gold actually came from further south, from the area which Arab travellers called Wangara, across the River Senegal, scene of the famous 'dumb bartering' described by the thirteenth-century geographer Yaqut, whose account was drawn upon by Rudyard Kipling for a memorable story in *Puck of Pook's Hill*.

The rewards of this trade were commensurate with its hazards. Ibn Hawkal tells us that

I have seen in Awdaghast a recognisance of debt by which a merchant of Awdaghast acknowledged himself a debtor of an inhabitant of Sijilmasa for the sum of 42,000 *dinars*. Nowhere in the east, neither in Iraq nor Fars nor Kurasan, have I heard tell of anything like this.

Elsewhere he named the merchant and referred to the witnesses to the document (which, incidentally, he referred to as a *sakk*, from which the word 'cheque' is thought to derive). There is no reason to disbelieve him. Comparisons of this sort are bound to be imprecise, but – very approximately – it looks as though this single debtor of a Sijilmasa merchant owed something like double the amount that at exactly the same time a king of England was leaving to his people in his will to be used for buying off the Vikings.

This long, frail line of communication supplied the Maghrib and al-Andalus with gold. As we have already seen, it was thence diffused to other destinations: the tributes paid to Christian Spanish kings, the annual subsidy rendered by Alfonso VI to the monastery of Cluny. When in 1095 Pope Urban II consecrated the mighty new monastery church built by Abbot Hugh, could he have known that this, the most ambitious building erected in Christendom since Roman days, rested in the last resort on cheques held in Sijilmasa and Awdaghast and on the labours of diggers and panners in the Senegal basin? One wonders.

The Gana and his subjects were Blacks of the Soninke group of tribes. The peoples of Awdaghast were white-skinned Berbers of the Sanhaja tribal confederation who had arrived from the western Sahara about a century before Ibn Hawkal's visit. They wore a *litham* or veil over their faces and were known to the Arabs as 'the veiled ones'. They had become nominal converts to Islam in the tenth century. One of the attractions of the faith may have been the notion of *jihad* or holy war against their neighbours, enemies and intermittent suzerains of the Gana. In about 1035 one of the Sanhaja tribal chiefs set out on a pilgrimage to Mecca which was to have momentous consequences. It may not be fanciful to suppose that something of the atmosphere of that journey from the western fringes of the Islamic world to the Holy City can be recaptured in an account of a similar journey made some eight centuries later. Ahmad b. Tuwayr al-Janna set out from Tishit, not far to the north-east of Awdaghast, for Mecca in 1829. The account of his pilgrimage which he later composed has a raw simplicity and unaffected charm which seems to reflect not just the author's character and piety but also the unsophisticated culture of the far west from which he came.

In the course of his return journey the eleventh century Sanhaja chieftain, whose name was Yahya ibn Ibrahim, encountered in Kairouan a famous religious teacher named Abu 'Imram. Yahya asked him for a man who might instruct his tribespeople in the true observance of the faith. Abu 'Imram had already been dismayed by Yahya's doctrinal ignorance and was horrified to learn that his subjects were more ignorant still. The difficulty was to find a man who was willing to undertake so distant and perilous a mission. Abu 'Imram, though living in Kairouan, was a native of Fez, and it was to his pupils in Morocco that he directed Yahya. Finally a pupil of a pupil of Abu 'Imram, a native of the Sijilmasa region named 'Abd Allah ibn Yasin, accompanied Yahya back to the Sanhaja country. The year was probably 1039.

Ibn Yasin's mission was not a success. His teaching was too austere for the Sanhaja tribesmen. Protected from molestation by Yahya's authority, after the latter's death his house was burnt down and he was expelled from the region. Fleeing with the few disciples he had been able to attract – tradition later said eight – he made his way to the Atlantic coast. Somewhere there, perhaps near the mouth of the River Senegal, he established his little community of believers in a *ribat*. (The nature of this *ribat* has stimulated much discussion. Ibn Yasin's *ribat* is best thought of as a community of quasi-monastic character whose inmates were dedicated to living a notably pure religious life; prepared, as they had to be in unknown territory, for self-defence and therefore with an inbuilt military capacity, but also with a role as Islamic missionaries to the peoples among whom they were established.) They came to be known as 'the people of the *ribat*', al-Murabitun, which among Romance-speakers in Spain was corrupted to *almoravid*. Hence the term by which they are generally known.

Ibn Yasin's *ribat* prospered. Large numbers of converts to Islam were made in the region and new members were attracted to the community. Ibn Yasin then, following the example of the Prophet, turned upon the Sanhaja tribes who had scorned his teaching. In the course of the years following 1042 tribe after tribe was defeated and compelled to acknowledge Islamic faith and Almoravide authority. In 1054–5, following an appeal from his former mentor, Ibn Yasin led his armies northwards to Sijilmasa. He was killed in battle in 1059 and military leadership passed to Abu Bakr ibn 'Umar, one of the original eight disciples. Abu Bakr, finding himself confronted by threats to his authority back in the south, delegated command of the northern sector to his cousin Yusuf ibn Tashufin. It was Yusuf who took the decision to lead his men over the Atlas and on to the plains of Morocco. There he founded a new base for his operations at Marrakech at a date variously given as 1062 or 1070. Thence the Almoravides fanned out to the north. Yusuf entered Fez in 1074–5 (AH467), Tlemcen in 1075–6 and Tangier in 1079.

The speed and extent of the Almoravide conquests, almost as remarkable as the original Islamic conquests of the seventh century, have never, like those, been satisfactorily explained. The rise of the Almoravides remains mysterious, largely owing to the paucity of original sources relating to them. The collapse of the Almoravide empire in the twelfth century was almost as sudden as its rise in the eleventh, and its destroyers took good care that as many as possible of the records relating to it should be destroyed. Sketchily documented, the Almoravides have not generally proved an attractive subject to the French scholars who have done so much for our understanding of the medieval Maghrib. One can point to certain factors which contributed to Almoravide success: for example, their control of the trans-Saharan gold trade, their ability to call upon the agricultural wealth of southern Morocco, and their good fortune in confronting the authorities of northern Morocco and western Algeria at a time when they were enfeebled by nomadic invasions from further east. It was no coincidence that Almoravide expansion occurred at a time when centralised political authority had collapsed in Spain. The tenth-century caliphs of Córdoba, like other prudent monarchs of Spain before and since, had kept a watchful eye on the Maghrib and had used diplomacy to 'defuse' any restiveness among the barbarians across the Straits: but this was beyond the capacity of the taifa kings.

All this may be said, but it does not really advance our understanding of the Almoravides. 'Abd Allah of Granada wrote of Yusuf that 'had I been able to give him my flesh and blood, I would have done so'. This gives us a clue. Ibn Yasin and Yusuf are best interpreted as leaders of 'a new force of revivalist Islam' of an intensity that was not to be seen again in North-West Africa, it has been claimed, until the nineteenth century. This force operated like a spark upon peoples characterised by a distinctive religious culture and social structure. What took place was 'a kind of relatively rare crystallisation of authority by means of religious charisma which enabled them to fuse tribal support into a unified force'. This religious charisma – the Berbers called it *baraka* – was the power behind the Almoravide movement.

Yusuf's armies presented as great a threat to the settled cultures of the Western Mediterranean as did, at exactly the same time, the armies of the Seljuk Turks to those of the Eastern Mediterranean in Byzantine Asia Minor and Fatimid Syria. In both instances the cultural divide between invaders and invaded was wide. Among the cultivated princes of al-Andalus Yusuf was perceived as a barbarian. He came from beyond the pale of civilisation, from (in Moroccan terms) the *bled es siba*, 'the lawless land' beyond the Atlas. His Marrakech was not a city but a camp. In Yusuf's day it consisted of no more than a stone fortress or *ksar*, a mosque and the tents of his followers; and it would have been surrounded by stockades of thorn, *Zizyphus lotus*, which is equipped with 'double sets of thorns, one pointing forward and the other curved back', of the sort that may still be seen in the Moroccan countryside for enclosing live-stock. Marrakech's walls came later, perhaps about 1100, and it was Yusuf's son Ali who was responsible for dignifying the city with elegant public buildings, of which regrettably only one survives, the exquisite Koubba el-Baroudiyin built in about 1130. Yusuf was not illiterate, but stories circulated about his lack of literary culture. When al-Mu'tamid wrote a flattering letter to him in the winter of 1086–7 asking him to come back to Spain he quoted the famous lines of the poet Ibn Zaydun (d. 1071) on the parting of friends:

> You left, and I left: yet my longing was not
> calmed in my heart, nor dry were made my tear-ducts;
> my losing you completely changed my days
> and turned them black: with you my nights were white.

It was said that Yusuf's knowledge of classical Arabic was not enough to enable him to grasp the allusion. 'Oh I see,' he said, 'he wants us to send him black and white slave girls!' *Ben trovato*, perhaps, but the story tells us something of the contempt in which Yusuf was held.

There is another story about that same exchange of letters. The taifa rulers, like others, were accustomed to give lavish presents in the course of diplomatic exchanges. When Yusuf corresponded with al-Mu'tamid of Seville he sent him shields of hippopotamus-hide, unprocurable in al-Andalus, and therefore rare and precious; but austere and military, a statement of priorities, even of intent.

Once this grim, ascetic zealot had reached the Straits the prospect of his intervention in Spanish affairs loomed large. It was solicited soon after his conquest of Tangier. It seems to have been in the autumn of 1079, after Alfonso VI's acquisition of Coria, that al-Mutawakkil of Badajoz wrote to Yusuf lamenting the perilous situation of al-Andalus and seeking help. Another embassy seems to have been sent a couple of years later. Al-Mu'tamid assisted Yusuf to complete his conquest of the Maghrib by sending a naval squadron from Seville to help in the blockade of Ceuta. After Alfonso VI's punitive raid on the taifa of Seville in 1083 al-Mu'tamid implored Yusuf's intervention.

But Yusuf continued to delay. It was the fall of Toledo which precipitated matters. As 'Abd Allah was to recall a few years later, it 'sent a great tremor through all al-Andalus and filled the inhabitants with fear and despair'. As we saw at the end of the last chapter, it induced a belligerent mood in Alfonso VI. In addition to installing al-Qadir at Valencia, laying siege to Zaragoza and demanding the surrender of Seville, it seems likely that the Christian king also sent a boastful letter to none other than Yusuf himself. If the text that has come down to us may be believed – and some have doubted it – Alfonso taunted Yusuf with cowardice in delaying to come and even offered to fight him in Morocco if Yusuf would provide him with the ships to ferry a Christian army across the Straits. As well as these exchanges at the highest diplomatic level, Yusuf was also receiving deputations from the *faqihs* and *qadis* – the guardians of Islamic law and the judges who administered it – of al-Andalus. They complained of features of the government of the taifa rulers which had been causing disquiet for some time. Prominent among these grievances was taxation. In order to pay the tributes demanded by Alfonso VI the taifa kings had been compelled to lay new fiscal burdens on their subjects. No one likes paying taxes, but the crucial objection was that the novel expedients went beyond what was sanctioned by Islamic tradition. Additional taxes were not simply burdensome to the people; they were also, and far more seriously, displeasing to God. The fall of Toledo sharpened the focus of discontent. Was it not a judgement from on high? An anonymous poet lamented the loss of Toledo:

> If we say, 'punishment has reached them
> and rejection by God has come to them',
> then we like them, and more than they,

deviate [from religion]; and how can someone who deviates be safe?
Can we be sure that vengeance will not fall upon us,
When corruption has combined with licence among us?

Events in Toledo itself contributed to the mounting alarm in Andalusi society. Among the terms of surrender agreed in May 1085 Alfonso VI had guaranteed to the Muslim inhabitants their continued use of the city's main mosque for worship. He had entrusted the government of the city to one of his principal lieutenants, Sisnando Davídez. Sisnando's unusual career made him suitable for this difficult assignment. He was a native of Portugal who had been captured as a young man in a raid and carried off to Seville. He entered the service of al-Mu'tatid of Seville (d. 1068–9) and rose high therein, being employed on diplomatic missions to King Fernando I of León-Castile. At some point, and for reasons unknown, he returned to Christian lands and took service under Fernando I who appointed him governor of Coimbra upon its conquest in 1064, charged with its defence and resettlement. (The appointment might have been made a few years later, and by Alfonso VI rather than Fernando I; but the point is of no great consequence in this context.) He continued prominent in the service of Alfonso VI: we have already met him hearing a law-suit at Oviedo with Rodrigo Díaz in 1075, and going on an embassy to Zaragoza a little later. He was respected by the Muslim authorities with whom he had dealings, such as 'Abd Allah of Granada, and the chronicler Ibn Bassam praised his shrewdness, tolerance and regard for justice. A man of such talents and experience was well-fitted to take on the sensitive task of governing Toledo.

Sisnando's conciliatory policy towards the Muslims of Toledo in 1085 was given little chance. Its main opponent would appear to have been Archbishop Bernard, who was appointed to the see of Toledo shortly after its conquest. Here was a man cast in a very different mould. Bernard was a Frenchman, a monk of Cluny, who had been sent to Spain in about 1079, quite possibly in the entourage of or at the request of Constance, niece of Abbot Hugh of Cluny, who married Alfonso VI in that year. By May of 1080 Bernard had become abbot of Sahagún, an old and distinguished monastic house which enjoyed close ties with the royal family and had recently become in effect the head of the Cluniac network in Spain. From this position, already one of eminence, he was promoted by the king to be metropolitan archbishop of Toledo and primate of the whole Spanish church. Bernard was forceful and energetic. His mind had been formed far from the lands where men such as Sisnando met and mingled with the Muslims. He grew up in that period when crusading ideas were slowly taking shape in, among other places, the monastery of Cluny. One of his fellow monks there was

Odo of Châtillon who later, as Pope Urban II, was to proclaim the First Crusade. Furthermore, Bernard was very ambitious for his see. Toledo must once again, as under the Visigothic kings, shine forth as the premier ecclesiastical beacon of the Iberian peninsula. Among other things, Toledo's archbishop should have a cathedral fitting to his dignity which should call to mind the triumph of the Cross over the Crescent.

At some point in 1086 Sisnando's policies were over-ridden, the terms of capitulation were flouted, and Toledo's principal mosque was turned into a Christian church. We cannot tell exactly what happened, nor exactly when, for much legend accrued about the incident and the reports of later chroniclers cannot be trusted in detail. One thing we can be certain of is that the move had Bernard's approval. The new cathedral was consecrated on 18 December 1086 and in the charter of endowment, probably drafted by the archbishop or a member of his staff, the king was made to observe that the building, 'once the abode of demons' had now become 'a tabernacle of celestial virtue for all Christian people'.

At about the same time Sisnando Davídez was replaced as governor of Toledo by the stricter Pedro Ansúrez. This change suggests that more was at stake there than the ambitions of an over-zealous archbishop. There was a conflict of views about the proper policy of a Christian ruler towards the Muslims which must have given rise to heated debates at court. In 1086 it seems to have been the hard-liners who gained the king's ear. The panic-stricken Andalusians could have known nothing of these divided counsels. All they could see was a Christian government which could not be trusted to honour agreements, and the conversion of the Toledan mosque strengthened the hand of those who sought Almoravide intervention.

There were divided counsels among the taifa princelings too. Doubtless they were aired on such occasions as the Zaragoza wedding of January 1085 which Rodrigo Díaz may have attended. We are told, for example, that al-Rashid, one of the sons of al-Mu'tamid of Seville, was opposed to the policy of looking to the Almoravides for help and urged instead a course of accommodation with Alfonso VI. (It is perhaps relevant that he had spent some time as a captive in Barcelona a few years earlier.) The trouble was that the taifa rulers were trapped. A stark choice faced them: would they go under to the Christian king, or would they run the risk of seeking Almoravide aid with all the peril for themselves that might ensue? Al-Mu'tamid is said to have led the way in deciding with the remark that he 'would rather be a camel-driver in Morocco than a swineherd in Castile'. Final negotiations were opened with the Almoravide leadership in the winter of 1085–6.

'Abd Allah's account of these negotiations and of subsequent events down to the Sagrajas campaign is of great interest. He shows how little trust there was between the Almoravide leaders and the taifa princes. He also shows that Yusuf was extremely cautious in his movements. Immediately after his victory over Alfonso VI he took his army back to Morocco. The most likely reason for this failure to exploit his triumph was the news of the death of his cousin Abu Bakr. Yusuf had to get back to Marrakech to cope with a succession crisis. It also seems likely that at this stage Yusuf had no further designs on al-Andalus. 'Abd Allah reports that when critics of the taifa rulers approached to complain to him, Yusuf would say, 'We have not come here for this kind of thing. The princes know best what to do in their own territories.' He was not to be so mild when he returned in 1089.

Sagrajas, one might say, was Alfonso VI's Manzikert. The significance of events which historians like to call 'decisive' is rarely perceived at all quickly by contemporaries. Yusuf's intervention and the battle of Sagrajas in 1086 form a case in point. The lengthening of Yusuf's shadow over al-Andalus was to be a gradual affair, not a sudden one. As for Alfonso VI, the defeat was humiliating, but it did not bring him to his knees. It invited a riposte; it highlighted the vulnerability of Toledo. Just as the taifa rulers had been urged by Yusuf, in 'Abd Allah's words, 'to agree among ourselves, to co-operate with one another and to close our ranks', so Alfonso set about mending fences in the winter of 1086-7. This brought Rodrigo Díaz back on to the Castilian scene.

We left Rodrigo in the service of al-Musta'in, presumed to have been defending the city of Zaragoza against the army of Alfonso VI in the summer of 1086. Shortly after Sagrajas Rodrigo and the king were reconciled, perhaps in November or December. (The formal reconciliation occurred at Toledo, and we know that the royal court was there in December for the consecration of the cathedral.) We do not know who took the initiative. What is fairly clear is that Rodrigo could make his own terms. The king was desperate, and was prepared – or could be brought – to pay Rodrigo handsomely for returning to his service. The author of the *Historia Roderici* tells us that

the king gave him the castle of Duáñez with its dependents, and the castle of Gormaz, and Ibia and Campóo and Eguña and Briviesca, and Langa which is in the western parts, together with all their territories and inhabitants.

He may have been quoting from a royal charter. The word 'gave' (*dedit*) is probably to be taken as meaning 'entrusted the defence and/or administration of' to Rodrigo. The king was not alienating chunks of territory but giving his vassal responsible and lucrative employment. Duáñez, Gormaz and Langa were important strong-points in the network of defences which guarded the Duero valley. Ibia, Campóo and Eguña were districts in the extreme north of Castile. Briviesca, to the north-east of Burgos, was contiguous to the Riojan territories of Count Garcia Ordóñez.

This was not all. His biographer goes on thus:

> Furthermore, King Alfonso gave him this concession and privilege in his kingdom, written and confirmed under seal, by which all the land or castles which he himself might acquire from the Saracens in the land of the Saracens should be absolutely his in full ownership, not only his but also his sons' and daughters' and all his descendants.

This remarkable concession has caused much perplexity to commentators. Some have rejected it outright, and used it to cast doubt on the credibility of the work as a whole. Others have expended ingenuity in elaborating possible explanations, all of them in the last resort implausible. I do not see why the passage should not be accepted at its face value, as a summary of – possibly a quotation from – a royal charter granting to the Cid a very unusual gift. We should remember that the circumstances were unusual. Alfonso needed skilled commanders, and in the hard bargaining which was the essence of the lord-vassal relationship he held a weak hand. It was a vassal's market. Rodrigo could call the tune.

We must also, as always, remember that Rodrigo was not the only man to be bargaining with Alfonso in the months after Sagrajas. On the eve of the campaign the king had sought help from France. His appeal had gone primarily to his wife's relatives in Burgundy. Duke Eudes (or Odo) of Burgundy, the nephew of Queen Constance, gathered an army which set off for Spain early in 1087. It included among its commanders Eudes's cousin Raymond. (It also included contingents from other areas of France under such leaders as William, known as 'the Carpenter', viscount of Melun near Paris.) In the absence of any Almoravides to fight, the French troops settled down to besiege Tudela, on the upper Ebro, as it turned out, unsuccessfully. After the siege had fizzled out in the spring Raymond went to the court of Alfonso VI and Queen Constance – and stayed there. Shortly afterwards he was betrothed to Alfonso's only legitimate child, the *infanta* Urraca, and made count of Galicia. It was later believed that he had been promised the succession to the throne. Whatever the truth about this – and we shall never discover it – it remains that Raymond's advancement was astonishing. It shows what sort of pickings were to be had in León-Castile in 1086–7 and thereby renders the reported terms of Rodrigo Díaz's reconciliation with his king more credible.

We know nothing whatsoever of Rodrigo's doings in the two

years following the reconciliation. Our only trace of him is in the witness-lists to a couple of royal charters of 21 July 1087 and 11 March 1088. Speculation about his activities is fruitless. If no news is good news, then we may presume that Rodrigo fulfilled his duties as a loyal servant of the crown. The case is different with the years 1089–92. They are well documented, and extremely turbulent.

In the spring of 1089 Rodrigo set out at the head of an army in a south-easterly direction. He crossed the Duero near Gormaz and went on to Calamocha where he celebrated the feast of Pentecost on 20 May. There he received a deputation from Abu Marwan, ruler of the taifa principality of Albarracín, with whom he negotiated a treaty by which Abu Marwan became a tributary of King Alfonso. After this he went on through the mountains of the modern province of Teruel until he reached the shores of the Mediterranean at Murviedro to the north of Valencia. It will be recalled that Alfonso VI had installed the ex-king of Toledo, al-Qadir, as ruler of Valencia. Al-Qadir had quickly shown himself as incompetent there as he had at Toledo. The governor of Játiva had risen against him, calling on the assistance of Mundhir al-Hayib, ruler of the double principality of Lérida and Denia, with whom Rodrigo had crossed swords in 1082 and 1084. Al-Hayib in his turn had sought the help of his Catalan ally Count Berenguer of Barcelona.

The Catalan political settlement of 1086 had permitted Berenguer to resume an active policy in the Spanish Levante. It was based upon a protectorate over – and the concomitant exaction of *parias* from – Mundhir al-Hayib and the exploitation of every means to 'destabilise' al-Qadir's régime, with a view to detaching Valencia from the protectorate of Alfonso VI, possibly to its ultimate annexation as the Castilian king had annexed Toledo. Valencia was a thriving city: a prize worth having. The allies had ravaged the countryside round Valencia in 1086; in 1088 they had unsuccessfully besieged the city itself. They were back in 1089. Berenguer established fortified bases at Cebolla and Liria and was once more besieging the city. At Rodrigo's approach he made off inland to Requena and from there made his way back to Barcelona. Rodrigo had an interview with al-Qadir and received the tribute which the latter owed to King Alfonso. He stayed on in al-Qadir's principality in order to pacify the territory, establishing himself for this purpose at Requena.

It was while he was at Requena that alarming news reached him. Yusuf and the Almoravides were back in Spain.

To place the return of the Almoravides in context we must retrace our steps a little way. One of Alfonso's moves in the aftermath of the conquest of Toledo was to place a garrison in the castle of Aledo, between Murcia and Lorca. Aledo lay far beyond the southernmost point of the king's effective dominion. At first sight the decision to instal a garrison in such a distant outpost appears foolish. On the other hand, Aledo was a convenient base from which to harry the lands between Denia and Murcia ruled by al-Hayib, who was troubling Alfonso's tributary al-Qadir in Valencia. At the time, again, the town of Murcia was rebelling against Sevillian over-lordship: Aledo, nearby, could offer assistance to the rebels, thus putting pressure on al-Mu'tamid of Seville and perhaps thereby assisting in keeping his tribute flowing northwards. Furthermore, a point to which 'Abd Allah drew attention in his memoirs, the inhabitants of the area round Aledo were for the most part Christians who were willing to supply the garrison with necessities. So far from being hasty and ill-considered, Alfonso's decision to establish a base at Aledo was bold and shrewd.

The Christian garrison at Aledo had exactly the disruptive effect upon the area which the king had hoped for. A poet from the court of al-Mu'tamid, 'Abd al-Jalil, was killed while travelling between Lorca and Murcia in 1088. There were Christian losses too. One of the miracles of St Domingo de Silos concerns a Castilian knight named Pedro de Llantada who was captured by the Saracens near Aledo and kept in captivity in Murcia for two years until the saint organised a miraculous escape. The story of his capture is introduced casually, in words that convey vividly the spirit of the operations round Aledo: Pedro had left the safety of the castle 'for a few days' ravaging' (*per dies aliquot ad predandum*).

In the winter of 1088–9 al-Mu'tamid of Seville crossed the Straits to appeal in person to the Almoravide leader. Yusuf heeded the cry and crossed to Spain for the second time in March 1089. He was joined by the rulers of Seville, Granada and Almería. The combined Muslim force marched to Aledo and laid siege to it. In response, Alfonso VI raised an army to go to its relief. Needing to maximise his military capacity he sent a summons to Rodrigo at Requena, ordering him to come with his troops to reinforce the royal army.

Something went wrong and the two Christian contingents failed to converge. As far as the campaign was concerned this did not matter, for the Almoravide forces withdrew at the approach of the royal army and the king was able to relieve and reinforce Aledo as he had planned. But as far as Rodrigo's personal fortunes were concerned it mattered very much. His enemies were quick to claim that his failure to join forces with the king was deliberate and that he had thereby treacherously endangered the royal army. Alfonso believed the accusation. He confiscated all Rodrigo's property and imprisoned, though only for a short time, his wife and children. Rodrigo drafted an elaborate justification of his actions, transmitted verbatim by his biographer, and offered to defend himself not only by oath but also by the judicial process of trial by combat: a mode of proof recently introduced from France into Spain, associated especially with accusations of treason in the circles of the military aristocracy.

His case was that Alfonso had ordered a rendezvous at Villena but had subsequently changed his mind about the route which the royal army was to follow. While Rodrigo waited at Onteniente, near Villena, the king and his army passed through Hellín, on a more westerly route to Aledo. By the time Rodrigo learned of the changed plan Alfonso was already on his way back to Toledo.

At this distance of time, and given the nature of our sources, it is impossible to judge who was in the right. Certain features of Rodrigo's defence make it difficult to believe that he was as completely innocent as he claimed. As against this, the junction of two armies is always a testing operation, especially when communications are poor, speed and secrecy are at a premium, and the route of march lies through broken, mountainous country. Whatever may have been the truth about the Aledo campaign, Rodrigo's enemies were ready to accuse him and the king ready to accept his culpability. In a very revealing aside his biographer lets slip that after the campaign was over and Rodrigo had settled into winter quarters at Elche, between Murcia and Alicante, 'he allowed certain of his knights whom he had brought with him from Castile to return to their homes'. Decoded, this means that some of his own followers thought that he was finished.

Down he may have been, but he was not out. Reunited with his family, Rodrigo spent Christmas at Elche and laid plans for the coming year of 1090. The first essential, as always, was cash wherewith to hold together his following. To lay his hands on it there was only one direction in which Rodrigo could turn. Any moves towards the south were ruled out partly by the presence of Alfonso's garrison at Aledo, partly by uncertainty over the intentions of the Almoravides. But to the north lay the rich lands of the Spanish Levante whose vulnerability he had probed in the previous year. Mundhir al-Hayib's principality of Denia was the obvious prey. Rodrigo moved first on Polop and helped himself to al-Hayib's caveful of treasure: the passage in the *Historia* relating this was quoted in Chapter 7. Then he moved on to Ondara, just outside Denia, where he spent Lent and Easter (6 March–21 April 1090). Al-Hayib 'agreed a peace' with him there, which almost certainly means that he bought Rodrigo off. Al-Qadir of Valencia was the next victim to be visited. Rodrigo and his army passed northwards through the principality of Valencia, exacting 'very great and innumerable gifts of money' from al-Qadir. For good measure he also 'accepted many and innumerable tributes and gifts' from those who were rebelling against al-Qadir – such men, presumably, as the governor of Játiva. Having thus profitably extorted his way up the

Levante coast Rodrigo established himself at Burriana, a few miles to the south of the modern city of Castellón.

Reprisals would not be long in coming. In taking tribute from al-Hayib and al-Qadir, Rodrigo was supplanting their 'protectors', respectively Count Berenguer of Barcelona and King Alfonso of León-Castile. Berenguer was perhaps the more dangerous, as the nearer of the two and the less distracted by other commitments. Al-Hayib had appealed to Berenguer for help after Rodrigo's passage through the Denia region. Together they planned to assemble a coalition against him, to consist of Castile, Zaragoza, Aragon and Urgel. The count of Urgel and King Sancho of Aragon would not come in. Al-Musta'in of Zaragoza affected to accede but secretly leaked news to Rodrigo of his enemies' plans. As for Alfonso VI, although Berenguer and he met for discussions at Orón, near Miranda de Ebro in the county governed by García Ordóñez, he too stood aloof: the defence of Toledo against yet another Almoravide attack – of which more presently – had to take first place.

So Berenguer was on his own; but he was still formidable. He gathered a large army, staffed by some of his most experienced commanders – such men as Guerau Alemany (Giraldo Alamán) de Cervelló, who had been one of the leaders of the Catalan army which had campaigned in the Levante in 1086, and Deudat Bernat (Deusdedit Bernaldi) de Claramunt, who had recently been entrusted with the defence and resettlement of Tarragona. Rodrigo, watching the preparations with misgiving, retreated from Burriana into the mountainous region near Morella. He established his camp there in a position of great natural strength 'in a place called Iber' as the *Historia Roderici* put it. The place-name cannot be identified and it may be that it has been corrupted in transmission. The *Poema de Mio Cid*, whose account of this episode is full though fantastic, referred to the place as *el pinar de Tevár*, 'the pine wood of Tévar', and it is assumed that the poet had access to reliable information. On the basis of a charter of Pedro II of Aragon of the year 1209 Menéndez Pidal was able to establish that the wood of Tévar probably lay between the villages of Herbés and Monroyo (on the boundary between the modern provinces of Castellón and Teruel).

Count Berenguer followed Rodrigo into the mountains and encamped nearby. There followed an exchange of letters between the two leaders. Their texts, apparently reliable, are preserved in the *Historia Roderici*. Berenguer taunted Rodrigo with treachery (to Alfonso VI, presumably), accused him of violating churches in the course of his campaigns and alleged that he put more trust in auguries – particularly the reading of omens in the flight of birds – than a good Christian should. (Is it coincidental that the author of the *Poema de Mio Cid* shows Rodrigo reposing trust in auguries drawn from birds?) The general sense of the count's letter was that Rodrigo was a boor and a thug. Its point was to provoke him into abandoning his position on the mountainside and coming down to fight on the flatter ground where Berenguer was encamped. Rodrigo's reply accused the count of being a braggart and a coward, reminded him of his humiliation in 1082 and turned the accusations of treachery back upon him by hinting darkly at his alleged fratricide. There was no question of Rodrigo abandoning his position.

During the following night Berenguer sent a detachment of his troops to take possession of the ground even higher up the slopes of the mountain above Rodrigo's lines. They succeeded in this undetected. At dawn Rodrigo was attacked simultaneously by these men from above and by Berenguer's main army from below. He was taken unawares. Rodrigo rallied his men and fought back. It is a testimony to his leadership, and to their discipline and morale, that they shifted and broke the main Catalan formation with their first charge. But in the skirmish which followed it Rodrigo himself fell from his horse and was wounded as he lay on the ground. His men fought on. One presumes that the advantage of the slope gradually told in their favour. The battle ended in a victory for Rodrigo's army. Not only that: Count Berenguer himself was taken, as at Almenar in 1082, and all his leading vassals – Guerau Alemany, Deudat Bernat, Ramón Mir, Ricart Guillem, 'and many other most noble men'. It was, as his biographer pointed out, 'a victory ever to be extolled and remembered'.

The Catalan camp was plundered. The count and his men were ransomed for enormous sums of money. The diplomatic advantages gained were even more important than the pecuniary. After the count's release Rodrigo made his way up the Ebro valley towards Zaragoza and then struck off south to Daroca where he was detained by illness, possibly as a result of his wound at Tévar. From there he entered into further negotiations with Count Berenguer, who had come to the court of al-Musta'in of Zaragoza for the purpose, the Muslim ruler apparently acting as an intermediary. After protracted exchanges terms were agreed. Berenguer came to Rodrigo's camp where

> peace and friendship between the two of them were proclaimed, and the count placed in Rodrigo's hand and protection that part of *Hispania* which had been subject to his overlordship.

Among the writers of this period the term *Hispania* was used to designate Muslim as opposed to Christian Spain. What the count was doing, therefore, was surrendering to Rodrigo his claims to lordship over the taifa principalities of the Spanish Levante. Of course, neither man could have deceived himself that such an arrangement would be permanent. However, it was Berenguer's recognition that the victory at Tévar had temporarily checked Catalan ambitions south of the river Ebro. The death of Mundhir al-Hayib, Count Berenguer's ally, at about the same time as the Tévar campaign, also played into Rodrigo's hand. He left a young son, Sulayman, whose regents divided up his principality of Lérida, Tortosa and Denia.

After his recovery and the completion of the negotiations at Daroca, Rodrigo led his army down to the Mediterranean at Burriana. He spent Christmas at Cebolla (now El Puig de Santa María) only a few miles north of Valencia, doubtless collecting more tribute from al-Qadir at the same time. Then he moved inland to lay siege to Liria where, says his biographer, 'he handed out very generous wages to his troops'. Well could he afford to. A year earlier, at Elche, repudiated by Alfonso VI and with his knights deserting him, Rodrigo had faced a bleak future. By the end of the year 1090 he had become the arbiter of the Levante coast from the mouth of the Ebro to the promontory on which Denia stands.

What he might do next would depend partly on his own exertions, partly on any moves made by Alfonso VI, but perhaps most of all on Yusuf and the Almoravides.

Yusuf had crossed to Spain for the third time in June 1090. While Count Berenguer and the Cid were engaged at Tévar the Almoravides were unsuccessfully besieging Toledo. By early September Yusuf and his army were back in the south, encamped outside Granada. Angered by the failure of the taifa rulers to participate in the recent campaign, and bruised by his failure to recapture Toledo, Yusuf was in a vengeful mood.

The breakdown of the fragile relations between the taifa princes and the Almoravides can be followed in 'Abd Allah's vivid account of the years 1089-90. In the course of the Aledo campaign 'subjects came in droves to lay their complaints against their rulers'; and this time Yusuf listened. 'Abd Allah was frank about his own apprehensions: 'I nearly died of worry . . . I was gripped by gloom and suspicion . . .' Opposition to non-canonical taxes such as the qabalat – an excise tax on sales, from which Spanish alcabala and French gabelle derive – became more vocal. When the town of Lucena rebelled against him in the winter of 1089-90 it was partly because he had imposed a supplementary tax on it. About this time 'Abd Allah embarked on a programme of refortification with an eye to possible Almoravide attack. He was suspected of negotiating with Alfonso VI, who was still taking tribute from Granada in 1090, for military aid against the Almoravides. When he wrote to Yusuf in justification of his actions he received a reply full of menace: 'I well know your conniving ways and mendacious utterances . . . Do not pin your hopes on the long-term. The near future is what matters to you.' Another town, Loja, rebelled. The general who was sent against it defected to the Almoravides. A leading jurist, Ibn Sahl, who was sent on an embassy to Yusuf in the spring of 1090, also defected. Fond of quoting proverbs, 'Abd Allah reflected ruefully that 'a tent cannot stand without pegs'.

So when Yusuf summoned 'Abd Allah to his camp in September, the ruler of Granada had no choice but to go. He was placed in captivity, stripped of all his treasure and then despatched to exile in Morocco. Yusuf moved next against 'Abd Allah's brother Tamim, ruler of Málaga: he too was deposed and exiled. The tiny principality of Baza went the same way before the year was out, and Almería followed early in 1091. Then the Almoravides under Yusuf's cousin and deputy Sir ibn Abu Bakr, turned upon the most formidable of the taifa states, Seville. The city of Córdoba fell to him in March 1091. Its governor Fath al-Ma'mun, one of the sons of al-Mu'tamid of Seville, was killed defending it. (His widow Zaida shortly afterwards became the mistress of Alfonso VI.) Seville itself was invested in June and fell to the Almoravides in September. Al-Mu'tamid in his turn was sent into exile in Morocco where he composed a number of moving laments over his lot which rank among the finest poems in Arabic literature.

> I wept upon seeing a flock of desert partridges flying past me;
> They travelled freely, unhampered by jail and fetters!
> This was not, so God help me, because of envy,
> But due to my longing that I might be like them:
> Freely moving about, not torn from my family, my heart
> Not tortured by grief, my eyes not weeping over lost children!
> May they enjoy their not being torn from each other,
> Nor may any of them ever grieve o'er a far-away parent,
> And may they never live like me, their heart leaping
> With pain when the jail door opens or the chains rustle.
> My soul ardently wishes soon to meet death;
> Let another, not I, love to live with feet in chains.
> May God protect the partridge and its fledglings!
> My own fledglings were betrayed by water and by shade.

Alfonso VI made two attempts to check the advance of the Almoravides in 1091. He sent an army under Alvar Fáñez to break up the siege of Seville but it was defeated at Almodóvar del Rio. He himself undertook an expedition seemingly designed to expel the Almoravides from Granada, but it had no success. Doubts have been expressed as to whether this latter campaign ever took place, but they seem ill-founded. The campaign is of interest as being the last recorded occasion on which the Cid and King Alfonso had any direct personal dealings.

As told by the author of the *Historia Roderici*, Rodrigo received letters from Queen Constance and from friends in Castile while he was besieging Liria in the winter of 1090–1. They urged him to join forces with the king for a campaign against the Almoravides. He followed their advice. He joined the king at Martos and together they went on to camp near Granada. The enemy did not offer battle, so after six days the king ordered his army back to Toledo by way of Ubeda. The reconciliation with the king did not last long. Outside Granada there was a quarrel over precedence – a matter of where Rodrigo chose to pitch his tents in relation to the king's. Alfonso was supported by his courtiers. At Ubeda the king launched a verbal attack on Rodrigo, accusing him of 'many and various things – but untrue ones'. He was planning to place him under arrest but Rodrigo got wind of this and escaped. Prompted by Rodrigo's enemies, Alfonso refused to accept his subsequent protestations of innocence. The king went back to Toledo and Rodrigo returned to the Levante. Christmas 1091 found him at Morella.

The story is plausible, even if it has its dark corners. Although banished in 1089, Rodrigo was still Alfonso's subject. Since then he had usurped the king's position as protector of al-Qadir and had diverted tributes due to the king into his own pocket. There would indeed have been 'many and various things' to accuse him of. Rodrigo's provocation of the king near Granada may have been deliberate; a bid, perhaps, to claim equality of status. Alfonso may not have wanted any reconciliation – it may be significant that the approach came from the queen – but his need for experienced commanders was as desperate as it had been four years earlier after Sagrajas; more so, indeed, as Almoravide plans to reunite al-Andalus under their own authority had emerged more clearly. Conscious at once of dependence upon Rodrigo and of the inability to discipline him, smarting under his arrogance, goaded by courtiers, frustrated by the failure of the campaign, Alfonso found his endurance tested beyond bearing. At Ubeda his pent-up rage exploded. It is all too credible.

The royal anger was not just a flash in the pan. Rodrigo knew the king's tenacity, and his own actions in the early months of 1092 are best interpreted as responses to the possibility of an attack. He made his way to Zaragoza and renewed his alliance with al-Musta'in. Then he negotiated an alliance with King Sancho Ramírez of Aragon and his son Pedro. Finally, he acted as intermediary in bringing about peace between Zaragoza and Aragon: a triumph of diplomacy, this, because Sancho had conquered Monzón in 1089 and was continuing to exert pressure on Zaragoza's northern marches. King Alfonso was making alliances too. He approached the most prominent maritime cities of northern Italy, Genoa and Pisa, proposing a joint attack upon Valencia by land and sea. It is said that they furnished four hundred ships, presumably in return for trading privileges should the city be conquered.

Alfonso's campaign against Valencia in 1092 was designed to show who the master of the Levante really was. The recruitment of Italian shipping showed that Alfonso meant to gain possession, through blockade, of the city itself. It must also have been his aim to remind the Muslim rulers of Alpuente and Albarracín that they were his tributaries, and no one else's. The campaign was therefore directed as much against Rodrigo Díaz as against any Muslim ruler, to prise him out of his position of *de facto* power in the Levante which he had usurped from the king two years before.

But Alfonso had barely settled down to besiege Valencia before he was recalled to Castile by disturbing news. Rodrigo had invaded his kingdom. The invasion and devastation of the Rioja in 1092 was graphically and sorrowfully described by Rodrigo's biographer in a passage which has already been quoted in an earlier chapter. What Rodrigo did was to enter Alfonso's kingdom by the valley of the upper Ebro, laying waste and burning as far as Alberite and Logroño, before retiring laden with booty to the castle of Alfaro, near the most north-westerly outpost of his ally al-Musta'in at Tudela. The action was not directed simply at the king. The prime sufferer was García Ordóñez, whose county this was. Rodrigo's biographer tells us that he chose to devastate García's land 'because of his enmity (*inimicitia*) and his insult (*dedecus*)'. And there is no reason why we should disbelieve him. The words he used would have had an ampler resonance for his contemporaries than they do for us. *Inimicitia* implied rather more than feelings of ill-disposition toward someone else: it indicated the active prosecution of malicious intent, for example in the context of a feud. *Dedecus* carried meanings of shame, loss of honour, ridicule, public humiliation – things that eleventh-century noblemen dreaded. We cannot tell for sure what hurts Rodrigo had in mind. At this period Count García was the most prominent Castilian magnate. His advice to the king may well have lain behind the troubles suffered by Rodrigo over the last three years – the king's unwillingness to hear the defence of his conduct on the Aledo campaign, the imprisonment of his wife and children, the discussions at Orón between Alfonso and Count Berenguer in 1090, the king's wrath in the course of the Granada campaign of 1091 and finally the attempt to crush him in 1092.

Now it was Rodrigo's turn to show *inimicitia* and inflict *dedecus*. García's lands were ravaged, to his heavy loss. He was held up for all to see as failing in his public duty of defending his county and maintaining order in it. And when he did get an army together – significantly, summoning 'all his kinsmen' to uphold the honour of the family – he did not dare to fight.

So Rodrigo returned to Zaragoza, his honour vindicated and his design of warning Alfonso VI off Valencia achieved. The king had abandoned his siege. The Italian fleets drifted off up the coast to help the count of Barcelona in an abortive siege of Tortosa. In the south the Almoravides inflicted further humiliation on Alfonso VI by taking the castle of Aledo.

The fall of Aledo was but one incident in a steady Almoravide advance in south-eastern Spain in the course of 1092. The campaign was led by Muhammad ibn Aisa, one of Yusuf's sons. He took Murcia in the spring, then Aledo, and in the late summer and autumn Denia, Játiva and Alcira. The last-named place is only twenty-two miles south of Valencia. Meanwhile there were changes inside Valencia itself. Al-Qadir's rule there had been as ineffective and unpopular as it had been in Toledo. A group of influential citizens conspired to call in Almoravide help to rid themselves of him. They were headed by the *qadi* of the city, Ibn Jahhaf, a respected figure whose family had been prominent in Valencian affairs for over a century. Al-Qadir just had time to send his treasure away for safe-keeping to the castles of Olocau and Segorbe before shutting himself up in his palace. Shortly afterwards he tried to escape – disguised as a woman, it was said – but was captured and executed (28 October 1092) on the orders of Ibn Jahhaf. His executioner was the son of that Ibn al-Hadidi who had been murdered on al-Qadir's orders in Toledo in 1075. On the following day Ibn Jahhaf was proclaimed ruler of Valencia.

News of these developments was brought to the Cid in the taifa of Zaragoza. His dominant position in the Levante was threatened by the Almoravide advance and the coup in Valencia. He hastened south-eastwards and laid siege to Cebolla, about nine miles north of Valencia. It was soon captured. He refortified it and established a base for further operations there. It is clear that he had decided to move in on Valencia as Alfonso VI had moved in on Toledo a few years earlier.

Rodrigo's siege of Valencia began in July 1093. The *Historia Roderici* is curiously sparing in its account of it. We have a supplementary account in the chronicle of Ibn 'Alqama. Much fuller narratives are furnished by later chronicles but, as usual, their details cannot be relied on. While we do not know the size of the force which Rodrigo could put into the field, it is probable that his army was smaller than the royal army with which Alfonso VI had briefly besieged Valencia in 1092; and he had no Italian ships to help him. So a siege in the strict sense of the word was out of the question. Rodrigo's strategy was to cut off supplies to the city by systematic ravaging on the landward side from bases such as Cebolla to the north and Benicadell to the south; the latter being a strongpoint which he had occupied and refortified after the Granada campaign of 1091. He could wear down the morale of the citizens of Valencia by hit-and-run attacks on its suburbs and by the rumour, and perhaps the reality, of atrocities. He could hope to receive some assistance from his Aragonese allies and may indeed have done so, though the sources tell us nothing of it directly: but the Aragonese were campaigning in the northern half of the Valencia taifa in 1093, and these operations may have been co-ordinated with Rodrigo's further south.

Above all, Rodrigo could hope that no Almoravide force would come to the relief of Valencia. His luck held once more. Ibn Jahhaf implored the sending of a relief force and Yusuf did indeed send one (September (?) 1093) but it did not offer battle. The *Historia*, of course, assures us that it was 'huge' but perhaps it was not big enough. In the latter part of 1093 the Almoravides were committed in the western half of the Peninsula – early in 1094 they were to over-run the taifa of Badajoz, deposing and murdering its ruler al-Mutawakkil – and it may be that this prevented the sending of an adequate army to Valencia. It may also have been that Yusuf underrated the seriousness of the threat to Valencia.

An army of fitting size was finally despatched in 1094. But by then it was too late. Rodrigo had continued to press his blockade ever more closely in the winter months of 1093–4. Food shortages began to be felt in the city. No relief force appeared. About the end of May Ibn Jahhaf opened negotiations. Terms of surrender were agreed. Rodrigo Díaz had made himself the master of Valencia.

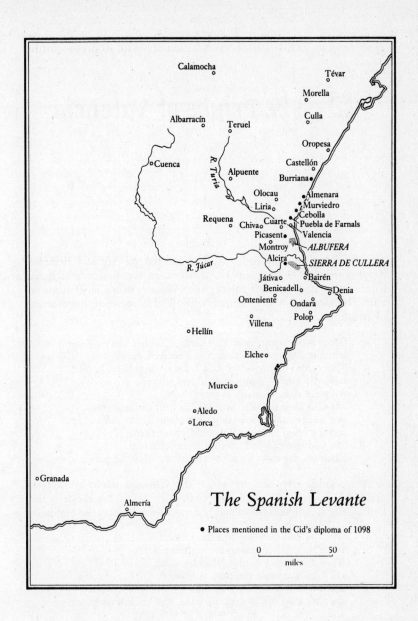

Calamocha

Tévar

Morella

Culla

Albarracín   Teruel

Oropesa

Cuenca

Castellón

R. Turia   Alpuente   Burriana

Olocau   Almenara

Liria   Murviedro

Cebolla

Requena   Cuarte   Puebla de Farnals

Chiva   Picasent   Valencia

Montroy   *ALBUFERA*

R. Júcar   Alcira   *SIERRA DE CULLERA*

Játiva   Bairén

Benicadell   Denia

Onteniente   Ondara

Polop

Villena

Hellín

Elche

Murcia

Aledo

Lorca

Granada

Almería

The Spanish Levante

● Places mentioned in the Cid's diploma of 1098

0   50

miles

II

✱ The Prince of Valencia

On Thursday, 15 June 1094, the Cid entered the city of Valencia as its conqueror. He took up his quarters in the palace which had formerly housed the taifa rulers. The *Poema de Mio Cid*, though not a strictly historical witness, must be allowed to speak of that moment of triumph:

> Great is the rejoicing in that place
> when my Cid took Valencia and entered the city.
> Those who had gone on foot became knights on horses;
> and who could count the gold and silver?
> All were rich, as many as were there.
> My Cid Don Rodrigo sent for his fifth of the spoils,
> in coined money alone thirty thousand marks fell to him,
> and the other riches, who could count them?
> My Cid rejoiced and all who were with him,
> when his flag flew from the top of the Moorish palace.

What was this city like, of which the Cid had made himself the master? Here is the *Poema de Mio Cid* again, describing the arrival of Doña Jimena and her children at Valencia shortly after the conquest.

> My Cid and they went to the fortress,
> there he led them up to the highest place.
> Then fair eyes gaze out on every side,
> they see Valencia, the city, as it lies,
> and turning the other way their eyes behold the sea,
> they look on the farmlands, wide, and thick with green,
> and all the other things which give delight;
> they raised their hands to give thanks to God,
> for all that bounty so vast and so splendid.

The visitor to Valencia today can repeat their experience by climbing the bell-tower of the cathedral known as the Miguelete (or, locally, the Micalet). His rewards will be in some measure greater than theirs; but there will be losses as well as gains. Greater, for the Miguelete, which was built in about 1400, is higher than any building which could have stood in Rodrigo's day; and when you have puffed your way up its steep steps to the platform some two hundred feet above the ground you are indeed rewarded with the '*panorama★ magnifique*' which your *Guide Bleu* has promised you. The losses lie in the size and uncontrolled ugly sprawl of modern Valencia. It is a big city today, with a population of about a million. From the city proper down to the port of El Grao a couple of miles to the east the country has been entirely built over. Inland to west, north and south featureless high-density housing blocks have invaded the farmland. Up and down the seaside high-rise hotels and holiday villas have comprehensively wrecked what was once an attractive coastline.

It is difficult but not impossible to make the effort to erase the developments of nine centuries and to see that landscape as Doña Jimena saw it; or as the poet Ibn az-Zaqqaq (d.1134) saw it:

> Valencia – when I think of her, and
> of her wonders – is the fairest in the land:
> the best witness for her is herself, because
> her beauty is apparent to the eye.
> Her Lord has dressed her in a robe of beauty,
> marked by two borders, the sea and the river.

The land has been steadily gaining on the sea in this part of the Mediterranean littoral. The line of the coast may have been as much as a mile closer to the city in the Cid's time than it is today. The rock of Murviedro, the modern Sagunto, which closes the plain of Valencia to the north, was probably almost on the sea instead of about a mile and a half inland as it is now. To the south there has been less change. Cullera, at the mouth of the River Júcar, with its lion-like sierra couched above it, is still on the coast; and the foothills of the inland ranges come right down to the sea near Denia where now the *autopista* from Valencia to Alicante bursts through them, affording asterisk-worthy views to the motorist. On the west side of Valencia the level land starts to rise gently after about ten miles. By the time you reach Liria, or Chiva, or Montroy you are in the foothills of the vast ranges to which you have already lifted up your eyes from the top of the Miguelete.

Huerta is the name given to the flat, rich, irrigated land which lies about Valencia. It is derived from the Latin *hortus*, 'a garden', and it is as a garden that it presents itself even now to the eye of the visitor. How the conquerors from bleak Castile must have gasped as they looked upon the ordered yield of that astonishingly abundant landscape: the paddy-fields of rice, the lustrous greens of the citrus groves, the chequerboard of fruit and vegetable plots; further to the west, on the rising ground, the vineyards, olive groves and cornfields; beyond them the pine forests on the slopes of the mountains. The garden has its lake, the Albufera, a shallow lagoon covering about twenty-five square miles, immediately to the south of the city, divided from the sea by a narrow strip of sand-dunes dotted with pines: source of food in the shape of wildfowl and eels; source of delight to the eye, particularly after rain, when the atmosphere becomes pearly and translucent, a watercolourist's dream.

Nothing structural survives of the city of which the Cid became the lord in 1094. We are dependent for our knowledge of it entirely upon what may be gleaned from literary sources and the layout of the streets in the oldest quarter. The situation and shape of the city were determined by the course of the River Turia, which here executes a loop to the north on its way to the sea. At a much earlier date the river seems to have had another arm which looped to the south at the same point. This southern watercourse had silted up, it seems, well before the Christian era, but was still clearly visible as a depression in the ground in the eleventh century. It may still just be discerned in almost imperceptible slopes in certain quarters of the city today, for instance near the Plaza Redonda and the marketplace or at the Plaza de Tetuán. Valencia grew up on the island between the Turia and the dried-up watercourse.

The site is level: there is no natural citadel. Accordingly the nucleus of the city in the Roman period and subsequently under Islamic rule was to be found at the intersection of the two principal roads which traversed it from north to south and from east to west. This crossing was situated in the region of what is now the cathedral. The city's principal mosque, which Rodrigo converted into a church for Bishop Jerónimo, underlay the existing cathedral. Next to it stood the palace of the taifa kings, from the top of whose tower Rodrigo is alleged to have shown the city and the country round about to his wife and daughters.

The city would have been defined to their gaze by its walls. We possess a contemporary description of them by the geographer al-'Udri who died in 1085:

Valencia has walls: 'Abd al-'Aziz, the grandson of Almanzor, took great pains in their construction. No city in al-Andalus has more perfect or more elegant walls. There are five gates. The Levante gate is called the Bridge Gate [Bab al-Qantara] and on passing through it one crosses the bridge. This also was built by 'Abd al-'Aziz. There is no finer bridge in al-Andalus: across it depart the caravans for Toledo, Zaragoza and Tortosa. Next on the Levante side is the gate called Bab al-Warraq: on going out of it you cross the river by a wooden bridge towards the suburb that lies beyond. In the direction of the Qibla, that is towards Mecca, there is the Gate of Ibn Sajar. On the northern side there is the Gate of the Snake [Bab al-Hanas]. On the southern side there is the gate called Baytala, and next to it on the west the Gate of the Silk Exchange [Bab al-Qaysariya]. Through these two gates go out the caravans for the west of al-Andalus and for Denia, Játiva and Alcira.

Al-'Udri thus lists six rather than five gates. To them we can add a seventh, not mentioned by him but attested in a record of the year 1088: the Bab al-Sari'a on the eastern side.

There are interesting continuities here. The Gate of the Silk Exchange was on the site of the future Lonja de la Seda, or silk exchange, a handsome fifteenth-century building which still stands and is now a museum. Silk was traded there for many hundreds of years. The main market of the city in the eleventh century was nearby: it still is. The other main focus of commercial life was by the Bridge Gate, where there was a custom-house, warehouses and lodging-houses. Whether any shipping made its way up the Turia as far as Valencia in the Cid's day we do not know. Perhaps then, as now, ships were unloaded downstream at the port of El Grao (which was closer to the city then than now, as we have already seen) and their cargoes transported to the city on the backs of camels, donkeys or slaves. In any case, the Turia shrinks so far as to be unnavigable during the summer months. Yet the river was always one to be treated with respect. Heavy thunderstorms, particularly in the autumn, could produce sudden flash-floods – and can do so still, despite elaborate hydraulic engineering. The handsome stone bridge built by 'Abd al-'Aziz was badly damaged in just such an inundation in October 1088.

On the north-eastern side of the city, across the river, was the Almunia, the royal gardens also laid out by 'Abd al-'Aziz. Nothing now remains of them and the area has long been built over. On the other side of the city it is likely that there was a good deal of extramural settlement. We are told, for example, that the Jewish quarter in the south-east was situated both inside and outside the walls. This is an indication that the intra-mural area was densely settled.

A poem by al-Muranabbi (fl. 1090–1130) was inspired by the sight of a girl coming out of the Bab al-Hanas at Valencia. It starts thus:

> The one I saw at the Gate of the Snake is
> a full moon arising from darkness . . .

The girl's beauty emerges into light at the gateway from the darkness beyond. One senses narrow streets, crowded tenements, much bustle and noise. We have no contemporary description of what

Valencia was like within its walls, but we do possess an account of Seville at this period. Of course, no two cities are exactly alike: but it is reasonable to suppose that Valencia and Seville had something in common.

Ibn 'Abdun's treatise on the administration of Seville was composed about the year 1100. The author was probably a municipal official. His book seems to have been prompted mainly by a concern with the correction of bureaucratic and commercial fraud, the maintenance of cleanliness and moral standards, and the prevention of crime. These ends, admirable though they are, tend to encourage a puritanical streak in those who urge them: Ibn 'Abdun is no exception to this rule. He comes across as a fussy, interfering, humourless killjoy. He wanted to ban chess because it was a game of chance (sic) and distracted from religious observance; he thought that the sale of truffles should be forbidden because of their aphrodisiac properties. But we should not complain: his treatise casts a flood of light into the dark corners of Seville's crowded streets.

Crowded they certainly seem to have been. We can sense cramped conditions in several of his recommendations. Sellers of firewood, for example, should not frequent marketplaces: their bundles trip people up and snag their clothes. The angles of butchers' stalls which stick out into the street ought to be sawn off because the meat dangling from them fouls the clothes of passers-by. There was not much 'public space'. At Valencia the marketplace was perhaps the only considerable open space within the walls; and we shall see to what a grim use Rodrigo would put it. Public places tended to be enclosed rather than open as in the cities of the ancient world: the mosques, the bath-houses. In Seville it was on the wall of the great mosque that standards of the sizes of wood to be used in construction, for instance as joists or beams, were displayed. As for the baths, Ibn 'Abdun had grave reservations about some of the goings-on there: bath attendants, masseurs and barbers must not frequent them without wearing trousers. Disorder and crime were, predictably, matters of concern to Ibn 'Abdun. We hear of pigeons trained to steal, of fortune-tellers visiting private houses to spy out the land for burglars, of pickpockets who acted in collusion with itinerant perfumers. Police patrolled the city of Seville by night but so did troublemakers such as mercenary soldiers from the garrison. Ibn 'Abdun thought that the watermen should be forbidden to ferry Berbers and Blacks into the city – there being then no bridge over the Guadalquivir – because they were notoriously disorderly.

The city may have been turbulent but we can also sense its solidarity in the face of a frightening world outside: the countryside. Although Ibn 'Abdun has a few perfunctory words of sympathy for the peasantry who suffered the rapacity of tax assessors and collectors, he regarded the rural hinterland with apprehension. Arms should never be sold to countrymen and – a revealing observation – every village should contain a watchman charged on oath to protect the rural properties of town-dwellers from the hostile attentions of the peasantry. And yet he was uneasily aware of the dependence of the city upon the countryside. There are hints of demand pressing upon its resources. The country people of the Marismas, the swampy land in the river delta, should be compelled to grow reeds for making baskets. There was anxiety about the food supply of the city.

If Valencia was anything like Seville there are hints here of the problems that would preoccupy its rulers, be they Muslim or Christian.

Rodrigo Díaz could have spared no time for reflection on the civil administration of his new conquest. In the summer of 1094 the first imperative was defence. The Almoravide army summoned by Ibn Jahhaf had apparently dispersed. However, Yusuf, fresh from the conquest of the taifa of Badajoz, was in no mood to abandon his designs on Valencia. He appointed his nephew Muhammad to the command of an enormous army recruited in both Morocco and al-Andalus. Muhammad's instructions were to take Rodrigo alive and bring him to Yusuf in chains.

Rodrigo probably hoped for assistance from his ally the king of Aragon. By December 1093 at the latest there was a southern Aragonese outpost at Culla, in the mountains to the north of the modern city of Castellón de la Plana. Culla was a long way from Valencia, about seventy miles over difficult country, but it was the nearest source of Christian help. However, at this critical juncture Rodrigo's luck failed him. Only a few days before his entry into Valencia, King Sancho Ramírez of Aragon had died (4 June 1094). It is likely that Rodrigo at once opened negotiations with his son and successor Pedro I (1094–1104) for a renewal of the alliance. The two men met at Burriana, on the coast just to the south of Castellón, and the pact was reaffirmed. But on this occasion the new king could offer Rodrigo nothing more tangible than words. The early months of a new king's reign were always politically perilous; in any case Pedro was committed to continuing the siege of Huesca initiated by his father: it was no time to lead an army outside his kingdom. Seen from Aragon, Rodrigo was an adventurer precariously holding an isolated city deep in enemy territory. Whatever his personal inclinations, the king of Aragon could never have persuaded his baronage to embark on a relief operation so distant and so hazardous. Aragon was Rodrigo's best bet and it had failed him. Given his recent encounters with Count Berenguer of Barcelona, it was useless to look for help from Catalonia. There remained the kingdom of León-Castile. A contemporary, Ibn 'Alqama, tells us that Rodrigo sought help from Alfonso VI and that the king did set out at the head of an army to go to his aid. Rodrigo must have swallowed his pride thus to turn to the king, and Alfonso's response showed generosity. The trouble was that the king's hands were tied. In the centre of the Peninsula Toledo had to be defended. Further west he had just lost to the Almoravides the territories of central Portugal – Lisbon, Santarem and Cintra – which al-Mutawakkil of Badajoz had ceded to him as the price of an alliance in 1093: the autumn of 1094 had to be given over to preparations for an attempt, in the event abortive, to recover them. So the royal army which set out for Valencia was probably a small one. But the question of its size is irrelevant, since it did not get to Valencia in time.

So Rodrigo found himself on his own. His situation somewhat resembled that in which the armies of the First Crusade found themselves four years later at Antioch: locked up inside a lately conquered city, anxiously awaiting the approach of a big and determined enemy relief force. How big the Almoravide army was we do not know. The author of the *Historia Roderici*, who was not disposed to underestimate its size, offers us 'nearly 150,000 mounted men'. This is obviously an exaggeration. Even if, as has been suggested, there is a textual corruption here and the original reading was '50,000' this still seems far too high. No Almoravide army is ever likely to have exceeded half this figure. We can be sure that Rodrigo's troops were outnumbered, but by how much we can only guess.

It was a time of gravest crisis for Rodrigo and his men. The atmosphere can be sensed from the reports of Ibn 'Alqama. It was put about that if the Almoravide army approached to lay siege to the city the Muslim population would be put to the sword – a revealing indication of how little the Christian conquerors believed that they could trust the citizens of Valencia. Panicky measures for defence were taken. All tools of iron were to be surrendered to the Cid on pain of death and sequestration of property, an order (presumably unenforceable) intended at once to disarm the inhabitants and to add to the weaponry of the defenders. A trick was used to entice the able-bodied male population out of the city to the coast, and then those who were judged to be potential troublemakers were sent off to fend for themselves elsewhere.

The Almoravide army drew closer. By the end of the month of Ramadan (early October) it was concentrated outside the city walls on the level plain named Cuarte, where Valencia's airport now is, a place whose name survives in the nearby suburb of Cuart de Poblet. Hostilities began in earnest after the fast of Ramadan was over, on the first day of the following month of Shawwal (14 October). Here is the author of the *Historia Roderici*:

The Almoravide army lay about Valencia for ten days and nights . . .

Every day they used to go round the city, shrieking and shouting with a motley clamour of voices and filling the air with their bellowing; and they often used to fire arrows at the tents and dwellings of Rodgrigo and his soldiers ... But Rodrigo, stout of heart as ever, comforted and strengthened his troops in a manly fashion and constantly prayed devoutly to the Lord Jesus Christ that He would send divine aid to his people. There came a day when the enemy were as usual going about the city yelling and skirmishing, confident in the belief that they would capture it, when Rodrigo the invincible warrior ... courageously made a sortie from the city accompanied by his well-armed followers. They shouted at the enemy and terrified them with threatening words. They fell upon them and a major encounter ensued. By God's clemency Rodrigo defeated all the Almoravides. Thus he had victory and triumph over them, granted to him by God. As soon as they were defeated they turned their backs in flight. A multitude of them fell to the sword. Others with their wives and children were led captive to Rodrigo's headquarters. Rodrigo's men seized all their tents and equipment, among which they found innumerable money of gold and silver and precious textiles. They thoroughly plundered all the wealth they found there. Rodrigo and his men were greatly enriched thereby – with much gold and silver, most precious textiles, chargers, palfreys and mules and various sorts of weaponry. They were amply stocked with quantities of provisions and treasures untold.

Ibn 'Alqama furnishes us with a little more detail about the battle. Rodrigo had divided his forces into two parts. A sudden sortie in strength was made by one of them in such a fashion as to suggest that he himself led it. Meanwhile, commanding the other body of troops, Rodrigo left the city by a different gate and fell upon the defenceless camp. The defeat quickly became a rout.

It was the classic tactic of feint followed by attack from a different quarter, carefully planned and boldly executed. It sounds as though Rodrigo achieved surprise: perhaps the thirteenth-century compilers of the *Primera Crónica General* were correct in reporting, or at any rate implying, that the operation started at dawn. It was a most remarkable victory: as one of Rodrigo's followers put it a few years later, it was 'incredible' (*ultra quam credi potest*). Its fame spread far and wide. It was *the* event of the year. An Aragonese notary could date a charter 'in the year when the Almoravides came to Valencia and Rodrigo Díaz defeated them and took captive all their troops'. The scribe's judgement was sound. The battle of Cuarte was the first occasion on which an Almoravide army had been defeated. Rodrigo had shown that they were not invincible. It gave a boost to the morale of all the Christians in Spain in somewhat the same way that victory over Kerbogha of Mosul outside the walls of Antioch restored the morale of the armies of the First Crusade.

For Rodrigo himself, a soldier with his back to the wall, his objective simply survival, it gave a breathing space. His lordship of

Valencia had stood its first test. Nothing could have been more certain than that it would have to submit to further challenge. We have a precisely contemporary witness to this. 'Abd Allah, the dethroned ruler of Granada, completing his memoirs in the winter of 1094–5, observed that

> were I to leave the writing of this work until the conclusion of the Valencia story, I would approach my task with a Muslim victory already attained. That is why a lacuna has been left in this book in expectation that a long-cherished hope might be realised.

'Abd Allah was well-placed to know what was in the minds of the Almoravide leaders. What was Rodrigo to do with the precious time he had gained?

Valencia and those parts of the *huerta* adjacent to the city were an island in an ocean of hostile territory. Once more a comparison with the First Crusade is apt. Edessa, Antioch and Jerusalem, conquered by the crusaders in 1098–9, were isolated and vulnerable until additional territorial consolidation took place. After his victory at Cuarte Rodrigo headed off to the north of Valencia and took the castle of Olocau. It guarded one of the northern approaches to the plain of Valencia and had been one of al-Qadir's treasuries. The acquisition of Olocau staked out a claim about the northern extent of Rodrigo's principality. It made clear to the ruler of the little taifa kingdom of Alpuente, to the north-west, that Rodrigo meant business. The acquisition of al-Qadir's treasure stored at Olocau replenished Rodrigo's war-chests and enabled him to reward his followers.

Mopping-up operations of this sort are occasionally referred to by the author of the *Historia Roderici* and may be inferred from other evidence, such as the list of endowments granted to the bishopric of Valencia in 1098 (of which more later). Routine and unspectacular, such policing manoeuvres were the daily fare of Rodrigo's soldiers while his domination lasted in Valencia. This was probably true in a literal sense. The staples on which the conquerers depended had to be sought in the country round about. Corn and meat, oil and wine had to be collected and transported to Valencia. Castles such as Olocau had a role here. Their garrisons were there not simply to fight Muslims but also to over-awe villagers, confiscate their produce, requisition their draught animals; and we need not suppose that they were too squeamish about how they got their way. Their leader, after all, could have given them lessons in how to lay waste a tract of countryside. There was nothing pretty or romantic about the Cid's rule in Valencia.

On occasion these operations could escalate into something more serious. This happened in the winter of 1096–7. Rodrigo's ally,

Pedro I of Aragon, had conquered Huesca in November 1096 and came south presumably in the first instance to inspect his outposts near Castellón. (The *Historia Roderici*, predictably, presents his only motive as a wish to help his ally.) Pedro went on to meet Rodrigo at Valencia where they decided to use the large force thus assembled to reinforce the southern frontier fortress of Benicadell, in the foothills of the sierra of that name between Játiva and Denia. This was the castle which Rodrigo had rebuilt and strengthened in 1091. It was of prime strategic importance, guarding as it did the principal southern approach to Valencia by the inland route. As Rodrigo and King Pedro were advancing southwards near Játiva they ran into an Almoravide army under Yusuf's nephew Muhammad, the commander whom Rodrigo had defeated at Cuarte two years before. They contrived to stock the castle and then turned hastily eastwards towards the Mediterranean, hoping to swing north along the easier terrain of the coastal strip back to the relative safety of the Valencian *huerta* on the far side of the distantly visible hump of Cullera. But the Almoravides could move fast too. When the Christian armies reached Bairén they found Muhammad's troops occupying the higher ground which there extended close to the sea; much closer then, it should be remembered, than now. The Almoravides had brought ships up the coast from the harbours they controlled further south, such as Almería. Rodrigo and the king found themselves pinned between the rising ground and the water, subjected to arrow fire from the ships and cavalry attacks from the slopes, compelled to fight at a disadvantage on ground not of their choosing. Laconic as ever, the *Historia* tells us that 'they were not a little afraid'. Rodrigo rode among his troops delivering a rousing harangue to raise their morale. Then battle was joined.

> At the middle of the day the king and Rodrigo with all the Christian army fell upon them and engaged them in strength. At length by God's clemency they defeated them and turned them in flight: some were killed by the sword, some fell in the river and enormous numbers fled into the sea where they were drowned.

Once again, as at Cuarte in 1094, Rodrigo had shown that Almoravide armies could be defeated. The allies returned to Valencia loaded with plunder and 'glorifying God with full-hearted devotion for the victory which He had given them'.

It was later in the same year of 1097 that Rodrigo had to confront another, albeit lesser Almoravide initiative. The governor of Játiva, in a move of insolent daring, led a force across the *huerta* of Valencia and established himself at Murviedro on the coast to the north of the city. Rodrigo managed to dislodge him and pursued him further up the coast to Almenara, to which he laid siege. The siege of

Almenara lasted for three months, at the end of which time it fell to Rodrigo (autumn (?) 1097).

The coastline from Valencia northwards to Murviedro secured, and Almenara beyond it in his hands, Rodrigo determined on a necessary but more arduous project: the conquest of Murviedro itself. If raids could be led by a governor of Játiva right across the heart of Rodrigo's principality, to find temporary sanctuary at Murviedro, then Murviedro must be taken into Rodrigo's hands. So much was clear, but the task would not be easy. Murviedro was no ordinary castle. The rock on which it stands is the strongest natural fortress on the coast of the Spanish Levante. Art had assisted nature. It was on top of this rock that the Iberians planted the city of Saguntum. Entering into treaty-relationship with Rome towards the end of the third century BC, Saguntum became the target of Hannibal's attack in 219 BC Heroically and tragically defended by its inhabitants, it eventually fell to Hannibal, and the event precipitated the Second Punic War. In 212 it was recaptured by the Romans, rebuilt and refortified. The name by which it was known in the lifetime of the Cid refers to the Iberian and Roman fortifications: Murviedro is derived from the Latin *muri veteres*, 'old walls'. (In modern times it has readopted its ancient name and is now known as Saguntum.) They have been patched and added to since, have suffered from the weaponry of modern war in 1811 and 1938, have been prettified for the tourist and pulled about by the archeologist; but there they still stand. The visitor can see at a glance why the celebrated travel-writer Richard Ford in his *Handbook for Travellers in Spain*, published in 1845, called it 'this most important and almost impregnable fortress'. Ford also called it 'rambling and extensive'. Indeed it is. The fortifications on top of the rock enclose an area of some nine acres. Cisterns constructed during the period of Islamic rule ensure an ample water supply. On all sides of the rock the drop to the plain below is precipitous. Copious stocks of Roman masonry provided the defenders with missiles to hurl down upon assailants.

Direct assault was out of the question. A siege it would have to be. It must have been with a sinking heart that Rodrigo reached this decision. An effective blockade would be difficult without a far larger body of troops than he could call upon, and without ships to prevent the sending in of relief supplies by sea. (Did Rodrigo attempt to enlist naval help from the obvious source, the maritime cities of Genoa and Pisa? We do not know. If he did, it is a fair guess that his request was turned down because Italian fleets were already committed in the Eastern Mediterranean, assisting the armies of the First Crusade.) Besieging armies get bored and restless, are given to complaining about the food and the lack of booty. Reduced by desertion and disease, they are the more vulnerable to relieving forces. However, Rodrigo had no choice. He laid siege to Murviedro early in 1098.

He pressed the siege as effectively as he could. His biographer tells us that 'he altogether prevented entry to or exit from the castle', which is just credible, and also that he used artillery, which is likely to have made more dents in the morale than the fabric of the defence. By the end of March the defenders of Murviedro were rattled. If the effectiveness of Rodrigo's siege was in part bluff, the bluff had worked. Scare-stories were circulating inside the fortress about the fate of the inhabitants of Valencia and Almenara. They opened negotiations with Rodrigo and asked for a term of truce: if they were not relieved within thirty days they would surrender. Rodrigo granted their request. This stay once granted, the defenders of Murviedro at once appealed for help to Yusuf and the Almoravides, King Alfonso VI, al-Musta'in of Zaragoza and Abu Marwan, the ruler of the taifa principality of Albarracín. The author of the *Historia Roderici* reports their answers, or makes up answers that seemed appropriate. Alfonso VI reasonably enough answered that he preferred that Rodrigo, rather than a Muslim ruler, should have Murviedro. Al-Musta'in, who had previously been leant on by Rodrigo, told the Murviedrans to look to their own defence. The count of Barcelona, who had received a massive bribe along with the appeal, undertook to attempt to draw Rodrigo away from Murviedro by laying siege to the more northerly castle of Oropesa. Rodrigo was so unimpressed by this that he did not even bother to go to Oropesa, but put it about that he would come soon and the count slunk home in terror. (Oropesa was held at this time on behalf of the king of Aragon, so the count of Barcelona in attacking it was opening hostilities with King Pedro rather than with Rodrigo. Were Aragonese troops perhaps assisting Rodrigo at the siege of Murviedro?) The elderly ruler of Albarracín – he had been governing his principality for fifty-four years – simply said that he could not help. What Yusuf said we do not know: but the Almoravides did not come.

When the term of thirty days was up the Murviedrans asked for more time, claiming deceitfully that they had not yet received answers to their appeal. Rodrigo was aware of the deception but nevertheless granted them twelve further days. Perhaps he judged that an assault would be too risky. He linked his offer with a threat to burn alive or torture and then execute as many of the defenders on whom he could lay hands if the surrender was not made promptly at the expiry of the new term. But even this was not enough and Rodrigo was compelled to offer another stay, until 24 June, the feast of the Nativity of St John the Baptist. He insisted that the inhabitants of Murviedro should evacuate the place before then. Most of them seem to have done so. When the appointed day came, Rodrigo sent his troops ahead of him to take possession of the almost deserted fortress. Shortly afterwards he made his own formal entry and celebrated an open-air mass to mark the occasion. A new garrison was installed, such booty as could be found was seized, and the remaining inhabitants were rounded up: three days later Rodrigo assembled them, stripped them of their possessions, chained them together and sent them back to Valencia. Murviedro was his.

We do not know what became of the captives. Perhaps we can guess what sort of people they were who had not heeded the call to evacuate Murviedro in June 1098: the elderly and the infirm, the stubborn, the despairing and the confused. Not the sort of folk, we might think, who would command big ransoms. Slavery was probably their lot. Some forty years later the poet al-Higari, a teacher of rhetoric in Granada, had the misfortune to be captured by the Navarrese while accompanying a raiding-party commanded by his friend al-Mustansir ibn Hud of Rueda (a descendant of Rodrigo's friends the ruling dynasty of Zaragoza). One sympathises with the plight of this donnish figure, described in a poem sent to a friend:

> A captive I became in cold Vizcaya,
> among fierce foes, no Muslim do I see!
> Obliged to do what is beyond my strength,
> tied by a rope, yelled at, subdued by force:
> they want me to perform hard labour, and
> woe to me, I am compelled to yield.

Comparable fates no doubt awaited those who trudged in irons from Murviedro to Valencia in the summer of 1098.

Rodrigo had done all he could to secure his conquests by force of arms. He could also use the methods of diplomacy. His two daughters were now of marriageable age. Like other girls of aristocratic rank they could expect to be disposed of in a manner calculated to forward their father's ambitions. In the event they made extremely distinguished matches. Cristina married Ramiro, the grandson of King García III of Navarre (d. 1054) and son of Ramiro, lord of Calahorra, who had perished at Rueda in 1083. This Ramiro the younger was one of the most prominent noblemen in the kingdom of Aragon and was to serve as the lord of the important place of Monzón from 1104 until his death in 1116. The marriage (which could have taken place at any time between 1094 and 1099) should be interpreted as a move on Rodrigo's part to strengthen his Aragonese alliance. Ramiro and Cristina had a son, García, who became king of Navarre when that country regained its political independence in 1134. The other daughter, María, married Ramón Berenguer III of Barcelona. (It has been suggested, though unconvincingly, that she made a first marriage to the *infante* Pedro, son of Pedro I of Aragon, who died after a long illness in 1102 or 1103.) This marriage was presumably designed to allay Catalan hostility, most recently displayed at Oropesa in 1098.

The other child of Rodrigo's marriage to Jimena who survived to adulthood was a son, Diego. (We do not know the order in which the children were born.) This Diego is a shadowy character, his very existence attested in only one source, and that a late one, an Aragonese text of c.1200 known as the *Liber Regum*. This evidence, such as it is, tells us that Diego was killed at the battle of Consuegra, south-east of Toledo, in August 1097. Now Consuegra was an Almoravide victory over Alfonso VI. Diego had therefore been fighting in the royal army. Whatever might be the implications – and the possibilities are wide – it prompts one to wonder what were the relations between Rodrigo Díaz and King Alfonso during the last, Valencian period of the former's life. Did Rodrigo's diplomacy look eastward to the kingdom of Castile, his homeland, as well as north to Aragon and Catalonia?

Ramón Menéndez Pidal had no doubts on this score. In his opinion, eloquently and persuasively argued, Rodrigo conquered Valencia for the king and held it as his vassal. But this is in fact very doubtful. The case relies upon reposing trust in late sources which were not concerned to record strictly historical truth, notably the *Poema de Mio Cid* and its derivative the *Primera Crónica General*. As against this testimony we must set that of two early sources. First, the author of the *Historia Roderici* never suggests that Rodrigo was acting on behalf of the king. Indeed, between Chapter 50 (set in 1092) and Chapter 75 (set in 1102, after Rodrigo's death) Alfonso is mentioned only once, and that in Chapter 70 when the defenders of Murviedro thought it appropriate to try to enlist the king's help *against* Rodrigo. Secondly, we have testimony which is exactly contemporary and almost certainly reflects Rodrigo's own views. It consists of the long preamble to the charter by which he endowed the cathedral church of Valencia in 1098. This would have been drafted by one of the bishop's clerks but we may take it that the views expressed would have been acceptable to Rodrigo as the donor; indeed there is every likelihood that he would have vetted the text in person. In it Rodrigo, styled prince (*princeps*) of Valencia, is presented as fighting God's battles, but not the king's. There is no reference to King Alfonso in the preamble nor anywhere else in the document. It is a sound maxim of historical method to prefer early and reliable testimony to late and unreliable. The inference is inescapable that between 1094 and 1099 Rodrigo was no man's but his own. Of course, it is possible that he and the king were well-disposed towards one another. They had after all a common interest in combating the threat of the Almoravides. Rodrigo's willingness to allow Diego to go and fight in the royal army may be symptomatic of this mending of fences.

One might like to entertain the thought that the private tragedy of the loss of his son in 1097 could help to explain Rodrigo's harsh treatment of the inhabitants of Murviedro in the following year. Perhaps it did contribute to it. But Rodrigo had already shown himself a stern ruler. The survivors of Murviedro were not the only ones who had cause to mourn Rodrigo's conquests.

We know little of the administration of Valencia between 1094 and 1099, but that little suggests that Rodrigo's government was harsh. In so far as he had anything which might be termed a policy it was propelled by an unceasing quest for money. It was this which occasioned his most barbaric act, the burning alive of the qadi Ibn Jahhaf in 1095. The event is not in doubt but the circumstances which led up to it are far from clear, and our understanding of them has not been assisted by those historians who have sought either to condemn or to justify Rodrigo's conduct. What seems to have happened is as follows. Shortly after Rodrigo had made himself master of Valencia he imprisoned Ibn Jahhaf and all the members of his family on whom he could lay hands. At issue was the whereabouts of al-Qadir's treasure. Before his murder in 1092 al-Qadir had managed to send some of his wealth away to places of safety such as Olocau; but much of it had fallen into the hands of Ibn Jahhaf, who had promised at the time of the capitulation of the city to surrender it to Rodrigo. Suspected of holding some of it back, he was tortured to force him to reveal its whereabouts. Opinion was evidently divided about the treatment meted out to Ibn Jahhaf. Even Ibn Bassam, normally hostile to Rodrigo, judged that through his deceit he had forfeited any claims upon Rodrigo's mercy. Ibn 'Alqama tells us that some form of trial took place in which Ibn Jahhaf was charged with the murder of al-Qadir. Rodrigo is said to have claimed that 'according to our law' a regicide must be burned alive. What law he had in mind we do not know. At any rate, this was the dreadful end of Ibn Jahhaf. A pit was dug, probably in the marketplace, in which he was secured by burying him up to the armpits and then a fire was lit about him. 'An eye-witness told me,' wrote Ibn Bassam, 'that when the fire had been lit round him he reached out to pull the burning brands nearer to his body in order to hasten his end and shorten his sufferings.' Rodrigo was with difficulty restrained from inflicting the same fate upon his victim's wife and children.

The execution of Ibn Jahhaf was only the most savage of Rodrigo's acts. After the battle of Cuarte he assembled all the richest citizens of Valencia at his palace and announced that they would remain imprisoned there until they had ransomed themselves for 700,000 gold *mithqals*. So breathtaking a sum was altogether beyond their capacity and it was subsequently reduced to 200,000. The money seems to have been raised and paid over.

Rodrigo's agents in the government of the city were Jews. By the autumn of 1094 he had appointed a Jewish vizir (whose name we do not know) as his principal deputy. These are the comments of Ibn 'Alqama:

> The Jew subjected the Muslim population to the greatest vexations: others of his co-religionists exerted themselves against the Valencians, who suffered the most bitter humiliations. It was from among the Jews that there were chosen the fiscal officials charged with the collection of taxes, the civil servants, the drafters of documents, the clerks for the armed forces. The Jewish vizir took upon himself the role of prefect of the city (*sahib al-madina*), ordering arrests and administering punishments. Each Muslim had at his heels a police agent who accompanied him every morning to ensure that he contributed something to the treasure-chests of the master of Valencia. If he failed to do this he was killed or tortured.

How much of this is credible as the literal truth it is hard to tell. The author was hostile to Rodrigo. He may have exaggerated the sums of money demanded or exacted. It is impossible to believe that 'every Muslim' could have been shadowed in the manner described – though the richer ones might have been. However, the account is plausible in its general lines. It can be confirmed from an unimpeachable witness. Muhammad ibn Ahmad ibn Tahir had ruled the taifa state of Murcia from 1063 until 1078 when he was dethroned by Ibn 'Ammar. The ex-king settled in Valencia where he lived through the disturbances of the years between 1085 and 1092 and Rodrigo's siege and conquest. In its wake he was imprisoned, and we possess the text of a letter which he wrote to a friend from prison in February 1095:

> We have become prisoners after a train of misfortunes so serious as to be without parallel. If you could see Valencia – may God favour her with His care and shed His light upon her – if you could see what fate has done to her and her people, you would lament, you would weep for her calamities . . . At the moment, I am compelled to purchase my freedom by paying a ransom, after surviving dangers which have almost cost me my life. My only trust remains in the goodness of God.

The old man presumably managed to pay his ransom, for he was released at some point and allowed to leave Valencia.

He was not the only emigrant. As we have already seen, Rodrigo expelled what seems to have been a fair number of people in the autumn of 1094. In the following year there seems to have been some sort of rising against him – we are ill-informed about the details – after Ibn Jahhaf's execution: it was suppressed and expulsions followed. Further emigrations took place in 1097 after the battle of Bairén. One of those who left in 1095 was the poet al-Waqqasi, who settled at Denia where he died in the following year: before his death he composed a celebrated lament over Valencia. Another who mourned Valencia's fall in verse was Ibn Khafaja, who lived nearby at Alcira:

> Swords have wrought ruin in you, oh dwellings,
> your beauties were wiped out by fire and decay.
> When one looks at you, over and over again,
> one's thoughts are stirred, one weeps and weeps.

Ibn Tahir and Ibn Khafaja were both to celebrate the recovery of Valencia for Islam in 1102. But back in the 1090s, as Rodrigo inflicted defeats on the Almoravides, captured fortresses and oppressed his subjects, such an outcome was not to be foreseen.

Rodrigo's biographer tells us nothing of his government of Valencia. He does, on the other hand, have a very little to tell us about his restoration of an ecclesiastical establishment in the territories he had conquered. When Rodrigo conquered Almenara he ordered a church to be built and he did the same at Murviedro. As these were presumably places with no existing Christian communities, the churches commissioned by Rodrigo were designed for the religious needs of the new garrisons and any Christian settlers who might be attracted. The case with Valencia was different. Here was a big city, with a Christian community headed by a bishop. The last 'Mozarabic' bishop of whom we have any certain knowledge died in about 1087 at Bari in Apulia while on his way to Jerusalem as a pilgrim. The Christians of Valencia must have had a church building, perhaps in one of the extra-mural suburbs. Rodrigo decided that a better one was needed and converted the principal mosque of the city into a cathedral dedicated to St Mary. In doing so he was following in the footsteps of Archbishop Bernard of Toledo who had converted Toledo's mosque into his cathedral church. It may be that Rodrigo's similar action in Valencia was prompted by one of Bernard's protégés, another French Cluniac monk, Jerónimo, who became bishop of Valencia.

Jerónimo was a native of Périgord who as a young man became a monk at Moissac. In 1096 he was invited to Spain by Archbishop Bernard who was passing through south-western France (of which he too was a native) on his way back from the papal court. Bernard was assembling a *kindergarten* of promising young clerics to whom he could hold out the prospect of preferment in the Spanish church over which, as primate, he presided. They served him well and he was a generous patron: at least seven of them ended up as bishops or archbishops; one of them even contended unsuccessfully for the papacy. After a short spell as a canon of Toledo Jerónimo joined the Cid at Valencia, apparently in 1098. (The *Historia Roderici* says that the mosque of Valencia was converted to Christian use after the fall of Murviedro in June 1098. The charter of endowment implies that Jerónimo's promotion to the bishopric occurred after that; though it also shows that Jerónimo had received some land from Rodrigo before his appointment. The chronological point is laboured because it establishes that Rodrigo's steps to restore the bishopric of Valencia were leisurely ones. Of course, there may have been good reasons for delay, such as the continued survival until 1098 of a 'Mozarabic' bishop of whom we know nothing.)

It is a reasonable inference that the initiative in putting Jerónimo forward was taken by the archbishop of Toledo. (It is very likely that the king would have been consulted as well – another glancing indication, it may be, of harmonious relations between Alfonso and Rodrigo.) Bernard was an empire-builder. To job 'his' man into the re-created see of Valencia was to extend Toledan ecclesiastical influence, hitherto confined mainly to Castile, into the eastern, Mediterranean zone of the Peninsula. He believed, probably correctly, that this was in accordance with the ancient administrative arrangements of the Spanish church. He could produce records of the Visigothic period which showed that the church of Valencia should be subject to the metropolitan of Toledo. In view of this, it is surprising that Bernard did not himself consecrate Jerónimo a bishop in unambiguous assertion of Toledan rights. However, our source is categorical that Jerónimo was consecrated in Italy by Pope Urban II. It also tells us that on the same occasion he was 'elevated by the liberty of a special privilege' (*specialis privilegii libertate*). This is the technical language of canon law. What it probably means is that the bishopric of Valencia was placed under the *direct* supervision of the papacy without the interposition of any other ecclesiastical authority. In other words, the Pope overruled Toledo's claims. The initiative could hardly have come from Toledo's man, Jerónimo. From whom, then? Surely, from Valencia's secular prince, Rodrigo Díaz. His success in detaching Jerónimo from Toledo by turning to the fountainhead of authority in the Western church is further evidence of his determination to be master of his own household.

If there was awkwardness over the re-establishment of the bishopric of Valencia in 1098 this might explain the surprising fact that the author of the *Historia Roderici* does not mention Bishop Jerónimo. Indeed, he does not even refer explicitly to the restoration of the bishopric. All he does is tell us of Rodrigo's gifts to the cathedral church: a golden chalice worth 150 marks and 'two very precious hangings woven in silk and gold thread the like of which had never been seen in Valencia'. The reflection is perhaps unworthy, but irresistible, that the conqueror who had seized al-Qadir's treasure, extorted huge sums of money from the citizens of Valencia and plundered the Almoravide camp at Cuarte, might have done better than this. Rodrigo's charter of endowment for the bishopric furnishes details of the lands which were granted to Bishop Jerónimo after his return from the papal court. It reads like a roll-call of his recent conquests: 'the market-garden which is next to the church of St Mary . . . twelve *pariliatas* of land within the bounds of Murviedro . . . a further twelve within the bounds of the castle called Almenara . . .' Some of the places cannot now be identified. For example, we do not know the whereabouts of 'the fortress which men call Almunia de Sabaleckem' and can only surmise that it had been acquired in one of the unrecorded minor campaigns of the years 1095–8. Not all the donations were to take effect at once: 'after my death we grant the garden which is within the bounds of the castle of Cebolla, a part of which our excellency had made over to the lord bishop Jerónimo before he rose to episcopal rank'.

The landed endowments granted and promised in 1098 were modest. This is not intended as a reproach. Newly restored bishoprics at this period tended to be poorly provided for, simply because donors had so little to give. The see of Toledo, later so fabulously wealthy, remained very hard-up for a century after its restoration in 1086. The restored see of Coria was so miserably endowed by Alfonso VII in 1142 that its bishop found it impossible to carry on there. Rodrigo's apparent stinginess where land was concerned serves to remind us how restricted his territorial dominion was.

Rodrigo's charter also conceded to those persons who had received grants of property from him the freedom to dispose of it to the bishopric of Valencia. This is our only tantalising glimpse of Rodrigo's attempts to encourage settlement in and round Valencia by rewarding his followers with land. The resettlement of lands conquered from Islam throughout Mediterranean Europe was to present Christian authorities with formidable problems for several centuries to come. It is unlikely that Rodrigo could have done much in this direction in the few years at his disposal. The 1090s were not the time to attract the peasantry of Castile or Aragon to come and settle in the Valencian *huerta*: the presence and the plans of the Almoravides made sure of that.

Rodrigo's leading men (*obtimates*) are referred to more than once in the text of the 1098 charter. At its foot it bears the autograph subscription of the grantor – 'I Rodrigo together with my wife confirm what is written above' (*Ego Ruderico simul cum coniuge mea afirmo oc quod superius scriptum est*) – and this is followed by the names of a number of witnesses: Ramiro, Nuño, Rodrigo, Martín, Diego, Fernando. Presumably these were the members of the inner circle of Rodrigo's *obtimates*. It is unfortunate that the scribe did not see fit to add their patronymics, for that would have made attempts to identify these men at least possible. As it is, there is really nothing we can do with such a list.

The *Poema de Mio Cid* and the chronicles of the later Middle Ages derived from it furnish us with the names of several who were said to have been among Rodrigo's followers in Valencia, the members of his *mesnada* or retinue. Where we can check on the whereabouts of genuinely historical personages among them during the last decade of the eleventh century we usually find that they were somewhere else. For instance, Alvar Fáñez was principally occupied with the defence of Toledo from his base on the Tagus at Zorita. Once again, the *Poema de Mio Cid* is unreliable as a source of historical information. The one member of the *mesnada* in the poem of whom it can be suggested with any degree of plausibility that he actually was in the Cid's following in the 1090s is Martín Múñoz, 'he who commanded Montemayor' as the poet called him. Martín was the son-in-law of Sisnando Davídez, under whom he held Montemayor in central Portugal and whom he succeeded as count of Coimbra. Ousted from this command in 1094, perhaps through the agency of Raymond of Burgundy, Martín disappears from the historical record until he turns up in the service of the king of Aragon early in the twelfth century. It is a fair if unprovable assumption that he entered the following of the Cid in Valencia and later moved into Aragonese service after Rodrigo's death. Possibly he is the Martín who subscribes the charter of 1098.

Rodrigo had done all he could to consolidate his hold on Valencia and its hinterland. He was not given time to do more. Just five years after his conquest of the city he died there, in his bed, in July 1099. Much later sources were to give the date of his death as 10 July. Five days later the armies of the First Crusade mounted their final and successful assault on Jerusalem.

Contemporaries recognised that in Rodrigo's passing the world had lost a hero. Ibn Bassam, who detested him, wrote of him that 'this man, the scourge of his time, by his appetite for glory, by the prudent steadfastness of his character, and by his heroic bravery, was one of the miracles of God'. His biographer ended his account of him as follows: 'While he lived in this world he always won a noble triumph over his enemies: never was he defeated by any man.' The chronicler of Maillezais, in Poitou, noted under his entry for the year 1099 that 'in Spain, at Valencia, Count Rodrigo died: this was a great grief to the Christians and a joy to their pagan enemies'.

Who was to succeed to the principality of Valencia? Rodrigo's only son had pre-deceased him in 1097. His two sons-in-law would have claims, Ramiro the Navarrese and Ramón Berenguer III, count of Barcelona. King Pedro of Aragon, his ally, would be interested. So too would Alfonso VI of León-Castile. All were fully committed elsewhere. The defence of Valencia devolved upon Rodrigo's widow Jimena. She would have to fight, that was certain. Yusuf was absolutely determined that Valencia should be repossessed for Islam. Jimena turned for help possibly to the Catalans and Aragonese, certainly to Alfonso VI. On 14 May 1100 he dated one of his charters 'on the road to Valencia, when I was going to put myself at the head of the Christians'. Whether or not he got there on that occasion we do not know. Doña Jimena's spirit was indomitable. In a charter of 21 May 1101 by which she confirmed and amplified Rodrigo's grants to the cathedral church of Valencia she spoke bravely of future conquests 'which, with God's help, we shall make by land or sea'. But the game was nearly up. In the late summer of 1101 the Berber general Mazdali, one of the most experienced Almoravide commanders, approached Valencia with a large army and settled down to besiege it. As the siege wore on through the winter Jimena sent Bishop Jerónimo to Alfonso's court to implore his help. In March 1102, as soon as the campaigning season opened, he came. Mazdali's forces withdrew to Cullera at his approach. Alfonso spent some time in reconnoitring the situation. His decision was for evacuation. Valencia was too far from his kingdom, he could not spare the troops and he had no commander of the calibre of the Cid. It was a prudent decision, though it must have pained him to make it. For Jimena it was the end of all that Rodrigo had fought so hard for, which she had striven to maintain.

During April the preparations for departure were made. The spoils of war, the weaponry and the household goods were packed up; the cathedral treasures and title-deeds, to be carefully preserved in readiness for a future reoccupation; most precious of all, the body of the Cid, which could not be abandoned to be dishonoured by his enemies. The long caravan of carts and litters, camels, horses, mules and donkeys, jolted off over the level lands of the *huerta* with its escort of troops. The king had detailed some of his soldiers to stay behind and fire the city. As Mazdali's men watched from the higher ground to the south they would have seen wreaths of smoke arise, soon to billow into thick black clouds. By the time they re-entered the charred remnants of Valencia, Rodrigo's body would have been well on its way home to Castile.

12

✳ My Cid of Vivar

Doña Jimena reinterred her husband's body in the monastery of Cardeña, and lived out the remainder of her life nearby. She was still alive in 1113, in which year she sold a church at Valdecañas – one of the estates which Rodrigo had settled on her at the time of their marriage – to two purchasers who may have been canons of the cathedral church of Burgos. The deed of sale was witnessed by Bishop García of Burgos, Abbot Pedro of Cardeña, and a bevy of other distinguished Castilians. This is our only glimpse of her during her widowhood and she probably died not long afterwards. (A late set of annals gives 1106 as the date of her death: on the assumption that an X has dropped out of the date through a copyist's error, this has been emended to 1116.) As to her daughters, we know nothing of them after their marriages. María must have died young, in or before 1107, for in that year her husband Count Ramón Berenguer III of Barcelona married for the second time. We have no idea how long Cristina lived.

The years of Jimena's widowhood were troubled ones in the public life of the kingdom of León-Castile. Almoravide pressure on its southern frontiers was maintained throughout the first quarter of the twelfth century, threatening the conquests of Alfonso VI. On his death in 1109 the king left no male heir and bequeathed the kingdom to his daughter Urraca, who was married off to Alfonso I of Aragon, known as *el Batallador*, 'the Battler'. But the marriage and the union of the crowns that went with it did not work. War between Aragon and León-Castile soon broke out. The Aragonese invaded Castile, and large tracts of land round Burgos and Palencia remained under their control for the rest of Queen Urraca's reign. (It is not impossible that it was financial difficulty occasioned by the

187

disturbed state of the country that compelled Doña Jimena to raise capital by the sale of property in 1113.) In the far west the queen's sister Teresa and her husband Count Henry of Portugal were restive vassals, gradually drifting into a *de facto* independence: in due course their son would style himself king of Portugal. There were times in Urraca's reign when it looked as though Galicia might go the same way. The kingdom seemed to be falling apart. In addition, this was a time of economic hardship. When the Almoravides took over the taifa kingdoms and cut off the payment of *parias* to the Christian rulers they precipitated a crisis of the first magnitude in the financial affairs of the largest of those kingdoms and the most reliant upon Muslim gold, León-Castile. A major source of revenue was cut off. Among the expedients to which Alfonso VI's and Urraca's governments turned in desperation was debasement of the coinage; and this brought in its train, as it always does, inflation and loss of confidence.

It is to Urraca's son Alfonso VII (1126–57) that the credit must go for restoring the fortunes of the kingdom. Almoravide pressure on the frontier slackened, the Aragonese were chased out of Castile, a settlement with Portugal was reached, fiscal stability was attained. It all took time: it was not until after 1135, when the king was crowned emperor at León in a ceremony which seemed to herald an optimistic mood, that buoyancy and confidence returned. During the 1140s and early 1150s Alfonso VII and his nobility resumed the advance to the south which had been halted since his grandfather's day. In 1147 he conquered Almería, and for the first time the rulers of Castile had a window on to the Mediterranean.

In the uncertain days of Queen Urraca people looked back to the glorious reign of Alfonso VI. This was the mood, for example, of the author of the *Historia Silense*, writing at León in about 1120, who meant to write a biography of the king but never got round to it. It was also the mood of Bishop Pelayo of Oviedo in his brief account of Alfonso VI, and of the authors at Santiago of the *Historia Compostellana* commissioned by their bishop, Diego Gelmírez. Perhaps people also looked back nostalgically at the great deeds of Rodrigo Díaz, the ever-victorious conqueror of Valencia. Those who had served with him were still about: Bishop Jerónimo lived until 1120, and young men who had fought at Bairén or Murviedro could have lived far into the reign of Alfonso VII.

How, in this period, legends about kings and heroes germinated, sprouted, flowered and multiplied, is a topic which has been long and inconclusively debated. One assumption often made is that there must be an appreciable timelag before historical reality can be transmuted into legend. But the timelag need not be long. As we saw in Chapter 6, legends about Roger of Tosny's cannibalistic feasts in Spain were committed to writing, by a chronicler who was a monk of Limoges, within at most fifteen years of the time when they were supposed to have occurred. An equally fantastic story was woven about the imprisonment – historically attested – of Bohemond of Antioch after his capture in a Turkish ambush in 1100. It was said that Melaz, the daughter of his captor – beautiful, it need hardly be said – brought about his release by a series of ruses, was subsequently baptised a Christian and was married to one of Bohemond's kinsmen. The story was written down in the form in which we have it in the tenth book of the *Ecclesiastical History* of the Anglo-Norman chronicler Orderic Vitalis in 1135; but it had probably reached northern France as early as 1106 when Bohemond, after his release, visited Western Europe to recruit troops for service under his command in Antioch. A last example also comes from Orderic's *History*. In Book Thirteen, composed probably in 1137, he provides an account of the battle of Fraga, fought in 1134, in which Alfonso *el Batallador* of Aragon was defeated by the Almoravides. Orderic's account can be checked against independent sources and much of his detail can be shown to be accurate. But his account of the battle's aftermath is sheer fantasy. He has Alfonso pursuing his (victorious!) enemies and slaughtering hundreds of them to avenge his defeat. (In reality Alfonso was severely wounded in the battle and died a few weeks later.) There is no reason to suppose that Orderic invented the story of the king's revenge. It probably came to him through the medium of Normans who had been in Alfonso's service. At all events it shows how even in the space of three years the growth of legend could obscure reality.

The earliest datable reference we possess to the circulation of tales about the Cid occurs in a Latin poem, referred to briefly in Chapter 1, which celebrates Alfonso VII's conquest of Almería in 1147. The poet has been calling to mind the great exploits of Alvar Fáñez, hero of the defence of Toledo against the Almoravides in 1110, who died in 1114. He goes on:

> Ipse Rodericus, Meo Cidi saepe vocatus,
> de quo cantatur quod ab hostibus haud superatur,
> qui domuit Mauros, comites domuit quoque nostros,
> hunc extollebat se laude minore ferebat,
> sed fateor verum, quod tollet nulla dierum:
> Meo Cidi primus fuit, Alvarus atque secundus.
> Morte Roderici Valentia plangit amici,
> nec valuit Christi famulus ea plus retinere.

Literally translated, this means:

Rodrigo, often called 'My Cid', of whom it is sung (*cantatur*) that he was never defeated by the enemies, who subdued the Moors and also subdued our counts, himself used to praise this man (i.e. Alvar Fáñez) and used to say that he himself was of lesser reputation: but I proclaim the truth, which the passage of time will not alter – my Cid was the first, and Alvar the second. Valencia mourned at the death of (her) friend Rodrigo, neither could the servant of Christ (bishop Jerónimo? Alfonso VI?) hold on to her any longer.

These lines, and in particular the crucial word *cantatur*, have given rise to reams of scholarly debate. Much of it has been more ingenious than convincing. The composition to which the author seems to allude – was it in the vernacular, as the term *Meo Cidi* might suggest, or in Latin? If the latter, could it be that the author, who was possibly a Catalan and conceivably acquainted with the contents of the library of Ripoll, was referring to the *Carmen Campi Doctoris*? Was the composition recited or chanted or sung? Was it orally transmitted or written down? Does the word *saepe*, 'often', indicate that the Cid was so-styled often in a single poem, or often in several poems? Was there another poem devoted to the exploits of Alvar Fáñez, yet another which treated Alfonso VI's evacuation of Valencia, yet another about Bishop Jerónimo?

There can be only one answer to all these questions: we do not know. The irreducible minimum with which we are left is this: that an author composing a Latin panegyric on Alfonso VII in or soon after 1147 could allude in passing to *Rodericus, Meo Cidi*, a famous hero of the recent past, confident that his audience would know whom he meant and be aware at least of the existence of verbal compositions – I choose as neutral a phrase as possible – devoted to his exploits.

What nearly all scholars are now agreed about is that Menéndez Pidal was mistaken in his conviction that the composition referred to was the vernacular epic which we know as the *Poema de Mio Cid*. The poem is important to us because in it for the first time there steps forth a Cid who has moved some way from the Rodrigo Díaz of history. He is not unrecognisably different. Yet the fact remains that in the epic the first and most decisive step – judged only of course on the evidence of surviving texts – from history into myth has been taken. This, its principal historical interest, pales into insignificance besides its literary interest: the *Poema de Mio Cid* is one of the masterpieces of European literature. Already mentioned frequently in the course of this book, but always skirted round, it is time to close with it. What is this poem?

The best advice in answer is to buy a copy, sit down and read it, and find out. For those to whom this course of action may not be practicable, a summary is offered here with the usual caution that this can be no substitute for the real thing. The poem is divided into three sections, conventionally referred to as the *Cantar del desti-*

erro ('Poem of the exile'), the *Cantar de las bodas* ('Poem of the marriage') and the *Cantar de la afrenta de Corpes* ('Poem of the insult of Corpes'). At the opening of the first section the Cid, accompanied by his retinue which includes Alvar Fáñez, is departing into exile from Castile on the orders of Alfonso VI. He leaves his wife and daughters in the care of the abbot of Cardeña and then sets out in a south-easterly direction, leaving the king's dominions at the crossing of the River Duero. Military operations undertaken by him against the Moors are then described in some detail. They take place partly in the valley of the Henares between Sigüenza and Alcalá, partly on the other side of the watershed near Medinaceli in the valleys of the Jalón and the Jiloca round Calatayud. (The poet appears to know this region well.) Successful in all his enterprises and enriched by booty, Rodrigo sends presents to his lord, King Alfonso, by the hand of Alvar Fáñez. The king's rancour towards the exile begins to cool. After Alvar's return from the royal court the Cid moves east and has his victorious encounter with the count of Barcelona at Tévar. The first *cantar* ends with the Cid magnanimously releasing his illustrious captive.

The second *cantar* concerns the Cid's campaigns in the Levante and his conquest of Valencia. Following these exploits his wife and daughters are permitted to join him, escorted to Valencia by the ever-faithful Alvar Fáñez. Jerónimo is made bishop of Valencia. After defeating Yusuf's army from Morocco the Cid sends further gifts to Alfonso, after which he is pardoned and restored to the royal favour. Meanwhile, two brothers of exalted birth but mean character, the *infantes* of Carrión, ask for the Cid's daughters in marriage. Pressed by the king but against his own better judgement, Rodrigo permits the marriages to take place. This section of the poem concludes with the celebrations which accompanied the double wedding.

At the opening of the third *cantar* the *infantes* are shown up as cowards and ridiculed by the Cid's followers in an incident when a captive lion escapes from its cage in the Cid's palace in Valencia. Further mockery is provoked by their failure to distinguish themselves in a battle against the Moroccan ruler Búcar. The *infantes* plan to avenge these slights. They depart for Castile with their brides. On their way they stop for the night in the forest of Corpes. On the following morning, having sent away all their servants, they strip their wives of their clothes, beat them senseless with their belts and spurs, and leave them for dead. The women are discovered and rescued by the Cid's nephew. Rodrigo decides to avenge his family's honour by seeking legal redress. He appeals to the king, who responds by summoning a solemn meeting of the royal court at Toledo. In court the Cid successfully claims restitution of his daughters' dowries. The *infantes* are subsequently defeated in judicial duels by the Cid's champions. The honour of the Cid has thus been vindicated and he is rendered even more illustrious by the subsequent remarriage of his daughters into the royal houses of Aragon and Navarre.

All critics have drawn attention to the mixture of history and fiction in the poem. Many of the events and persons are 'real', in the sense of being historically verifiable. The Cid of history was indeed exiled by Alfonso VI, he did defeat the count of Barcelona, he did capture Valencia, he was victorious over the Almoravides. In the same way Doña Jimena, Alvar Fáñez and Bishop Jerónimo were all, as we know, people who really did live in the late eleventh and early twelfth centuries. The poet has taken certain liberties with history: for example, he calls the count of Barcelona Ramón when his real name was Berenguer, and refers to the abbot of Cardeña as Sancho though he was actually called by the resoundingly Visigothic name of Sisebut. Changes such as this were perhaps made because of the demands of the poem's metre. Other departures from historical record were more radical. Though the *infantes* of Carrión really existed, they never married the Cid's daughters. The dreadful scene in the forest of Corpes never took place. Literary, aesthetic reasons dictated the artifice of the marriages, for we the audience are to know more of the Cid in witnessing his reactions to them and his subsequent conduct. The poet evidently knew a good deal about the Cid of history and his times – and there has been much discussion about how he could have come by this knowledge – but he re-shaped his materials with considerable literary skill in accordance with the ends he had in mind. Who was he? Where and when did he write? What were those ends?

The poem has come down to us in a single manuscript, now in the Biblioteca Nacional in Madrid, copied in a hand of about 1350. At the very end of the text there is a sentence, now almost illegible, which appears to read: '*Per Abbat le escrivió en el mes de mayo en era de mill e CC xlv años*', that is, 'Per Abbat wrote it in the month of May in the Era 1245.' The Spanish Era 1245 is equivalent to the AD year 1207. These words have provoked even more scholarly debate than the references to the Cid in the Latin poem on the conquest of Almería.

On the assumption that the fourteenth-century scribe copied correctly from the exemplar in front of him, it is plain that the epic existed in the form in which we have it by the year 1207. No one disputes this. Difficulty arises over the interpretation of the word *escrivió*, 'wrote'. Does it mean 'wrote down' in the sense of 'made a copy of' (an existing text) or 'took down' (from dictation of an orally transmitted poem)? Or does it mean 'wrote' in the sense of 'composed' (for the first time)? Was Per Abbat a copyist or was he an author? Opinion has been sharply divided. The authorship of Per

Abbat, in the year 1207, has been powerfully urged by Professor Colin Smith in his sparkling book *The Making of the 'Poema de Mio Cid'*, which appeared in 1983, and in a number of articles published before and after that date. His case is forcefully and elegantly argued but it has not persuaded all critics. There are those, myself among them, who though full of admiration for Smith's work are not quite convinced by it and would prefer to opt for a date of composition somewhat before 1207. But how much before? Very few would now agree with Menéndez Pidal that the poem was in existence by about 1140. During the last thirty-odd years separate but convergent lines of research on such matters as the language of the poem, its references to legal and bureaucratic procedures, its apparent indebtedness to Old French epic of the twelfth century, have tended to suggest that the work is unlikely to be earlier than about 1175. As a cautious answer to the question, 'when was the *Poema de Mio Cid* composed?', some such formulation as 'by 1207 – perhaps in the last quarter of the twelfth century' will suit for present purposes. The question of where the epic was composed is less controversial. Its language is the Spanish of Castile. The geographical focus of the poem is upon such Castilian places as Burgos, Cardeña and Toledo (apart from the necessary excursion to Valencia). The poet seems particularly well-acquainted with the topography of eastern Castile. All critics are agreed that the work was composed by a Castilian for a Castilian audience.

There are three important features which differentiate the Cid of the poem from the Rodrigo Díaz of history. In the first place he is emphatically Castilian. His origins in Vivar are repeatedly stressed. One of the pains of exile is separation from 'beloved Castile'. It is to the cathedral church of Burgos that the exile sends a boot filled with gold and silver to pay for a thousand masses. The poem begins in Castile with its moving account of Rodrigo's departure from Burgos into exile, and this is balanced by the ending with his return to Castile for the hearing before the king's court in Toledo. The geographical emphasis of the poem is therefore quite different from that of the author of the *Historia Roderici*. As we have seen, that writer seems to know and care little about the Castilian quality of his subject: nearly all his attention is directed to the campaigning in the Ebro valley and the Levante.

Secondly, the Cid of the poem is uncompromisingly Christian. It is not simply a matter of portraying Rodrigo as devout, though the poet frequently does this – we see the hero praying, invoking Santiago, being vouchsafed a vision of the Archangel Gabriel, desiring to regain Valencia for Christendom, repeatedly thanking God for his good fortune, and so forth. What is more significant is that the poet says nothing – perhaps knew nothing – of Rodrigo's activities as a mercenary captain in Muslim pay. The Cid is never portrayed as fighting alongside Muslims, only against them. It is true that he is on terms of friendship with Avengalvón (Ibn Ghalbun), the Muslim governor of Molina – 'my friend with whom I am at peace' – but this is because Avengalvón is his tributary: he is a friend who can be given orders. The governor of Molina has an important literary function in the poem as showing up the treacherous behaviour of the Cid's wicked sons-in-law, but otherwise plays hardly any part. His role is to be nobly submissive to the Cid – a mood nicely caught by the sculptor who executed in the 1940s the statues of personages in the poem to flank the bridge over the River Arlanzón at Burgos, who portrayed Avengalvón in just such an attitude. The same artist's version of Bishop Jerónimo, a churchman militant and triumphalist, is likewise faithful to the poem (as well, perhaps, as an intriguing sidelight on the self-image of the Spanish church of some fifty years ago). For the poet, Jerónimo joined the Cid because he wanted, in his own words, 'to kill a few Moors' and when the Cid hears this he hails Jerónimo as 'a good Christian'. Jerónimo offers the crusader's indulgence of remission of sins to those who fall in battle with Yusuf, and requests the privilege of himself striking the first blow. In the course of the battle the bishop loses count of the number of Moors he has killed.

Finally, the Cid is presented by the poet as consistently loyal to his lord, King Alfonso. Although the king treats him unjustly his loyalty never wavers. 'I have no wish to fight against my lord Alfonso.' From exile he sends gifts to Alfonso, and battle-trophies such as Yusuf's tent. Having conquered Valencia he pledges lifelong loyalty to the king. Despite his misgivings he defers to the king's wish that his daughters should marry the *infantes* of Carrión. After they are dishonoured the Cid shows his respect for the king's peace and his confidence in the king's justice by seeking legal redress rather than personal revenge by violence. The tone of his relations with the king is neatly summed up in the line, 'whatever the king may wish, the Campeador will do it'. The independent, insubordinate, arrogant Rodrigo Díaz of history has been wrapped in a cloak of royalist pieties.

A Cid presented as a Castilian, a Christian and a loyalist, as embodying virtues at once martial and civic, a law-abiding citizen as well as a good family man and a brave soldier, in a poem composed towards the end of the twelfth century, was a Cid who could appeal to – whom? Let us look for a moment at the changes in the Spanish political scene during those years. Alfonso VII's territorial gains such as the conquest of Almería had been made possible in large part because of the collapse of Almoravide dominion in al-Andalus in the 1140s and 1150s. But they did not long survive his death. A new sect of Islamic fundamentalists, the Almohades, had grown up in the Maghrib from the 1120s onwards in reaction against what they saw as the increasing corruptions of the Almoravide régime: the Almoravide leadership had 'gone soft' and betrayed the movement's original ideals. Almohade intervention in Spain began in the later years of Alfonso VII's reign, and by 1173 it had brought the whole of al-Andalus under its sway. Meanwhile, Alfonso's dominions were divided on his death in 1157 into separate kingdoms of León and Castile for his two surviving sons. The eldest, Sancho III of Castile, died young in 1158 leaving an infant, Alfonso VIII, to succeed him. The early years of the child's reign were extremely disturbed as rival aristocratic factions fought for power in the regency, sometimes appealing for aid to the boy's uncle, Fernando II of León. This period of instability, indeed of intermittent civil war, coincided of course with a time when the Almohades were pressing hard on the southern frontiers of Castile. (One recent historian, María Lacarra, has sought to relate the composition of the *Poema de Mio Cid* directly to this time of aristocratic turbulence.) It was not until after the young Alfonso VIII achieved his majority in 1169 that some measure of stability was restored to Castilian public life. But the Almohade menace was still there, and at Alarcos in 1195 their forces inflicted a decisive defeat upon the Castilian king. But it proved to be their last throw. In 1212 Alfonso VIII won an even more decisive battle against the Almohades at Las Navas de Tolosa. His successor Fernando III, who reunited the crowns of Castile and León in 1230, built upon this victory to push a crusading reconquest deep into the south. In 1236 he conquered Córdoba and in 1248 Seville. This time the Christian gains were never to be reversed.

One can see how the Cid of the poem could have had a special resonance in the Castile of Alfonso VIII. Here was a kingdom imperilled by those who put sectional interest before the common good, who neglected their Christian patriotism and forgot their duties to the king. The poet reminded his compatriots of where their responsibilities lay. He also made it clear that interest coincided with duty. A theme sounded again and again in the poem is that the Cid and his followers bettered themselves and made themselves very rich by fighting the Moors. Perhaps this was a reminder that was needed in the dark days after Alarcos or in the run-up to Las Navas. This does not make the *Poema de Mio Cid* a 'political poem' in any crude sense of that phrase. However, one can understand how the Castilian 'establishment' could approve the figure of the Cid which the poet held out.

In the light of this it is no wonder that when Alfonso the Learned's team of scholars sat down under the royal eye to compose their national history, later on in the thirteenth century, they decided to give such prominence to the exploits of Rodrigo Díaz in the image which the poet had shaped for him. Their royal patron was able to present them with another literary work germane to their purpose which he had been given in 1272. In that year Alfonso X paid a visit to the Castilian monastery of Cardeña where, it will be recalled, the Cid and (so it was believed) his wife Jimena were buried. Somewhat surprisingly, their tombs were not provided with epitaphs. The king in person composed fitting lines to be carved on the tombs, and the grateful monks presented him in return with a volume devoted to the last days of the Cid, his death in Valencia, the subsequent transfer of his body to Castile and its eventual interment at Cardeña. (We cannot actually demonstrate that the work was given to the king on this occasion, but it seems overwhelmingly likely.) The work itself has been lost, but it – or at any rate a large part of it – was incorporated apparently verbatim by the Alfonsine chroniclers in their history. It is usually referred to today either by the title they gave it, the *Estoria de Cardeña*, or by the modern title *Leyenda de Cardeña*. What the work demonstrates is that the monks of Cardeña had elaborated a cult of the Cid focused upon his tomb in their abbey church. This was evidently in a flourishing state by the year 1272; for how long before that it had been flourishing we cannot tell.

The Benedictine monastery of Cardeña had been founded, as we saw in Chapter 5, at the end of the ninth century. From its earliest days it had enjoyed warm relations with the aristocracy of Old Castile. These relations brought it wealth and renown which were at their most ample during the lifetime of Rodrigo Díaz. The two centuries which followed saw a decline in the abbey's fortunes. The slow southward movement of the frontier shifted the centre of gravity of the kingdom from Old Castile to New or, to put it another way, from Burgos to Toledo – and beyond. New fashions in aristocratic piety, new religious orders, meant disdain for what the monks of Cardeña had offered so confidently for so long. First the Cistercian monks in the twelfth century, then the friars in the thirteenth, and the Spanish military orders such as the Order of Santiago, all proved more attractive to lay patrons than the creaking piety of old-fashioned Benedictinism. The monks of Cardeña were left stranded. As benefactions fell off, small but significant indicators of hard times and undermined confidence can be detected: no new buildings, economies in the monastic library and scriptorium, sales of land, abbatial rights challenged by tenants in the courts. There was nothing unusual about this. Several other old-established ecclesiastical foundations were suffering in the same way and for the same reasons. To take but one example, the churchmen of Oviedo never had it so good as when their city was the principal seat of government of the Asturian kings in the ninth century: but when the kings moved south to León in the tenth, Oviedo became the provincial backwater it has remained ever since.

But an additional misfortune befell the monks of Cardeña in the middle of the twelfth century which rendered their sufferings worse than those of comparable communities. In 1142 Peter the Venerable, abbot of Cluny, visited the court of Alfonso VII. At this time the famous Burgundian abbey was nearly bankrupt. This state of affairs had arisen, as it usually does, from a variety of causes, among them the prolonged financial embarrassment precipitated by the cutting-off of the annual *census* paid by the kings of León-Castile when the Almoravides stopped the flow of tributary gold to the north. Payments to Cluny had long since lapsed, and in the changed circumstances of 1142 it was obviously unrealistic for Abbot Peter to insist on their revival. What he could attempt to do, however, was to secure some compensatory settlement from Alfonso VII. Such a settlement was reached, and one of its terms was the cession by the king to Cluny of the monastery of Cardeña. Perhaps the two men acted in good faith, though it is hard to see what legality Alfonso's grant might have had or how Abbot Peter could have brought himself to encourage it. Abbot Martín of Cardeña had not be consulted. When bands of Cluniac monks descended on Cardeña to take it over Martín and his monks resisted but were overborne and forced to evacuate their monastery. They at once initiated suits at the papal curia – doubtless at great expense – in defence of their rights which were, eventually, upheld. The community returned to Cardeña in 1146, but found it bare. The departing Cluniac monks had stripped it of the accumulated treasures of two-and-a-half centuries before they left.

The Cluniac interlude of 1142–6 must have been a traumatic one in the life of the Cardeña community. It may have intensified the pressures to change and to adapt to altered circumstances which all the 'stranded' religious communities of northern Spain were experiencing at this period. Some of them were doing it rather successfully. The clergy of Compostela, for instance, were busy in the mid-twelfth century reshaping St James, hitherto not particularly martial, into Santiago Matamoros, St James the Moor-Slayer, patron saint of a crusading reconquest with his own military order. How and when it occurred to the monks of Cardeña that in the bodies of the Cid and his wife they possessed 'relics' of considerable potential we cannot tell. Kings were revered at other monastic houses where their bodies rested, for example King Sancho II – patron of the Cid – at nearby Oña. The hero Roland was remembered at Roncesvalles, where 'relics' of him were shown; many pilgrims who used that pass through the Pyrenees would afterwards travel close to Burgos and Cardeña; the Cid's name had been linked with Roland's in the Almería poem. It is probably fruitless to try to pin down the early growth of the Cardeña legends about the Cid. The cult of dead heroes at their tombs is too perennial (from Hector to

Elvis Presley), too enduring a human instinct for any individual manifestation of it to be neatly docketed and explained by the historian (or anyone else). Where there is the piety of friends or kinsfolk, the pride of neighbours, the cupidity of custodians, the gullibility of tourists, the blarney of guides, the limitless capacity of the human mind to suspend disbelief, what can be said but that legends are bound to flourish? At Cardeña the climate for their growth was propitious, and 1272 (at latest) marks a stage in their elaboration.

The *Estoria* (or that part of it preserved in the thirteenth-century chronicles) is a bizarre work. It opens with an account of an embassy to the Cid in Valencia from the 'Great Sultan of Persia'. The envoys bring with them a number of rare presents, among them 'one of the finest chess-sets in the world, which is still today in the monastery of San Pedro de Cardeña', and above all 'a pound of myrrh and balsam, which is the unguent they use for embalming the bodies of famous men when they die'. Shortly after this St Peter – patron of Cardeña – appears to the Cid in a vision and informs him of his impending death, which will occur within thirty days; he also announces, mysteriously, that 'God so loves you that He will grant you victory in battle even after your death'. The Cid makes the customary spiritual preparations for death and also some highly unusual physical ones. During the last week of his life he takes no food or drink, only a daily dose of myrrh and balsam, thus performing an act of auto-embalmment to ensure the preservation of his body after death. After instructing his followers what to do with his corpse and (of course) stipulating that his final resting-place must be at Cardeña, 'where he lies today', he dies. After this his body is further embalmed, the face is made up, the eyes opened, 'so that no one would take him for anything but alive'. In accordance with his deathbed instructions his body is clothed, booted and spurred, mounted on his charger Babieca and led off towards Castile by Bishop Jerónimo. Meanwhile, Alvar Fáñez defeats 'King Búcar of Tunis' with the help of St James. (The story that the dead body of the Cid actually led his troops into combat, so memorably rendered by Charlton Heston, is a later embellishment.) Alfonso VI hastens to Cardeña for the funeral, and wonders to find the body of his vassal to all appearance miraculously preserved; but when he is told about the embalmings 'he no longer took it for a miracle for he had heard tell that they treat kings thus in Egypt'. At any rate, he will not permit a normal burial to take place. So the Cid's body is placed in the abbey church near the high altar, seated on an ivory stool which the hero had once captured from the Moors, clothed in precious silk and holding his sword Tizon, in its scabbard, in his left hand.

The Cid's servant Gil Díaz – allegedly a Valencian *faqih* who had been converted to Christianity – cares for his horse for two years,

During this time he puts him out to stud so that he can sire a distinguished progeny, whose descendants 'are perhaps still with us today'. At the end of the two years Babieca dies and Gil Díaz buries him 'before the gatehouse of the monastery' where he plants two elms to mark the spot, 'and these elms stand there to this day'. In the course of time Gil Díaz dies in his turn and is buried by his own request next to Babieca. When Doña Jimena dies she is buried at her husband's feet. The Cid himself continues to sit on his ivory chair. Seven years after his death a Jewish intruder makes his way into the abbey church, alone, and attempts to pluck the hero's beard. Instantly the Cid's right hand seizes the hilt of his sword and pulls it a few inches out of the scabbard – to the terror of the intruder, who is subsequently converted to Christianity. After ten years the end of the Cid's nose drops off. The abbot decides that it is not fitting that the Cid's body should remain there any longer 'because it looks ugly'. So the hero is finally interred beside his wife.

Whatever one may make of all this, it is clear that by 1272 a cult of the Cid as a sort of saint had been successfully got up by the monks of Cardeña. The vision of St Peter and the description of the deathbed owe much to hagiographical literary convention. Relics are shown to the devout – the chess-set, the ivory stool. At least one quasi-miraculous tale is in circulation. After the cult had been launched, all that was needed was an occasional shaking-out of new sail or light nudge to the tiller. The tombs at Cardeña multiplied to include those of relatives of the Cid and of Jimena, that of their son Diego, and those of several of the Cid's companions-in-arms. In due course these persons were provided with fictitious armorial bearings. The chapel where they lay was rebuilt in the eighteenth century, and there the tombs are still shown today – except for those of the hero and his wife, whose supposed remains were moved to the cathedral of Burgos in 1921. The elms which marked Babieca's grave have long since gone, but a memorial stone now marks the spot. Incredible as it may seem, as recently as 1948 the duke of Alba commissioned an archaeological excavation to search for Babieca's bones: it was unsuccessful. Relics multiplied: the Cid's two treasure-chests, his swords, his standard, his crucifix (which was borrowed by Alfonso XI in the fourteenth century to carry into battle). An early offshoot of the Alfonsine chronicles, apparently composed before 1312, was printed at Burgos in 1512 by the then abbot of Cardeña under the title *Crónica del famoso cavallero Cid Ruy Díez Campeador*: further editions followed in 1552 and 1593. When the Cid's tomb was opened in 1541 to move the remains to another part of the abbey church a fragrant smell arose from the coffin – a sign of sanctity – and rain fell, ending a long drought, and this was attributed 'to the merits of the holy knight Rodrigo Díaz'. Evidently the monks of Cardeña regarded the Cid as a saint. They were not alone. In 1554 Philip II petitioned for his canonisation: the process was initiated at Rome but later interrupted and never resumed.

Little would be gained by a relentless survey of the various manifestations of the legendary or cultic Cid. In the fourteenth century an epic devoted to his youthful exploits, the *Mocedades de Rodrigo*, was composed. Ballads celebrating his exploits circulated during the later Middle Ages. They proved enduringly popular: the *Romancero del Cid*, a collection of hundreds of such ballads published at Lisbon in 1605, was twenty-six times reprinted. Ballads and woodcuts kept the Cid firmly in the consciousness of Spaniards at home or scattered about their far-flung empire. The dramatic potential of the ballads was first realised by Guillén de Castro, who successfully adapted some of them for the stage in 1618. His play was the inspiration for Corneille's *Le Cid*, which was rapturously received in Paris on its first performance in 1636.

The single manuscript of the *Poema de Mio Cid* was discovered – oddly enough, at Vivar – in 1596 but was not printed until 1779. It quickly aroused interest, particularly in the English-speaking world; partly because of the publicity given to it by Southey, who published a book on the Cid in 1808, partly because a strong British concern with Spain was triggered off by the Napoleonic invasion and the Peninsular War, partly because a Romantic interest in the Spanish past was stimulated by Lockhart's translations of Spanish ballads and such works as Washington Irving's tales in *The Alhambra* of 1832. Among the travels of the manuscript in the nineteeth century was a journey across the Atlantic to Boston so that it could be consulted by the distinguished Hispanist George Ticknor for his *History of Spanish Literature*, which appeared in 1849.

The year 1849 was notable for another event in the growing literature devoted to the Cid. This was the publication at Leiden of the first edition of a collection of essays modestly entitled *Recherches sur l'histoire et la littérature de l'Espagne pendant le moyen âge* by a young (only twenty-nine) Dutch orientalist named Reinhardt Dozy. Under the innocuous title 'Le Cid d'après de nouveaux documents', or as we might translate it 'New light on the Cid', Dozy tossed a bomb into the cosy arena of national hagiography and Romantic blather. By this date the Cid of history had long been completely obscured by the Cid of legend. Dozy was not quite the first writer to attempt to release the historical Rodrigo from his cocoon of myth, but he was the first to bring to this task the combination of a formidable critical intelligence and a first-hand knowledge of such Arabic texts bearing upon the history of the Cid as were then available. (Dozy himself had discovered the text of Ibn Bassam relating to the Cid in 1844.) His essay is marvellously fresh and lively, still very much worth reading. Its effect was devastating because he showed, painstakingly, courteously, but all too clearly, how different the real man was from the legendary one. Dozy dismissed the poem as having no value as historical evidence. The Cid of reality was a *condottiere*. He was neither humane nor loyal nor patriotic. On the contrary, he was a harsh man, a breaker of promises, a pillager of churches, only interested in pay and plunder. Cruellest cut of all, Dozy described the Cid in the last paragraph of his essay as 'more Muslim than Catholic'.

Dozy's views provoked a storm of criticism in Spain, for he was attacking one of the most cherished of national myths. The fact that he did this authoritatively, with a scholarship which no Spaniard of the day could match, only served to rub salt into the wound which he had opened. He defended his interpretation of the Cid in subsequent editions of his essays in 1860 and 1881. It gained currency abroad. In Spain Dozy and his work continued to be reviled – but not refuted.

The counter-blast to Dozy was not finally delivered until 1929, when Ramón Menéndez Pidal published *La España del Cid*. His interpretation of the work published in 1934 has proved more influential than any other. In essence, what Menéndez Pidal did was lovingly and reverently to resurrect as much of the legend as was consistent with what he took to be exacting scholarly criticism, and to present it as history. The result is less an interpretation than a vision. For Menéndez Pidal the Cid was a flawless character who personified what he saw as the virtues of the Castilians: brave and proud, pious and patriotic, chivalrous and generous, a loving husband and father, a vassal so true that even the capricious hostility of an unjust king could not unseat his loyalty. It was of critical importance to his vision that the Cid's specifically Castilian virtues were also national ones. His vision of the Cid dovetailed with another vision, already widely diffused but by no means universally shared, about the role of Castile in the whole sweep of Spanish history. Castile's historic destiny was to unify Spain. The Cid therefore offered a pattern for all Spaniards to follow. In the Preface to the first edition of *La España del Cid*, and in the closing chapters of the book, Menéndez Pidal candidly admitted that the work was one of piety as well as history, intended to have a didactic function. Menéndez Pidal had lessons for his generation, in much the same way, perhaps, as the author of the *Poema de Mio Cid* had had lessons – somewhat similar ones – for his.

That Preface, and the concluding two chapters in which the author elaborated most fully his vision of the Cid, take us into a moral and intellectual world which to the prosaic Anglo-Saxon mind will seem rather rum. The vision was central to Menéndez Pidal's life and thought. It is present in its essentials in his edition of the *Poema de Mio Cid*; though this was published in the years 1908–11, the major part of the work for it had been done in 1892 and 1893 as an entry for a prize offered by the Royal Spanish Academy (which Menéndez Pidal won). It is strongly present in the works of his old age, for example in the long essay 'Los Españoles en su historia' which he published in 1947 as a preface to the collaborative *Historia de España* of which he was the founding editor; and it looms in the background of his book on the *Chanson de Roland* and other medieval epics which he published at the age of ninety in 1959. The vision first glimpsed when he was a young man sustained him and was sustained by him for an active scholarly career of seventy years.

How and why did Menéndez Pidal come by his vision of the Cid and of Castile and of their place in Spain's history? Why did he communicate it so urgently and eloquently to his compatriots? A few guesses may be offered by way of an answer.

Ramón Menéndez Pidal was not by birth a Castilian: he was born in Corunna in 1869 to parents who were by origin Asturian. Although he had fairly distinguished family connections his parents were not affluent, and shortly after Ramón's birth they fell upon hard financial times and were reduced to a somewhat nomadic existence by reason of one of Spain's many nineteenth-century revolutions. His father lost his magistracy through refusal to swear allegiance to the new constitution – federal, anti-clerical and civilian – which was born out of the revolution of 1868. His father did not regain his post until 1876, and died four years later. The child Ramón was dragged from Oviedo to Seville to Albacete to Burgos and again to Oviedo. The family finally settled in Madrid in 1884.

Ramón's childhood, one might say, was overshadowed by the politically disastrous, domestically unsettling experiment of federalism. But it had not been an unhappy one. One of the relatives who influenced him was his uncle the Marqués de Pidal, who was a collector, a man of scholarly tastes. In 1863 he had bought the single extant manuscript of the *Poema de Mio Cid*. The young Ramón was introduced to his life's work at an early age. The move to Madrid – to the centre, to Castile – brought stability. It also brought success: a brilliant university career, his prize-winning edition of the poem, his first book on medieval epic (in 1896), a chair in Romance Philology and a marriage in 1900 which was to prove singularly happy. The newly-weds spent their honeymoon retracing on horseback the route of the Cid's travels in exile as recorded in the first *cantar* of the epic. One very important incident occurred in the course of this idyllic journey. At Osma, on 28 May 1900, Ramón and his wife heard a washerwoman on the river bank singing a ballad, hitherto unrecorded, about the death of the eldest son of Ferdinand and Isabella nearly four hundred years before. They recognised in it authentic historical information. The incident powerfully impressed Ramón and did much to fortify his conviction, which never subsequently wavered, that orally transmitted poetry could be a source of reliable historical evidence.

While studying at Madrid University between 1885 and 1890 Ramón had attended the lectures of the orientalist Francisco Codera, a fine scholar whose work on Hispano-Muslim history has not yet been superseded. Codera introduced his gifted student to the work of Dozy, lending him his own copy of Dozy's essays which had recently come out in a third edition shortly before the author's death in 1883. Ramón was pained by Dozy's treatment of the Cid. Something beloved had been desecrated. Years later he would accuse Dozy of 'Cidophobia', and devote twenty pages of the first chapter of *La España del Cid* to a point-by-point refutation of Dozy's views. Another influence on the young Ramón was Marcelino Menéndez y Pelayo (1856–1912), the foremost Spanish literary critic and historian of his generation, appointed to a chair at Madrid University at the age of twenty-one after a prime-ministerial request to the Cortes to waive the rule that candidates should be over twenty-five. Menéndez y Pelayo's legendary erudition and industry were harnessed to an interpretation of Spanish history of a violently Catholic and nationalistic kind. 'Spain, the evangeliser of half the globe; Spain, the hammer of heretics; Spain, the sword of the Pope. This is our greatness and our glory: we have no other.' There was no room for dissidents in a history so conceived. His *Historia de los heterodoxes españoles* (1880–2) was dedicated to the proposition that all deviants from official ecclesiastical teaching – be they medieval heretics, Moriscos, Jews, or the rationalists of the Enlightenment – were engaged in a plot to subvert that Catholic orthodoxy of which the Spanish nation was the guardian. Menéndez y Pelayo's views were widely accepted. When Menéndez Pidal accused Dozy of 'Cidophobia', of being 'led astray by rationalism', one can detect the tones of his master.

Personally fulfilling for Menéndez Pidal, the last decade of the nineteenth century was one of public humiliation for his country. The last tatters of transatlantic empire were torn from her after shaming defeats at the hands of the United States in 1898. National degradation gave birth to a mood of anxious self-examination. What had gone wrong? Historians contributed to the prolonged public debate which ensued. They could rediscover and delineate Spain's manifest destiny. They could identify the heterodox influences which had beguiled her into deviating from its imperatives. They could hold up ennobling examples from the past to comfort and instruct the present. These were the years when the 'spirit' of Castile was rediscovered, or invented; the years when Antonio Machado, a schoolmaster in the quintessentially Castilian town of Soria, composed poems celebrating the bleak landscape round about and the rugged virtues of its peasantry; the years when the hobnailed boots

of intellectuals crunched out from Soria across that same bleak landscape, their wearers to inspect the lately unearthed remains of
Numantia and contemplate with morally uplifting sorrow the scene
of the last stand of the Celtiberians – the true, the original, the Ur-
Castilians – against the invading foreigner.

'Though engaged in the study of our national past,' said Menéndez
Pidal in an interview in 1916, 'nothing concerns me so much as our
present and our future.' Later in the same interview he said:

> Throughout the history of Spain, Castile has played a unifying and
> anchoring role. Castile is not the whole of Spain, but her spirit *is* the
> unity of Spain. It has been so from her first appearance in history.

In 1929 *La España del Cid* was received with acclamation by the
public. Among the early reviewers of it was the influential critic
Azorín (1873–1967), who had published in 1899 a work entitled *La
alma castellana*, 'The Soul of Castile'. Azorín praised Menéndez
Pidal's work as 'a wonderful lesson in patriotism'. It is a revealing
phrase. Menéndez Pidal had given the Spaniards the Cid they
wanted. And his version was unassailable. The national hero whom
he presented so convincingly and so readably in the text of his
work was elaborately defended, walled by footnotes, buttressed by
appendices of meticulous scholarship, fortified by all the massive
intellectual authority of the Director of the Royal Spanish Academy,
the editor of the *Poema de Mio Cid* and the *Primera Crónica General*.
There could be no criticism of Don Ramón's Cid in his native land;
and there was precious little elsewhere.

Two years after its publication came the abdication of Alfonso
XIII and the proclamation of the Second Republic, five years after
that the outbreak of the Civil War and in 1939 the victory of the
Nationalists under the leadership of General Franco. The Catholic,
Castilian, crusading – but not the loyalist! – Cid of Menéndez Pidal
was irresistible to Franco's propagandists. Early on in the conflict
the Nationalists claimed for their movement the character of a 'crusade', and this was later enshrined in the title of the official history
of the struggle. Franco's connection with Burgos, like the Cid's,
was made much of. In 1937 a journal was established there entitled
Mio Cid: its first editorial proclaimed the aim of 'raising the standard
of the Cid throughout Spain'. In the same year a collection of
modern ballads was published in which the Cid and Franco were
explicitly compared. Towards the end of the war General Aranda
compared his advance from Teruel to the Mediterranean to the
Cid's campaigns in the Levante. Immediately after the war the huge
equestrian statue of the Cid which stands in Burgos was commissioned. *La España del Cid* became and for long remained a set book
for cadets at Spanish military academies.

The author must have found this extremely distasteful. Though by temperament conservative, Menéndez Pidal was genuinely neutral in politics. He distrusted the Nationalists, despised their rhetoric and was shocked by the more unsavoury doings of the Franco régime in the years immediately after the Civil War. He was ill-used by the government which had so crudely exploited his work. He was deprived of his presidency of the Academy and subjected to minor but vexatious persecutions such as, for a time, the freezing of his bank account. At one point he was denounced by an anonymous delator and for a period was compelled - this internationally renowned scholar in his seventies – to appear weekly before a tribunal charged to examine the political views of suspected dissidents. The tide turned from about 1947. Don Ramón was restored to the presidency of the Academy and – generously, in view of his recent sufferings – composed in his essay 'Los Españoles en su historia' a plea for national reconciliation. He lived out the remainder of his life full of years and honour. The Preface to the last edition of *La España del Cid* revised by him was written when he was ninety-seven. He died at the age of ninety-nine in 1968.

Since Menéndez Pidal's death, and indeed to some extent before it, students of literature, history and philology have criticised many facets of his work. His most famous book still stands, though now with somewhat the air of a medieval castle under siege: battered by artillery, some of its masonry cracked by the mines that the sappers have pushed into the foundations, morale sinking among the ravenous garrison as the prospect of the arrival of a relief force becomes daily more remote. Yet the bodies of those who tried to assault it too soon still lie among the débris of the scaling-ladders which failed to carry them over the battlements, a warning to the besiegers not to be too hasty. We still think of eleventh-century Spain as the Cid's Spain, and for this we have Menéndez Pidal to thank. It is now sixty years since the first publication of *La España del Cid*, a work long meditated beforehand and in part designed to refute a writer whose work was first published in 1849. What sort of Cid is wanted today? I should not presume to guess. The only presumption I make is to share the claim of his earliest biographer, the anonymous author of the *Historia Roderici*: 'What our limited skill can do we have done: written of his deeds briefly and in a poor style, but always with the strictest regard for truth.'

Bibliography

1 The Problem and the Method

The first (1929) edition of Ramón Menéndez Pidal's *La España del Cid* was translated into English by H. Sutherland under the title *The Cid and His Spain* (London, 1934). Users of this translation should bear in mind that it is shorn of all the scholarly apparatus – footnotes, appendices, editions of documents – of the original Spanish edition.

The *Poema de Mio Cid* has been many times edited. Two excellent editions have recently been published by English scholars, now Professors of Spanish at respectively Cambridge and Oxford. The earlier of the two to appear was Colin Smith, *Poema de Mio Cid* (Oxford, 1972), with a valuable introduction and notes. This was shortly afterwards followed by Ian Michael, *The Poem of the Cid* (Manchester, 1975), accompanied not only by admirable apparatus but also by a facing translation into English prose by Rita Hamilton and Janet Perry: this edition was reprinted in the Penguin Classics series in 1984. Smith's text of the poem has been reprinted, accompanied by a line-by-line translation into English, with commentary, by Peter Such and John Hodgkinson, *The Poem of My Cid* (Warminster, 1987). Of the many attempts to render the poem into English verse the most successful to my mind is that of W. S. Merwin (London, 1959), referred to in the text of this chapter.

A lively and up-to-date introduction to Cidian problems is provided by Peter Linehan in his article 'The Cid of history and the history of the Cid', *History Today* 37 (September 1987).

2 Al-Andalus

By far the best introduction to the history of Spain in the early Middle Ages is provided by Roger Collins, *Early Medieval Spain. Unity in Diversity 400–1000* (London, 1983). The standard history of Islamic Spain before the year 1031 is that of E. Lévi-Provençal, *Histoire de l'Espagne musulmane* (Paris and Leiden, 1950–5). The most important recent contribution to our understanding of the early social history of al-Andalus has been made by Pierre Guichard, *Tribus arabes et berbères en al-Andalus* (Paris, 1973). R. W. Bulliet's *Conversion to Islam in the Medieval Period* (Harvard, 1979) is a stimulating introduction to its subject, while T. F. Glick's *Islamic and Christian Spain in the Early Middle Ages* (Princeton, 1979) is full of new insights sometimes obscured by a rebarbative style. The economic history of the early Middle Ages has most recently been surveyed by R. Hodges and D. Whitehouse, *Mohammed, Charlemagne and the Origins of Europe* (London, 1983). This work may be supplemented by A. M. Watson, *Agricultural Innovation in the Early Islamic World: the Diffusion of Crops and Farming Techniques* (Cambridge, 1983), a mine of information on its subject, and A. Y. al-Hassan and D. R. Hill, *Islamic Technology* (Cambridge, 1986), a concise and well-illustrated survey.

Among original sources cited in this chapter, Ibn Hawkal may be read in the translation of M. J. Romani Suay (Valencia, 1971); Idrisi in the reissue of Saavedra's

and Blázquez's translations edited by A. Ubieto Arteta (Valencia, 1974); Ibn Waddah's poem is quoted from the translation of A. R. Nykl in his *Hispano-Arabic
Poetry* (Baltimore, 1946). Pascual de Gayangos translated al-Maqqari's great history
of al-Andalus (London, 1840–3) which is the source, among other things, of the
description of the Hall of the Caliphs and of the anecdotes about Almanzor. I have
gleaned incidental information from the epigraphical evidence assembled in Lévi-
Provençal's *Inscriptions arabes d'Espagne* (Paris, 1931) and from S. D. Goitein's
fascinating selection of *Letters of Medieval Jewish Traders* (Princeton, 1973) from the
Cairo Geniza.

3   THE BREAKING OF THE NECKLACE

The best analysis of the period of the taifa states is to be found in D. Wasserstein,
The Rise and Fall of the Party-Kings, Politics and Society in Islamic Spain 1002–1086
(Princeton, 1985). For Valencia see A. Huici Miranda, *Historia musulmana de Valencia*
(Valencia, 1969); for Granada the best guide is 'Abd Allah himself in the recent
translation by A. T. Tibi (see references for Chapter 7); for Zaragoza there is only
the laborious compilation of A. Turk, *El reino de Zaragoza en el siglo XI de Cristo/V
de la Hégira* (Madrid, 1978).

Ibn Salim's anecdote about the ecstatic swoon of Abu Muhammad is told by al-
Maqqari. For poetry I have turned to A. R. Nykl's work cited in the references
for Chapter 2 and to J. T. Monroe, *Hispano-Arabic Poetry: a Student Anthology*
(Berkeley, 1974). Ibn 'Ammar's famous panegyric on al-Mu'tadid is quoted from
the translation of A. J. Arberry, *Moorish Poetry. A translation of 'The Pennants', an
anthology compiled in 1243 by the Andalusian Ibn Sa'id* (Cambridge, 1953): there is a
more literal rendering into prose in Monroe's selection.

For the Jewish communities of al-Andalus at this period see most recently E.
Ashtor, *The Jews of Moslem Spain*, vol. 3 (Philadelphia, 1984), who is also the
source of the information about Toledo's monastic wine-bars.

4   THE HEIRS OF THE VISIGOTHS

Excellent introductions to the history of Christian Spain are provided by Roger
Collins's *Early Medieval Spain* (see Bibliography for Chapter 2) and its comple-
mentary volume Angus MacKay, *Spain in the Middle Ages: from Frontier to Empire
1000–1500* (London, 1977). No really satisfactory book on the Asturo-Leónese
kingdom has yet been written. For its neighbours to the east see Roger Collins,
The Basques (Oxford, 1986) and T. N. Bisson, *The Medieval Crown of Aragon. A
short history* (Oxford, 1986).

Ibn Hayyan's account of the Pamplona campaign of 924 may be found in the
Crónica' del Califa 'Abdarrahman III an-Nasir entre los años 921 y 942, translated by
M. J. Viguera and F. Corriente (Zaragoza, 1981). I have elsewhere offered a few
reflections on 'Reconquest and Crusade in Spain, c.1050–1150', *Transactions of the
Royal Historical Society*, 5th series, 37 (1987). Relations between Christians and
Muslims are surveyed by N. Daniel, *Islam and the West, the Making of an Image*
(Edinburgh, 1960) and *The Arabs and Medieval Europe* (London, 1975); by T. F.
Glick (see Bibliography for Chapter 2); and by B. Z. Kedar, *Crusade and Mission.
European Approaches Toward the Muslims* (Princeton, 1984). Gerbert's letters have
been translated by H. P. Lattin (New York, 1961). Walcher of Malvern is quoted
in the translation by R. W. Southern, *Medieval Humanism and Other Studies* (Oxford,
1970), pp. 166–7. For the trans-Saharan gold trade and for Ibn 'Abdun see the

Bibliographies for Chapters 10 and 11 respectively. R. A. Fletcher, *Saint James's Catapult* (Oxford, 1984) surveys the origins and growth of the cult of St James at Compostela. J. Pérez de Urbel's *Sancho el Mayor de Navarra* (Madrid, 1950) is the only detailed study of its subject though it is insufficiently critical.

5   A Few Men in a Small Land

The standard work on early medieval Castile is J. Pérez de Urbel, *Historia del Condado de Castilla* (2nd ed., Madrid, 1969), but it badly needs to be replaced by something more up-to-date. Much good work is now being done on early Castilian history: for example, C. Estepa Díez has recently written on 'Burgos en el contexto del nacimiento de la ciudad medieval castellano-leonesa' in *La Ciudad de Burgos. Actas del Congreso de Historia de Burgos. MC Aniversario de la Fundación de la Ciudad 884–1984* (Madrid, 1985); and R. Collins has some helpful pages on the legal system of early Castile in his paper on 'Visigothic law and regional custom in disputes in early medieval Spain' in W. Davies and P. Fouracre (eds.), *The Settlement of Disputes in Early Medieval Europe* (Cambridge, 1986). A new synthesis of early Castilian history is required. L. Serrano, *El Obispado de Burgos* (Madrid, 1935) ranges widely but not always critically over the early ecclesiastical history of Castile.

Among original sources cited in this chapter I have drawn freely upon four groups: first, the surviving documentation of the monastic houses of Old Castile, most of it printed by L. Serrano, especially that from Covarrubias and Cardeña (Madrid, respectively 1907 and 1910); secondly, the early *fueros* of Castile in the comprehensive if uncritical edition of T. Múñoz y Romero (Madrid, 1847); thirdly, the early charters of the cathedral church of Burgos, now available in the edition by J. M. Garrido Garrido (Burgos, 1983); and finally two hagiographical texts, the *vitae* of St Domingo of Silos now available in the edition by V. Valcarcel (Logroño, 1982) and of San Juan de Ortega printed by the Bollandists (*Acta Sanctorum, Iunii*, vol. I).

On the mechanics of the salt industry, and generally on the economy of a great monastery, see S. Moreta Velayos, *El Monasterio de San Pedro de Cardeña* (Salamanca, 1971). On the relations between monasteries and aristocracy I have found M. Chibnall, *The World of Orderic Vitalis* (Oxford, 1984) useful.

The charters of King Fernando I have been edited by P. Blanco Lozano in *Archivos Leoneses* 79–80 (1986) and she is working on a study of the reign. For the operations of the 'protection racket' – the phrase is Angus MacKay's (see Bibliography for Chapter 4) – the best starting-point is in the collected essays of J. M. Lacarra, *Colonización, Parias, Repoblación y otros estudios* (Zaragoza, 1981). The count of Barcelona's fiscal affairs, among much else, are investigated in the commanding study by P. Bonnassie, *La Catalogne du milieu du Xe à la fin de XIe siècle* (Toulouse, 1975); Count Gómez Díaz's may be reconstructed from *Documentación del Monasterio de San Zoilo de Carrión* (Palencia, 1986). C. J. Bishko has produced an elaborate study of 'Fernando I and the origins of the Leónese-Castilian alliance with Cluny' in his *Studies in Medieval Spanish Frontier History* (London, 1980), though not all his conclusions are acceptable. The life of St Adelelmus is to be found in *Acta Sanctorum, Januarii*, vol. II. On the distinctiveness of the so-called Mozarabic liturgy I have found two works by A. A. King useful: *Notes on the Catholic Liturgies* (London, 1930) and *Liturgies of the Primatial Sees* (London, 1957). Much has been written about its abrogation: see most recently the collection of essays edited by B. F. Reilly under the title *Santiago, Saint-Denis and Saint Peter: the Reception of the Roman Liturgy in León-Castilla in 1080* (New York, 1985) and references therein.

6 CONTEMPORARIES

The materials of which this chapter is constructed have been assembled from sources too diverse to be individually cited in a short bibliographical note of this kind. Consider by way of example the paragraph beginning 'The list could be extended . . .' on page 82. For Domnal Déisech see *The Annals of Innisfallen*, ed. S. Mac Airt (Dublin, 1951), p.219; for the Greek bishop in Spain see *Colección de Documentos de la Catedral de Oviedo*, ed. S. García Larragueta (Oviedo, 1962), No. 41; for Ulf and Madselin see *Anglo-Saxon Wills*, ed. D. Whitelock (Cambridge, 1930), No. XXXIX; for the Jewish boy from Przemysl see I. A. Agus, *Urban Civilisation in pre-Crusade Europe* (Leiden, 1965), pp. 104–5; for Guynemer see S. Runciman, *A History of the Crusades*, vol. I (Cambridge, 1951), pp. 199, 201, 217–18, 238, 255.

For better or for worse I have decided not to refer the reader to the individual pieces of the mosaic. To anyone wishing to become acquainted with the aristocracy of the eleventh century the best course is prolonged immersion in the *Ecclesiastical History of Orderic Vitalis*, superlatively edited, translated and annotated by Marjorie Chibnall for the series 'Oxford Medieval Texts', especially Books III–VI in volumes 2 and 3 (Oxford, 1969, 1972), which – despite the title Orderic gave to his great work – are really a leisurely account of the nobility of southern Normandy in the eleventh century. The best modern account of the aristocracy of this period, at any rate a section of them, is Karl Leyser's *Rule and Conflict in an Early Medieval Society: Ottonian Saxony* (London, 1979), a dense, rewarding and thought-provoking study. Though he austerely eschews the anecdotal, Georges Duby's essays translated under the title *The Chivalrous Society* (London, 1978) are the work of a scholar who has done much to enlarge our understanding of the feudal nobility of France, following in the footsteps of his mentor Marc Bloch, whose *Feudal Society* (English translation, London, 1961) remains a classic.

There are good treatments of *Normandy Before 1066* by D. Bates (London, 1982) and of *The Byzantine Empire 1025–1204* by M. Angold (London, 1984). J. J. Norwich, *The Normans in the South* (London, 1967) is a lively and readable account of its subject. The same cannot be said of R. B. Yewdale, *Bohemond I, Prince of Antioch* (Princeton, 1924); but it is painstaking and reliable.

7 THE SOURCES

The *Carmen Campi Doctoris* has most recently been edited by Roger Wright, 'The first poem on the Cid – the *Carmen Campi Doctoris*', in *Papers of the Liverpool Latin Seminar*, volume 2 (1979), pp. 213–48, which contains in addition an English translation of the text and an admirable discussion of the poem as a whole. For a different view of the poem see C. Smith, 'The dating and relationship of the *Historia Roderici* and the *Carmen Campi Doctoris*', *Olifant* 9 (1982), pp. 99–112: Professor Smith would place composition of the poem in the second half of the twelfth century.

The *Historia Roderici* was edited by R. Menéndez Pidal among the appendices to *La España del Cid* (7th edition, Madrid, 1969), pp. 921–71. No published translation into English exists.

Ibn 'Alqama's work is best presented in the French translation of E. Lévi-Provençal in his article 'La prise de Valence par le Cid', which is to be found in a collection of his essays, *Islam d'Occident* (Paris, 1948), pp. 187–238. The relevant extracts from the work of Ibn Bassam were likewise printed in a French translation by R. Dozy, *Recherches sur l'histoire et la littérature de l'Espagne pendant le moyen âge* (3rd edition, Leiden, 1881), pp. 8–28.

For the *Poema de Mio Cid* see the references for Chapter 1. The best introduction to the later chronicles is now to be found in B. Powell, *Epic and Chronicle. The 'Poema de Mio Cid' and the 'Crónica de veinte reyes'* (London, 1983), with copious references to earlier work on the subject.

Of the other narrative sources composed in Spain, Pelayo's chronicle was edited by B. Sánchez Alonso (Madrid, 1924), the *Historia Silense* by J. Pérez de Urbel and A. G. Ruíz-Zorrilla (Madrid, 1959), the *Crónica Nájerense* by A. Ubieto Arteta (Valencia, 1966) and the *Life of Sto. Domingo de Silos* by V. Valcarcel (Logroño, 1982).

'Abd Allah's autobiography may be consulted in the translation, very fully annotated, of A. T. Tibi, *The Tibyan. Memoirs of 'Abd Allah b. Buluggin, last Zirid amir of Granada* (Leiden, 1986).

The Oviedo law-suit of 1075 may be followed in *Colección de documentos de la Catedral de Oviedo*, ed. S. García Larragueta (Oviedo, 1962), No. 74. Sancho II's grant to Oña in 1070 is printed in *Colección diplomática de San Salvador de Oña*, ed. J. del Alamo (Madrid, 1950), vol. 1, No. 58: the pseudo-original is preserved in the Archivo Histórico Nacional in Madrid, Sección de Clero, carpeta 271, No. 6. Rodrigo's grant to the church of Valencia in 1098 was printed among the appendices to Menéndez Pidal's *Las España del Cid* (7th edition), pp. 868–71.

8   THE CAMPEADOR

For the original sources relating to the Cid from which I quote in this and the three subsequent chapters see the discussion in Chapter 7 and the Bibliography to that chapter. The most recent modern study of the period is Bernard F. Reilly's *The Kingdom of León-Castilla Under King Alfonso VI 1065–1100* (Princeton, 1988), which provides a detailed political history of Alfonso VI's long and important reign with full references to earlier literature on the subject.

Pedro Rúiz's charter of 1062 is printed in *Cartulario de San Pedro de Arlanza*, ed. L. Serrano (Madrid, 1925), No. lxiv. The passage on spear-management is quoted from Maurice Keen, *Chivalry* (London, 1984), p. 24. Useful comparative material is to be found in J. O. Prestwich, 'The military household of the Norman Kings', *English Historical Review* 96 (1981). Santiagan memories of Alfonso VI are to be found in the *Historia Compostellana*, ed. E. Flórez (Madrid, 1765), pp. 60, 65, 113, 140, 253. The record of the Cardeña-Orbaneja law-suit is printed in *Becerro gótico de Cardeña*, ed. L. Serrano (Madrid, 1910), No. XIV; that of the suit over Tol in *Colección de Documentos de la Catedral de Oviedo*,, ed. S. García Larragueta (Oviedo, 1962), No. 74, and for the background see Nos. 40, 46, 63, 70, 71. The royal diploma of 14 March 1075 (*ibidem*, No. 72) which describes the discovery of the Oviedo relics cannot be authentic as it stands but is probably based on genuine materials. Rodrigo's *carta de arras* for his wife has most recently been printed in *Documentación de la Catedral de Burgos (804–1183)*, ed. J. M. Garrido Garrido (Burgos, 1983), No. 25. His charter for Silos, illustrated in Plate 9, is printed in *Recueil des chartes de l'Abbaye de Silos*, ed. M. Férotin (Paris, 1897), No. 19.

9   EXILE IN ZARAGOZA

In general, see the opening paragraph of the Bibliography to Chapter 8. Turk's book on Zaragoza (see Bibliography for Chapter 3) is a guide to the political scene in the taifa kingdom where Rodrigo spent his exile. For Catalan affairs see S. Sobreques i. Vidal, *Els grans comtes de Barcelona* 2nd ed., Barcelona, 1970); for Aragonese, A. Ubieto Arteta, *Historia de Aragón* (Zaragoza, 1981); for Navarrese, J. M. Lacarra, *Historia del reino de Navarra en la edad media* (Pamplona, 1975). The chronology of events in the years 1079–81 is difficult to sort out: I follow what seems the most plausible sequence.

Al-Mutawakkil's invitation to Abu Talib is quoted from A. J. Arberry, *Moorish Poetry* (Cambridge, 1953), p. 40: for the cabbage leaf see A. R. Nykl, *Hispano-Arabic Poetry* (Baltimore, 1946), p. 173. On the frequency of frontier raids, the possible reactions of responsible opinion to Rodrigo's exploits and the evidence for Christian knights in Zaragozan service see *La 'Vita Dominici Siliensis' de Grimaldo*, ed. V. Valcarcel (Logroño, 1982), respectively pp. 392, 376–8 and 478. The characterisation of Rodrigo's actions as 'maverick' is that of Roger Wright in his discussion of the *Carmen Campi Doctoris*. For the Aljafería of Zaragoza see J. L. Corral Lafuente (ed.), *La cultura islámica en Aragon* (Zaragoza, 1986). Al-Muqtadir's couplet is quoted from H. Pérès, *La poésie andalouse en arabe classique au XIe siècle* (2nd ed., Paris, 1953), p. 152. The purchase of Caserras from Arnal Mir de Tost is recorded in the *Liber Feudorum Maior*, ed. F. Miguel Rosell (Barcelona, 1945), vol. I Nos. 151, 152. The will of Count Gonzalo Salvadórez is printed in *Colección diplomática de San Salvador de Oña*, ed. J. del Alamo (Madrid, 1950), No. 77.

Rodrigo's biographer (Chapter 24) tells us that his subject remained in the service of al-Musta'in 'for nine years': like other commentators I have assumed that this is a copyist's error for 'months'.

10   THE ALMORAVIDE INVASION

An additional source, which sheds a little light on Alfonso VI's Valencian campaign of 1092, is Ibn al-Kardabus, *Historia de al-Andalus*, trans. F. Maíllo Salgado (Madrid, 1986). Otherwise the sources remain as listed in the Bibliography for Chapter 7: 'Abd 'Allah and Ibn 'Alqama are particularly important.

In sketching developments in the Maghrib I have found the following works useful: J. Béraud-Villars, *Les Touareg au pays du Cid* (Paris, 1946); E. W. Bovill, *The Golden Trade of the Moors* (2nd ed., Oxford, 1970); J. F. P. Hopkins, *Medieval Muslim Government in Barbary, Until the Sixth Century of the Hijra* (London, 1958); E. Lévi-Provençal, *Islam d'Occident* (Paris, 1948); H. T. Norris, 'New evidence on the life of 'Abdullah b. Yasin and the origins of the Almoravid movement', *Journal of African History* 12 (1971); R. le Tourneau, 'Nouvelles orientations des Berbères d'Afrique du nord (950–1150)', in D. S. Richards (ed.), *Islamic Civilisation 950–1150* (Oxford, 1973); J. S. Trimingham, *A History of Islam in West Africa* (Oxford, 1962). E. Gellner, *Saints of the Atlas* (London, 1969) is a work of social anthropology rather than history; however, this fascinating book contains insights which historians should not neglect. J. D. Hooker and J. Ball, *Journal of a Tour in Morocco and the Great Atlas* (London, 1878) was a chance find which I owe to a shelf-clearing operation by the North Yorkshire County Library: the tour was a botanical one under the leadership of the celebrated botanist Sir Joseph Hooker of Kew (1817–1911) and it occurred before the interior of Morocco had been opened up to European visitors; the participants' scientific training in exact observation and description renders their account of the society as well as the flora of Morocco of great value. Another chance find was *The Pilgrimage of Ahmad, Son of the Little Bird of Paradise*, trans. H. T. Norris (Warminster, 1977): a remarkable story. Like many other English travellers to Morocco I have been enthralled by Gavin Maxwell's *Lords of the Atlas* (London, 1966), and I am grateful to his Bibliography for directing me to such delicious literary curiosities as Lady Grove's *Seventy-one days' camping in Morocco* (London, 1902).

For Ibn Hawkal, see the references for Chapter 2. The English king referred to was King Ealdred, grandson of Alfred, who died in 955: his will is translated in D. Whitelock, *English Historical Documents*, vol. I, (2nd ed., London, 1979), No. 107. A. MacKay and M. Benaboud discuss 'The authenticity of Alfonso VI's letter to Yusuf b. Tasufin' in *Al-Andalus* 43 (1978). For the career of Sisnando Davídez see E. García Gómez and R. Menéndez Pidal, 'El conde mozárabe Sisnando Davídez y la política de Alfonso VI con los taifas', *Al-Andalus* 12 (1947). R. Bartlett, *Trial by Fire and Water. The medieval judicial ordeal* (Oxford, 1986) discusses trial by combat in Chapter 6. Al-Mu'tamid's lament is quoted from A. R. Nykl, *Hispano-Arabic Poetry* (Baltimore, 1946). On Valencia see A. Huici Miranda, *Historia musulmana de Valencia* (Valencia, 1969), who corrects Menéndez Pidal on a number of points but is not always reliable himself.

11 THE PRINCE OF VALENCIA

Among the sources Ibn 'Alqama and Ibn Bassam are the most important. The *Poema de Mio Cid* is quoted from the verse translation of W. S. Merwin (see Chapter 1 and references). The charters by which the Cid and Doña Jimena granted endowments to the cathedral church of Valencia are printed among the appendices to Menéndez Pidal's *La España del Cid*. Ibn 'Abdun's treatise on the government of Seville has been translated under the title *Sevilla a comienzos del siglo XII* by E. García Gómez (Seville, 1981). Reilly's account of the reign of Alfonso VI remains indispensable. For Aragonese affairs see A. Ubieto Arteta, *Colección diplomática de Pedro I de Aragón y Navarra* (Zaragoza, 1951).

12 MY CID OF VIVAR

Colin Smith's *The Making of the 'Poema de Mio Cid'* (Cambridge, 1983) is an extremely stimulating treatment of its subject. Only slightly less so is M. E. Lacarra, *El Poema de Mio Cid: realidad histórica e ideología* (Madrid, 1980).

For the political history of the kingdom of León-Castile in the twelfth century see Bernard F. Reilly, *The Kingdom of León-Castilla under Queen Urraca 1109–1126* (Princeton, 1982); M. Recuero Astray, *Alfonso VII, emperador: el imperio hispánico en el siglo XII* (León, 1979); and J. González, *El reino de Castilla en la época de Alfonso VIII* (Madrid, 1960). The poem on the conquest of Almería is to be found in *Chronica Adefonsi Imperatoris*, ed. L. Sánchez Belda (Madrid, 1950). The most recent treatment of the development of the vernacular chronicles is that of B. Powell, *Epic and Chronicle: the 'Poema de Mio Cid' and the 'Crónica de Veinte Reyes'* (London, 1983). There is much of great interest to be found in A. D. Deyermond, *Epic Poetry and the Clergy: Studies on the 'Mocedades de Rodrigo'* (London, 1969).

On Cardeña's chequered history the study by Moreta Velayos, cited in the Bibliography for Chapter 5, may be consulted. For the literary activities of its monks see the seminal article by P. E. Russell, 'San Pedro de Cardeña and the heroic history of the Cid', *Medium Aevum* 27 (1958) and the further explorations of Colin Smith, 'The diffusion of the Cid cult: a survey and a little-known document', *Journal of Medieval History* 6 (1980); 'Leyendas de Cardeña', *Boletín de la Real Academia de la Historia* (1982); and 'Historiadores de Cardeña', in *Studia in honorem M. de Riquer* (Barcelona, 1987).

Ramón Menéndez Pidal has not yet been the subject of full-scale biography. In its absence I have found the following useful: C. Conde, *Menéndez Pidal* (Madrid, 1969); M. E. Lacarra, 'La utilización del Cid de Menéndez Pidal en la ideologia militar franquista', *Ideologies and Literature* 3 (1980); S. Hess, *Ramón Menéndez Pidal* (Boston, 1982).

Index

215